The European Heritage in Economics and the Social Sciences

Series Editor:
Jürgen Georg Backhaus

For further volumes:
http://www.springer.com/series/5902

DER OESTERREICHISCHE VOLKSWIRT

MIT DER BEILAGE: DIE BILANZEN

ERSCHEINT JEDEN SAMSTAG

RED. & ADM. WIEN IX. PORZELLANGASSE 27
TELEFON 22143 POSTSPARKASSENCTO. 21177

6. JAHR   WIEN, 1. AUGUST 1914   **NR. 44**

ABONNEMENT-EINLADUNG

Am 1. Juli hat ein neues Abonnement auf unsere Zeitschrift begonnen.

Das Jahresabonnement des **Hauptblattes** beträgt für **Österreich und Deutschland K 24**, des **Hauptblattes und der Beilage »Die Bilanzen« K 36**, für die Weltpostvereinsländer K 28, bzw. K 40.

Die Beilage wird **nur** an Abonnenten des Hauptblattes abgegeben.

Abonnements auf den „Österreichischen Volkswirt" und die Beilage können mittels Erlagschein der Postsparkasse oder Postanweisung bei unserer Administration, Wien, IX./1, Porzellangasse 27, bei jeder größeren Buchhandlung oder bei jedem Postamt unter Angabe der Zeitungsnummer 3418a erfolgen.

Einzelne Exemplare 80 Heller.
Probenummern auf Verlangen gratis.

Die Administration.

Dr. Gustav Stolper: Der Krieg.

Wenige Tage vor Überreichung des Ultimatums in Belgrad hat Graf Tisza im ungarischen Abgeordnetenhaus erklärt, daß eine ernste Wendung nicht als wahrscheinlich anzusehen sei. Wer je versucht hat, den Dingen auf den Grund zu sehen, hat sich durch diese Erklärung nicht über den Ernst der Situation täuschen lassen. Ob das, was geschehen, notwendig gewesen ist oder nicht, wird die Geschichte zu entscheiden haben. An dieser Stelle, wo seit nahezu zwei Jahren die Politik des Grafen Berchtold immer wieder den schärfsten Widerspruch hervorgerufen hat, muß betont werden, daß ihre Haltung seit dem Attentat in Sarajevo ruhig, geradlinig und bestimmt gewesen ist. Und das gibt auch die Überzeugung, daß die überraschenden Umstände, unter denen die befristete Note an Serbien gerichtet wurde, und der Ton dieser Note, der eine glatte Unterwerfung Serbiens forderte, in besonderen Erwägungen begründet gewesen sind. Allerdings hat diese Note die Monarchie dort, wo man sich an Äußerlichkeiten halten zu müssen glaubt, ins Unrecht gesetzt. In der französischen und russischen Presse ist ihr der Vorwurf gemacht worden, daß sie ein Ultimatum stellte, bevor verhandelt worden sei, und daraus wird gefolgt, daß es Österreich-Ungarn weniger um die Gewährung sachlicher Garantien gegen die großserbischen Umtriebe, als um die Demütigung Serbiens, bzw. seines Schutzpatrones Rußlands zu tun sei. Österreich-Ungarn hat, wie die Dinge einmal liegen, keinen Grund, diesem Gedankengang zu widersprechen. Daß es wirksame Garantien gegen die großserbische Idee nicht gibt, ist gerade in diesen Blättern immer wieder betont worden und auch die Forderungen, welche die befristete Note formulierte, bieten in Wirklichkeit keinerlei Schutz gegen die Fortsetzung der alten serbischen Politik. Die Unmöglichkeit, wirklich sachliche Garantien ohne Niederwerfung Serbiens zu verlangen, dürfte in der Tat die hiesigen leitenden Stellen dazu veranlaßt haben, die Forderungen an Serbien in eine Form zu kleiden, die die Ablehnung oder wenigstens die vollständige Annahme als höchst wahrscheinlich erscheinen ließ. Heute handelt es sich längst nicht mehr um die Anerkennung der österreich-ungarischen Forderungen durch Serbien. Heute steht weit Größeres auf dem Spiel.

„Die Monarchie setzt ihre ganze Existenz ein, wer ihr in den Weg tritt, muß den gleichen Einsatz bieten." So soll sich dieser Tage die maßgebende Stelle zum politischen Vertreter der „Frankfurter Zeitung" geäußert haben. Dieser elementare Satz zeigt, wie weit die Dinge gediehen sind. Die leitenden Kreise der Monarchie sind zur Überzeugung gelangt, daß jetzt die Stunde gekommen ist, in der die Monarchie die Probe auf ihre Lebensfähigkeit als Großmacht ablegen muß, und die Einmütigkeit, mit der die gesamte Bevölkerung ohne Unterschied der Nationalität bewußt oder unbe-

Jürgen Georg Backhaus
Editor

The Beginnings of Scholarly Economic Journalism

*The Austrian Economist
and The German Economist*

Springer

Editor
Prof. Dr. Jürgen Georg Backhaus
University of Erfurt
Krupp Chair in Public Finance and Fiscal Sociology
Nordhäuser Str. 63
99089 Erfurt Thüringen
Germany
juergen.backhaus@uni-erfurt.de

ISBN 978-1-4614-0078-3   e-ISBN 978-1-4614-0079-0
DOI 10.1007/978-1-4614-0079-0
Springer New York Dordrecht Heidelberg London

Library of Congress Control Number: 2011934797

© Springer Science+Business Media, LLC 2011
All rights reserved. This work may not be translated or copied in whole or in part without the written permission of the publisher (Springer Science+Business Media, LLC, 233 Spring Street, New York, NY 10013, USA), except for brief excerpts in connection with reviews or scholarly analysis. Use in connection with any form of information storage and retrieval, electronic adaptation, computer software, or by similar or dissimilar methodology now known or hereafter developed is forbidden.
The use in this publication of trade names, trademarks, service marks, and similar terms, even if they are not identified as such, is not to be taken as an expression of opinion as to whether or not they are subject to proprietary rights.

Printed on acid-free paper

Springer is part of Springer Science+Business Media (www.springer.com)

Preface

Introduction

The twin journals, *Der Österreichische Volkswirt* and *Der Deutsche Volkswirt* were created by Gustav Stolper, godfather of Joseph Schumpeter, first in Vienna and subsequently after the First World War, in Berlin. Schumpeter was to become a frequent contributor of the Berlin based journal, which combined a successful blend of economic analysis and political and business insider knowledge which Stolper gained with his famous and sought-after parties at his Wannsee based villa "with sausage and beer" (quoted from memory of an invitation card found in the Stolper estate in the Federal Archive). After Stolper had to sell the influential weekly to an Arian – he himself was Jewish – the paper lost its attractiveness and importance, which in post-Second World War Germany it would never regain, despite the stunning economic policies it could have reported.

But Stolper in New York could not repeat the successful business formula either, despite trying hard and although he established a similar network of brilliant personalities, many of whom had been likewise transferred from Berlin, some rising to power during the Roosevelt administration. In this sense, this volume reports a rather unique episode in European intellectual history.

The twin publications of the Austrian and the German Economist offer a kaleidoscope of many different ideas and concepts. It is therefore not surprising that a large number of different topics are addressed in this publication, as we try to reflect its variety. There are articles on the philosopher of culture – Michael Polanyi by Michele Cangiani and Alexander Ebner. In "a staggering world," Polanyi certainly signifies one of the leading transformations of the social sciences stemming from Europe. As Stolper tried to reflect the major intellectual developments in his publication, Polanyi also being an author was nevertheless referred to again and again. Despite the coverage of the intellectual developments in the Austrian Economist, the intriguing question posed by Jürgen Backhaus, what the emperors could have done in 1914 if one of their advisors had carefully followed the Österreichische Volkswirt has a stunning answer: nothing.

There are articles focusing on demography at the beginning of the twentieth century (compare the chapter by Gerhard Scheuerer); articles covering monetary aspects (compare the chapter on theories of hyper inflation by Gerrit Meijer); articles on foreign developments in countries such as Bosnia, Russia, China and Iran (for the latter compare the chapter by Ursula Backhaus); as well as articles on employment policies and stabilization, which are analyzed by Marcel van Meerhaeghe, who covers the political reactions to the Treaty of Versailles and on the reparation problems, and by Günther Chaloupek, who analyzes topics "From stabilization to depression. Comments in the Österreichische Volkswirt on economic policy in Austria between 1923 and 1929."

Perhaps the gem of the entire book is Sabine Wenhold's chapter on "Lilo Linke und Gustav Stolper." From being the secretary of Gustav Stolper, Lilo Linke develops into an influential political actor herself which has been overlooked in the scholarly literature so far. Her important role is described in the chapter in detail.

In 1932, Stolper organized a campaign against the launching of deficit based employment measures thought up by Lautenbach and Röpke, and this was actually published as a separate book. This activity certainly weakened the government and showed little understanding of Lautenbach's lucid concept. Details are put together by Hans Frambach, "How to fight unemployment?" – Review of the strategy discussion in "Der Deutsche Volkswirt."

After Gleichschaltung (equalization), the term refers to strict censorship, the journal totally lost its attractiveness. The poor Nazi bought it for good money after Gleichschaltung had acquired an empty shell. With the censorship, Stolper's project was mute, as can be read in the chapter by Helge Peukert, "Der deutsche Volkswirt after Gleichschaltung (1933–1935)."

Gustav Stolper could not relaunch his project in the United States, but the inexhaustible mover found new projects, about which Nicholas Balabkins gives a vivid account: "Gustav Stolper's Influence on U.S. Industrial Disarmament Policy in West Germany, 1945–1946."

The only account of Gustav Stolper which so far has found its way into international scholarly journals originally also should have been included into this volume for completeness, but Duke University Press did not give us permission to reprint: Hansjörg Klausinger (Graz), "Gustav Stolper, *Der deutsche Volkswirt*, and the Controversy on Economic Policy at the End of the Weimar Republic." History of Political Economy, Vol. 33, no. 2, 2001, pp. 241–267.

Contents

Preface v

1 "A Staggering World": Karl Polanyi's Contribution
  to *Der Österreichische Volkswirt* 1
  Michele Cangiani

2 Polanyi on Markets, Democracy and the Crisis of Liberalism 15
  Alexander Ebner

3 What Would the Emperors Have Done Differently
  in 1914 if One of Their Advisors Had Carefully Followed
  the *Österreichische Volkswirt*? 31
  Jürgen Backhaus

4 Demography in Germany at the Beginning of the Twentieth
  Century in the Light of *Der Deutsche Volkswirt* 39
  Gerhard Scheuerer

5 Issues of Economic Policy in Germany in the Interbellum 45
  Gerrit Meijer

6 On "The Europeanization of Persia" by N. Basseches 57
  Ursula Backhaus

7 The Austrian and German "Economist" in the Interwar
  Period: International Aspects 65
  Marcel van Meerhaeghe

8 From Stabilization to Depression: Comments
  in the *Österreichische Volkswirt* on Economic Policy in Austria
  Between 1923 and 1929 73
  Günther Chaloupek

9 Gustav Stolper: Mentor of a Young German Democrat 93
  Sabine Wenhold

10	**How to Fight Unemployment? A Review of the Strategy Discussion in "Der Deutsche Volkswirt", 1930–1932**............................ 109
	Hans Frambach
11	***Der Deutsche Volkswirt* After *Gleichschaltung* (1933–1935)**................ 125
	Helge Peukert
12	**Gustav Stolper's Influence on U.S. Industrial Disarmament Policy in West Germany, 1945–1946** 147
	Nicholas W. Balabkins

Index.. 163

Chapter 1
"A Staggering World": Karl Polanyi's Contribution to *Der Österreichische Volkswirt**

Michele Cangiani

1.1 Polanyi and the *Volkswirt*

Karl Polanyi (1886–1964) was a member of the editorial team of *Der Österreichische Volkswirt* from 1924 to 1938, when the journal interrupted publication as a result of the *Anschluss*. He was editor for foreign and world affairs, co-editor after Gustav Stolper's departure for Germany, "foreign editor" from 1933,[1] when he had to move to England for political reasons. According to Kari Polanyi-Levitt and Marguerite Mendell, "he was the most outspoken, left-wing member of the *Volkswirt* editorial team" and "was advised by his colleagues to emigrate" (Polanyi-Levitt and Mendell 1987, p. 24).[2] Polanyi himself comments the crisis and the turning point of March 1933, when the Dollfuss government assumed a "new attitude [...] amounting to a *coup d'état*", attempting to face the Nazi menace in Austria, after the German elections of that month and the collapse of Bavarian autonomy; among other things, "public meetings were forbidden and the press put under censorship" (Polanyi 1933, p. 578).

---

* Part of this paper is a reduced and revised version of M. C., "Prelude to *The Great Transformation*", in K. McRobbie, ed., *Humanity, Society and Commitment. On Karl Polanyi*, Montréal/New York/London: Black Rose Books, 1994, chapter 2.

[1] See below, attached to this paper, the advertisement of the *Ö. V.* in *The Economist*, May 26, 1934.

[2] Also the editor, founder and publisher of the journal, Walther Federn, had later to emigrate; he died on February 1, 1949, in New York. Polanyi was doing his job in that city since 1947, as visiting professor at the Columbia University; he wrote in German an "Eulogy for Walther Federn" (ms., Karl Polanyi Institute of Political Economy, Montreal, *K. Polanyi Archive Catalogue*, box 14, file 16) probably intended for a meeting of common friends in Vienna.

M. Cangiani (✉)
Università Ca' Foscari Venezia, Venezia, Italia
e-mail: cangiani@unive.it

Polanyi wrote 250 pieces for the *Ö. V.* – full-length articles, reports on foreign affairs and reviews.[3] There are also other unsigned short pieces and foreign news items that are probably written by him as well. This impressive body of journalism succeeds in highlighting the epochal change, which is epitomized in the title of the second chapter of Polanyi's book of 1944, *The Great Transformation*: "Conservative Twenties, Revolutionary Thirties". His analyses and comments for the Viennese weekly allow a better understanding of the premises and different forms of the "great transformation" of economic and political institutions, with which he deals in his book within a wider historical perspective. World politics and economy constitute the main themes of the articles, but the internal situation of several countries, the United Kingdom in the first place, is also analyzed.

His first emigration brought Polanyi to Vienna from Budapest in 1919. The periodical *Szabádgondolát* (*Free Thinking*), of which he was the editor since 1913, was closed down by the Communist government. In 1920, many Hungarians moved to Austria, escaping the White Terror, when, as Polanyi writes, "after a nine months' interval almost equally divided between a democratic and a Communist revolution, the feudal nobility regained political control" of Hungary (Polanyi 1937, p. 29). In Vienna, Polanyi's old familiarity with socialist ideas turned to full adhesion; his political–philosophical position is expounded in several articles he wrote for the *Bécsi Magyar Újság* (*Hungarian News in Vienna*) between 1919 and 1923. Most of his articles for this newspaper deal, however, with political events in foreign countries; this was, in fact, the premise of his job at the *Österreichische Volkswirt*.

The extremely stimulating reality of the *rote Wien* was as important for Polanyi's formation as the milieu of progressive-radical Budapest students before the war. The socialist municipality of Vienna became the seat of memorable intellectual and political advancements. In one of the "Notes on the sources" added to *The Great Transformation* Polanyi recalls with never-ending enthusiasm that "unexampled moral and intellectual rise in the condition of a highly developed industrial working class" (Polanyi (1944) 2001, p. 299). He maintained a fruitful relationship with Austrian socialists. An article he published in the journal of the latter (Polanyi 1925) has been included in the anthology *Austro-Marxistische Positionen* (Mozetic, Hg., 1983). Also very important was the link with Austrian economists, who were the main reference for Polanyi's economic studies, up to the second after-war period, when his research concerned the comparative analysis of economic systems and the method of economics (see e.g. Polanyi 1961). Polanyi's polemical confrontation with free-market ideas of second-generation Austrian economists, such as Ludwig Mises and Friedrich Hayek, is constant all along his life, and constitutes, in particular, a basic motive of *The Great Transformation*; but its beginnings are to be found in Vienna after the First World War. The discussion Polanyi entertained with Mises about the features and feasibility of a non-centralized socialist economy dates back to that period (Polanyi 1922, 1924).

From 1924 onwards, for 15 years, the *Ö. V.* required the greater part of Polanyi's work. In an issue of the journal, Richard Bermann, a member of the staff, describes

---

[3] Some have been recently republished in Polanyi (2002, 2003).

the meetings of the editorial team, every Tuesday morning at Porzellangasse 27. He mentions Polanyi's "truly cosmic briefcase" containing "every possible available piece of information relating to economic and political events reported anywhere in the world in the past week. Or not yet reported" (Bermann (1928) 2006, p. 325). That briefcase was an indispensable reference in the discussion; the purpose of the meetings was in fact, Bermann continues, "to monitor new developments, determine editorial policy, but most especially to select the themes of the economic and political Notes (*Glossen*)" (ibid.).

The next paragraph rapidly reviews Polanyi's contribution, the themes and type of which reflect the evolving historical situation; thus, some light is also shed on the vicissitudes of the journal. The rest of the study is dedicated to some significant issues dealt with in Polanyi's work; the choice of them is inevitably partial and reflects my own point of view.

1.2 Polanyi's Articles: An Overview

Approximately 10% of Polanyi's articles deal with the economic, social and constitutional innovations of the American New Deal, and with the political and constitutional contrasts that policy brought about. About 5% of the articles discuss Germany, the USSR, Austria and other countries, while the rest – some 85% – can be divided equally between two main themes: world politics and economy, and Great Britain. Sometimes these two themes overlap, in the sense that the writer deals with international problems from the point of view of British interests and diplomatic activity, as well as outlining the debate over such issues within Britain itself.

For a closer look at the contents and characteristics of these articles, it is best to divide them chronologically. Not many pieces were written between 1924 and 1932 (eight per annum at the most). A good part of these pieces deal with Great Britain, and in particular with the organization of the workers' movement, the question of the coal mines, the struggles culminating in the 1926 General Strike and the reforms proposed by the more advanced wing of the Liberal Party. Then there are international problems, which are often viewed through the work of the League of Nations. The main problem dealt with is that of peace. European states were continuing to negotiate on national security, war reparation and debts, border disputes, disarmament and the rights of defeated nations. But Polanyi considered that the very premises for a real and lasting peace were missing. Europe seemed incapable to settle its disputes, those open by the Peace Treaties included. The fact that victorious powers denied Germany the parity of status seemed to him as unfair as dangerous.[4] In general, in his view, only a wider and deeper democracy could ensure peace, but precisely neither a development of this kind was satisfactory within individual states, nor was there a supranational organization that could wield any effective power.

---

[4] Shortly before Hitler's rise to power, he dedicated two articles to this question: "Gleichberechtigung und Völkerbund", 25 June 1932, and "Gleichberechtigung un die deutsche Linke", 22 October 1932.

Along with the essay "Der Mechanismus der Weltwirtschaftskrise" (which the Viennese journal published in a special supplement), Polanyi wrote 14 articles in 1933. These deal with various topics: Hitler's rise to power and its political and economic consequences for Germany and Austria; the Soviet planned economy; the change brought about in America by Roosevelt's presidency; the difficulty of facing the current economic crisis, not only because of its scale and the fact that the remedies proposed were either obsolete or of dubious efficacy, but also because different countries failed to agree on a common policy (witness the failure of the World Economic Conference held in London[5]). By the end of the year Germany withdrew from the Disarmament Conference and the League of Nations ("Der 14 Oktober", October 21, 1933), and the world appeared to be more unstable, more staggering than ever ("Ein Welt im Wanken", 23 December 1933).

For Polanyi 1933 was a crucial year (it was a key year in his private life as well, the year of his second emigration, as we have seen). It had become impossible to ignore the fact that the tendency towards democracy and socialism had been defeated, that nations seemed inclined more towards war than peace, and that the great crisis was bringing about important institutional changes. The articles of 1933 – together with one written at the end of 1932 ("Wirtschaft und Demokratie", December 24) – deal directly with the main themes of *The Great Transformation*: the complex crisis within the liberal-capitalist system, a crisis involving liberal democracy, the economic system and the world power balance (i.e. peace). Two articles on the beginnings of Nazi regime ("Gegenrevolution", 11 February 1933, and "Hitler und die Wirtschaft", 29 July 1933) are as accurate in analyzing the ongoing events as illuminating on the deep nature of that "counterrevolution".

Polanyi considered 1935 to be another "milestone" ("Markstein 1935", 21 December 1935). The Italian Fascist war in East Africa ended all hope of peace. It was by now clear that international relations were determined by the conflict between the various forms of government (and even of social system), which resulted from the crisis of the liberal system. As we will see in greater detail below, most of the articles written the previous year (1934) deal with the corporative-democratic transformation within Great Britain. From 1935 onwards, Polanyi also dedicated several articles to the American transformation signified by the New Deal.

From 1936 to 1938, Polanyi wrote numerous short incisive pieces, almost always on diplomatic news or international events. The only question analyzed in depth is that of the New Deal and correlative developments of *démocratie en Amérique*. Clearly the need for self-censorship had become stronger than it had been in the past: symptomatic of this fact is that, after 1933, Polanyi did not publish any more articles on the subject of Fascism in *Der Österreichische Volkswirt*. He continued, however, to deal with that subject in his 1934 articles for the English periodical *New Britain*, in the 1935 essay *The Essence of Fascism*, and in numerous lectures and seminars held in Great Britain and in the USA, the manuscripts and outlines of which are conserved at the Karl Polanyi Institute in Montréal.

---

[5]See "Roosevelt zerschlägt die Konferenz", 8 July 1933. N. B.: from here on Polanyi's articles in the *Ö. V.* are referred to in the text by their title and date.

1.3 Social Struggles in England

A substantial number of articles in the pre-1926 period discuss the British workers' movement. There is also an article on the 1925 Socialist International Congress held in Marseilles ("Die neue Internationale", 12 September 1925). In this piece, Polanyi shares the position of the Austrian delegation, supporting a more open and fruitful relationship between different achievements and tendencies of socialism, and with the Communist International. This would also be the premise of the taking on of the international role of promoting peace, a role that, in Polanyi's view, only the socialist movement could successfully perform.

Polanyi's political position was close to "functional" socialism propounded by Otto Bauer in Austria and to the Guild Socialism "restated" by G. D. H. Cole in England (1920). He was therefore more sympathetic towards the Independent Labour Party and its "political-socialist perspective" than towards the Labour Party. He considered, however, the first Labour government an important achievement and a confirmation of the role of English Socialism as a reference point for all European Socialist parties, because of its democratic spirit, its "religious foundation", its willingness and ability to assume the responsibility of government, and its effective diplomatic initiatives in the cause of peace ("England und die Wahlen", 9 November 1924).

As G. D. H. Cole has written, British Socialism had become "a formidable force since the great labour unrest of 1910–1914" (Cole 1935, p. 36); at the end of the First World War it was strengthened even further. In 1924, the Labour Party formed a government that fell after a few months. In his comments upon this episode, one can see not only Polanyi's admiration for British democracy, but also his conviction that the experience of government had helped to transform the Labour Party into a "great popular socialist party", which could now act like a "political" rather than a "trade union" body. However, the Socialist Left, which was led by the Independent Labour Party and was pushing in this direction, was divided ("Zur Krise der englischen Arbeiterbewegung", 25 April 1925). The "possibilism" of the Labour Party's leadership, its government spirit and what G. D. H. Cole calls its "constitutionalism" were leading to an attempt to achieve social peace at any price, with the support of the Trade Unions, which formed the power base of the party.

In Polanyi's view, this weakened the Party's policy programme and the demands it made upon employers and government. Besides, at the base of the workers' movement, any attempt to pursue an overall programme in the general interest was impeded by "trade unionism" – that is, by the *petty bourgeois* defense of the economic interests of particular groups.

In the years to come Polanyi would carefully chart all the facts that gradually destroyed the illusions, though not the hopes, raised by English democracy and the socialist movement. In 1926, he tries to clarify the responsibilities of the Labour Party and Trade Union leaders for the failure of the General Strike, without neglecting, of course, to analyze the effective strategies adopted by employers and the government. He saw the Strike and its failure as the opportunity for the ruling class not only to put the Labour Party in a difficult position, but also, generally speaking, to conclude the counter-revolution by ending a long period of social struggle to its own advantage ("Probleme des englischen Generalstreiks", 29 May 1926). It is significant that after this date Polanyi ceased for many years to publish articles on the English workers' movement in the *Ö. V.* He will write further articles on the subject in 1934; but these articles are expressly designed to show just how much the situation had changed: the Labour Party and the Trade Unions were now involved in supporting the corporatist transformation of British society. Polanyi saw the 1926 Strike as the end of an historical period, one in which it had seemed possible that the growing political influence of the workers' movement operating within democratic institutions could lead to the gradual achieving of a real democracy in all spheres, including the economic.

Beyond Polanyi's analyses on England and the problems he raised about the socialist movement of that country, there was his interest for the vicissitudes of the tentative construction of a socialist democracy in Austria. Also 1926 was the year in which Otto Bauer, at the Linz Conference of the Austrian Social-Democratic Party, had admitted both the theoretical and practical difficulties of a gradual and peaceful development of democracy into Socialism. However, Bauer did not cease to believe in the continuity between the bourgeois and socialist revolutions, between the ideal affirmation of democratic principles, which characterized the beginning of modern society, and the implementation of those principles, which would be made possible by a move beyond capitalism (see Bauer 1934, 1936).

This idea of continuity is also central to Polanyi's thought. Like Bauer, he believed that the move beyond the institutions of liberal capitalism should protect, even strengthen, individual liberty and individual rights against arbitrary decisions of the powers-that-be. Both Polanyi and Bauer viewed Fascism as representing the very negation of the historical achievements of modern society. Seen in this way, Fascism is much more than a reaction against the real or feared political and economic gains made by the working classes. Fascist regimes went so far as to completely eliminate the very idea of free political agents, denying a right which had up to then been possessed (at least theoretically) by all individuals. This is what Polanyi is referring to when he talks of the abolition of "the political State" and the negation of the modern concept of society by Fascism.

The refusal to acknowledge the continuity between the affirmation of democratic principles in modern society and their implementation through socialism, the tendency to consider democracy as a merely illusionary superstructure of a capitalistic organization of the means of production, are things which Polanyi criticizes even in the official Marxism adopted by the Third International. He was of the opinion that such a position made Marxism incapable of understanding either the general characteristics of Fascism or the historical juncture of the Crisis of the 1930s, which enabled it to make its breakthrough to power in many countries, in a situation in which capitalism and democracy seemed to have become incompatible (see Polanyi 1934, p. 128, 1935, p. 391).

In the articles written during the 1920s, and again in *The Great Transformation*, it is pointed out that a socialist revolution very quickly ceased to be a real possibility after the Great War, if indeed it had ever been one. However, the political institutions of liberal democracy continued to admit the possibility of a "popular government", or at least the representation of the interests of the working classes. That representation, according to Polanyi, was the main – that is, the most feared and criticized – ground of the political-democratic "interference" with the functioning of the market economy. The conflict between classes resulted in a contraposition between politics and the economy, which ended by damaging the economy and discrediting democracy. The economic crisis and the crisis of democracy fuelled each other, creating a social and institutional *impasse*, in which Fascism made easily its way.

This understanding of the crisis was apparent long before *The Great Transformation*, and can be found in the 1932 article "Wirtschaft und Demokratie", in which Polanyi was most probably thinking in particular of the Weimar Republic. Another early expression of these ideas is the analysis of the crisis in Great Britain he published a year earlier ("Demokratie und Währung in England", 19 September 1931). This article discusses theories about the economic crisis and possible remedies; in particular it describes the position of the Committee on Finance and Industry, which was chaired by Harold Macmillan and included John M. Keynes amongst its members. According to Polanyi, the new ideas put forward were hampered by the attachment to classic economic theory in a country where, he says, "the Gold Standard was part of the Constitution". Of course, behind this attachment to the pound sterling there was the pressure from the City to reduce unemployment benefits and, in the future, wages themselves. Dominant industrial and financial interest groups were not even reassured by the fact that the Labour government seemed willing to accept the idea of defending the currency, and the consequences of this choice: such a government had to fall. Like others, English society was now at an *impasse*, and the severity of the crisis meant that the inevitable move to a new institutional arrangement could only be traumatic. A reform and new economic institutions were unavoidable, but the dominant interest groups feared that the change could be done at their disadvantage if a "popular government" was in charge, however moderate it was. Thus the Labour leader Macdonald formed a National Government with members of the Conservative and the Liberal parties. So doing, Polanyi writes in "Demokratie und Währung…", he "broke with the traditions of democracy – to the disadvantage of the working classes." Polanyi's interpretation of this historical turning point was confirmed by the fact that on September 21, immediately after the publication of his article, the Gold Standard was abandoned – one of the very first measures taken by the National Government.

The difference in tone between Polanyi's comment in this occasion and his confidence in the first Labour government, when he had still been full of faith in the future of democracy and of socialist movement, reveals just how much things had changed in the course of a few years. Also Harold Laski, among others, argued that any attempt to render social and economic structures congruent with political democracy would, even in the case of England, encounter a reaction aimed at hampering the achievement of such an end (see Laski 1933, 1934).

Polanyi's experience as observer and commentator of the situation in England had an undoubted influence upon the genesis of *The Great Transformation*.

One need only think of the real and symbolic importance this book attributes to the collapse of the Gold Standard, or to the evidence that a new economic policy had only become possible after the weakening of working class resistance and the collapse of socialist or socialist coalition governments, thanks also to the constraints imposed by the old-style economic policy. All in all, England was the home of the "market system", and the fate of such a system throughout the world was linked to the fate of British hegemony.

1.4 A Democratic-Corporatist Transformation

We may now turn to a subject that occupies a central place in Polanyi's articles but remains generally implicitly presupposed in *The Great Transformation*: the industrial reorganization of Great Britain, seen from a technical, economic and, above all, political point of view. Initially, Polanyi pays particular attention to the coal industry. Later, in 1934, he wrote numerous articles on the textile and steel industries, and on the new "managerial and self-sufficient" agricultural policy that cut the import from the Dominions, thus weakening the imperial link ("Agrarische Zwangswirtschaft in England", 3 March 1934; "Elliot oder Empire?", 19 May 1934). The Minister of Agriculture, Walter Elliot, and industrialists alike all put great reliance on the customs barrier, which had been set up in 1932. After a century of free trade, Great Britain too adapted itself to the "new wave of protectionism", the approaching of which Polanyi had already observed ("Neue Schutzzollwelle", 28 November 1931).

Polanyi never considered the technical-economic aspect of industrial problems in isolation; he always looked at the overall social context and the historical situation. When analyzing coal industry, in 1925–1926, he looked at the social struggles in which the miners had played a leading part, at wage and normative agreements, at government intervention and at the possibility of socialization (such socialist idea was encouraged in the post-war period also by the experience of the wartime economy; no need to recall the debate on *Sozialisierung* in German-speaking countries). As already pointed out, Polanyi would later realize the ways in which the situation changed. The period during which the workers' movement had been growing, and had been able to put forward solutions to the problems of an industrialized society, came to an end; the initiative lay henceforth with the other side.

In two 1928 articles ("Liberale Wirtschaftsreformen in England", 11 February 1928 and "Liberale Sozialreformer in England", 25 February 1928) Polanyi discusses the reforms proposed in *Britain's Industrial Future*, the report published by the Liberal Industrial Enquiry, which was set up under the auspices of Lloyd George and took advantage of the collaboration of J. M. Keynes. Polanyi points out that the "Liberal reformers' liberalism" goes beyond classic utilitarianism and individualism, beyond a pure and simple faith in market forces. It even envisages a sort of "social policy" rich in "psycho-logistic pragmatism" – that is, it pays careful attention to workers' ideas on their own situation, and it is founded on the conception that collaboration is to everyone's advantage. The problem of the reorganization of production within whole sectors of industry is faced head-on, and it is recommended that these sectors were provided with bodies for self-government. Furthermore, *Britain's Industrial Future* assigns an important role to the state, which should direct private investment, control trusts especially in case of oligopoly, and set up *public concerns* to supplement private initiative (or replace it in situations where a monopoly exists). Last but not least, the Enquiry recommends social "integration" of the working classes, in exchange for concessions and guarantees. With regard to this, more importance is given to questions of power and "control" than to wages. The password seems to be "industrial co-operation", and thus more effective and extensive joint committees are proposed, along with a prudent form of profit-sharing, "unconditional recognition of the Trade Unions in the interpretation and representation of workers' interests", and state involvement in the settling of industrial disputes. In his comment, Polanyi wonders if these are all signs of a move beyond "a society whose substance is the cash-nexus". He sees a clear intention to "raise wage work from being a mere contractual relation to being a legally guaranteed position with a clear social status"; but he does not see any intention of abolishing private ownership of the means of production or of limiting the managerial power of employers.

In these observations too comes out that typical Polanyi tension between a certain utopianism and an acute sensitivity to the actual historical and political context. On the one hand he had not been entirely able to give up his old hope of a democratic, socialist move beyond liberal capitalism; on the other, he was beginning to be aware of how distant the revolutionary years of the immediate post-war period had become, while also seeing that there were other kinds of "moving beyond". He notes, for instance, that the Works Councils proposed by the Liberals had nothing in common with those set up in 1915 by Clydeside workers during their struggle against the Ministry of Munitions. He notes also that *Britain's Industrial Future* does take up the line proposed in 1917–1918 by the Whitley Committee – except that the reforms are now put forward on the basis of the belief in *community* rather than *conflict* of interests between labour and capital. This new attitude is, according to Polanyi, even clearer in the ideas of Alfred Mond, Chairman of the Imperial Chemical Industries, who in 1927 argued for a dialogue between industrialists and the General Committee of the T.U.C. Polanyi immediately grasps, and explains to his readers, that such initiatives are decidedly innovative; they show a tendency towards a *corporate form* of reorganization of industry, industrial rationalization going hand-in-hand with new industrial relations.

The time was not yet ripe, however, for the passage from planning to effective implementation. One of the main themes of *The Great Transformation* is that the great crisis was a necessary catalyst. It was then that market society really moved beyond the liberal system, the "market system" *stricto sensu*, whilst preserving capitalism and the market system in the widest sense of the term. The move was realized by the "transformation", which could either be of a "democratic-corporative" type, or – where no sort of democracy survived – of a fascist type.

The two articles dedicated to *Britain's Industrial Future* show how keenly proposals and symptoms of innovation attracted Polanyi's attention, even before the outbreak of the slump. Convinced of the crisis of the liberal form of capitalist development, he tried to understand the new form – broadly speaking a corporative one – that was coming into being.

Such awareness was rare among observers of the day, divided in general between Marxist "catastrophism" and obsolete liberalism. One need only think of an economist much appreciated for his sociological and historical interests, and for his contributions to the study of the "dynamics" of the capitalist system: Joseph Schumpeter did not grasp the question of the *transformation* as a question of the various institutional structures assumed by capitalist society, passing through crises that are not reducible to the economic cycles of different periods nor to the demoralization of the entrepreneurs. It was not only in the Twenties, but even after the Second World War, as is evident in his last work, that Schumpeter expresses the fear that "the private-enterprise system" would not be able to endure, owing to such political interventions as stabilization policies, income redistribution, price regulation and anti-trust measures, public control over labour and money markets, and the creation of public enterprises for the satisfaction of social needs, together with security legislation (Schumpeter 1950, pp. 448–450).

Polanyi on the contrary – while remaining loyal, unlike Schumpeter, to the ideals of post-war "Red Vienna" – knew well that the diffusion of organized and managerial capitalism, and the forms of political intervention in the economy adopted, for instance, by the New Deal did not destroy the "private-enterprise system". He knew that the fears and disaffections of the ruling class counted for very little in comparison with its ability to involve the working class, and if necessary to fight and defeat it. Only the market system in the strict sense of liberal-competitive capitalism, together with liberal democracy, did come to an end. Polanyi had already understood all this in the period between the two wars. In one of his articles on the New Deal, he fully endorses the opinion of the Secretary of Agriculture, Henry Wallace, that Roosevelt's policy, and even the principle that "industry is a public matter", allowed capitalism to persist, reinforce itself, and develop ("Arbeitsrecht in U. S. A.", 13 February 1937). Schumpeter, by contrast, was hostile to the New Deal just because he could not understand this significance it had.

In another article ("Schmalenbach und Liberalismus", 30 June 1928) Polanyi explains that the aim of the British Liberals was to set up forms of coordination and control, without however eliminating "the principles of economic freedom" – that is, the capitalistic character of the economy. In the same article, Polanyi reminds us the ground where every proposal of managing economy, including that of British Liberals, is rooted: "free competition finally, and by nature, leads to monopoly"; this "is an old truth and a structural phenomenon characteristic of an epoch." And this is the main reason why by the 1920s the ideology of self-regulating market was out-of-date, except as a weapon serving deflationary policies at the expense of the working classes. Only after the great crisis, however, did some basic institutional features of liberal capitalism – such as free trade, the gold standard and liberal democracy implying a formal separation between economic and political institutions – undergo radical change. It was by then clear that one could no longer rely on market forces alone; the economic process had to be reorganized.

The changes actually carried out in Britain in the direction of corporatism fell far short of those proposed by the opposed ideologies of Guild Socialism and Oswald Mosley's Fascist corporatism, but they were significant all the same. Concentration of capital was accompanied by an attempt to rationalize production through negotiated agreements or the institution of cartels covering entire industrial sectors. During the 1930s, the state helped reorganization, whilst encouraging the trend towards concentration. There were the measures concerning the coal industry, and the 1936 and 1939 laws on the reorganization of the cotton industry. In his 1925–1926 articles, Polanyi already emphasizes that the fate of the coal mines depended on a three-cornered contest between employers, workers and government. In 1934, he analyses in several articles the Lancashire cotton industry, the crisis of which can be seen as the symbol of the decline of an economic system (liberal capitalism) and of an era (that of British hegemony).[6] Another sector in crisis, iron and steel, was helped out by the granting of special customs protection. However, the government measures were subject to the industrialists' association agreeing to a plan for the rationalization of production and export, the fixing of prices and the establishing of quotas to prevent excess production. Polanyi's first article on this industry deals with precisely these measures ("Englisches Stahlstatut", 28 April 1934), whilst the others deal with plans put forward by the Trade Unions, the Labour Party and the Conservatives.

A key figure amongst the latter was Harold Macmillan, whose argument was based on the premise that equilibrium could no longer "be preserved by an automatic reaction to the indicator of price fluctuation" (Macmillan 1933, p.16). Tending to look rather kindly upon the "Whitley System", he proposed a moderate planning policy and a moderate corporatism (understood as entailing the pluralistic representation of all interests and the systematic organization of relations between industry and state). His proposal envisaged the creation of representative bodies at all levels, culminating in a Central Economic Council (taking up the TUC-approved recommendation of a National Industrial Council, which had been one of the results of the Mond-Turner talks a few years earlier). Both Mond (Lord Melchett) and Lloyd George (another precursor, as we have seen) held positions close to that of Macmillan. However, as Polanyi notes, Macmillan had great difficulty convincing the Conservative Party and industrialists that the modest planning policy he proposed did not aim to weaken but "to consciously reinforce the bourgeois foundations of the economy", countering a socialist-type "socialization" with a plan for the "voluntary self-administration and self-defense of industry" ("Tory Planwirtschafter", 20 October 20 1934). Historians have confirmed Polanyi's view of the case: Macmillan's proposal of pluralistic corporatism (even though if it contained the guaranteed predominance of industrialists and only limited national direction) was defeated by the line put forward by the Federation of British Industry, arguing for independent and voluntary reorganization within each industrial sector.

---

[6]Four articles in the *Ö. V.*, vol. XXVI, 1934, amounting to a long essay: "Lohntarif-Bill für Lancashire", May 26; "Lancashire im Fegefeuer", June 2; "Lancashire as Menschheitsfrage", June 23; "Lancashire as Menschheitsproblem", June 30.

Certainly the industrialists could not consider the attitude of the working classes to be of no importance. According to Polanyi, one of the essential factors in the democratic-corporative transformation of Britain was the collaboration of the Trade Unions, which in effect meant the collaboration of the majority of the Labour Party. After the crisis of 1931, he notes, little was left of social struggles and "socialist tendencies". What then was the meaning of the TUC's plan for the nationalization of the iron and steel industry? It was "a sign of the growing tendency towards economic planning", a tendency interpreted by the Trade Unions as trying to meet the requirements of the organizations representing owners and management, and to gain the benevolent attention of the government.

So the Trade Unions did not put themselves forward as the representatives of a socialist tendency but of "the corporative interests of individual categories of workers" ("Labour und Eisenindustrie", 25 August 1934). Even if they really intended to nationalize the iron and steel industry, the result of their proposal would have been a managed economy, in which "the Trade Unions rather than the state would represent the collectivity". This would mean that social production would not be organized with the view of the *intérêt général* in mind, but on the basis of the (real or supposed) interests of different categories of workers, and within the limits set by the need to make profit and by the "technical" choices made at a managerial level. These group interests would be represented by Trade Unions, which would also choose managers and undertake to avoid industrial unrest and arbitrate conflicts. This concept was criticized on the Labour Left by Laski; Polanyi defines it as "democratic-corporative" and a good basis for meeting bourgeois theorists and politicians halfway ("Gewerkschaftstagung in Weymouth", 22 September 1934). The Labour Party approved the nationalization plan, in spite of the opposition of its left-wing headed by the Socialist League, which defined it "a corporative solution of the problem of nationalization". Interpreting the opinion of the Left, Polanyi goes so far as to say that, behind their apparently radical language, the resolutions of the majority revealed "a mental attitude of acquiescence to Fascism" ("Labour in Southport", 13 October 1934).

1.5 World Politics Transformed

Obviously Polanyi did not only have the experience of the situation in England to work on but also he could look at other types of transformation, such as the New Deal, the development of industrialization and collectivism in the USSR through the Five Years Plans, and the diffusion of Fascism throughout a large part of Europe.

The clear opposition of the alternatives and the depth of the consequent changes are reflected both in the conflict which was shaking the very basis of society and in the new shape of world politics. In "Markstein 1935" (21 December 1935) Polanyi outlines a key concept of his interpretation of the evolution of the international conjuncture in the inter-war period. The Italian aggression to Ethiopia seems to him to confirm that "the years of the Peace Treaties are finished", in the sense that Nations are no longer divided by the opposed attempts to assure peace and to revise Treaties.

Now, on the one hand, the worst aspects of "old-style policies of domination and territorial conquest" keep again the stage. The principal cause of this deterioration is the diffusion of Fascism and authoritarian regimes that, as Polanyi asserts some years before, consider war a natural outcome and fuel and exploit nationalism to this purpose ("Italien und Europa", 10 March 1928). But democratic regimes are not exempt from criticism. In 1933 Polanyi considers the "Pact" proposed by Mussolini and signed by France, Germany, Great Britain and Italy dangerous for disarmament and peace ("Viererpakt statt Abrüstung", 3 June 1933). Subsequently, he often deplores the acquiescence of Western Powers to fascist aggressive expansionism and, in particular, their suspect neutrality as to the Spanish Civil War. In the article of 1935, the United Kingdom seems to Polanyi too lukewarm in contrasting the Italian war against Ethiopia, probably because British colonial interests tend to prevail over "the principles of the League of Nations".

On the other hand, Polanyi acutely points out the true novelty of international politics in those times of crisis and transformation: what is now decisive is the clash of alternative forms of social organization. International alignments reflect now conflicting social options. This means "a tight intertwining of internal and external political events. It is not Italy but Fascism, not Germany but National-Socialism, not Russia but Bolshevism, not the United States but the new ideas of the Roosevelt age that are factors of the process. England tries to preserve democracy, Japan experiments an oriental type of industrial feudalism" ("Markstein 1935", 21 December 1935, p. 232). A development of this concept and a more detailed analysis of world politics in the interwar period can be found in the pamphlet *Europe To-Day*, where Polanyi observes that "the emergence of *social* alongside of *national conflict* in our time goes a long way to explain what is, perhaps, the most striking feature of contemporary history, namely the frequency with which *foreign wars* and *civil wars* intersect in the pattern of international events" (Polanyi 1937, p. 14).[7]

In *The Great Transformation* Polanyi relates "the distinction between World Wars I and II" to this historical change: "the former [war] was still true to nineteenth century type – a simple conflict of powers, released by the lapse of the balance-of-power system; the latter already is part of the world upheaval" (Polanyi (1944) 2001, p. 30). In the Thirties, and in the war to which they inevitably lead, "the fate of nations was linked to their role in an institutional transformation" (ibid. p. 28), to the diverse ways of getting over the crisis of the liberal system.

The conflict was essentially between Fascism and democracy. It is, however, necessary to take into account that for Polanyi democracy should have evolved and achieve fulfillment in socialism; this was the basic reason for the general crisis of democracy (in "democratic" countries as well), and was a basic factor in the reshaping of international relations. What made it impossible to stop Germany's and Italy's "new politics of *social interventionism*" (Polanyi 1937, p. 78) in Spain and elsewhere was that the conflict between democratic and fascist countries was made more complicated and contradictory by the overlapping of conflict between capitalism

---

[7] Apart from the obvious reference to Carl Schmitt's ideas, there is a close correspondence between Polanyi's interpretation of the history of the twentieth century and that recently expounded by Eric Hobsbawm 1994.

and socialism. In the article "Spaniens Blockade" (27 February 1937), for instance, Polanyi condemns as very dangerous the insensitivity to the destiny of Spanish democracy and to the fact that "the antithesis of internal policy in Spain has assumed the value of an axis of polarization of an inevitable international war". On the one hand, in Spain the alliance of "National Fronts" that would eventually lead to resistance and victory against Fascism was prefigured. On the other hand, the ambiguities and hypocrisy of the "non-intervention" policy failed to disguise the hostility of the so-called democratic governments towards any form of "popular government".

References

Bauer, Otto, 1934, "Demokratie und Sozialismus", *Der Kampf*, n.1.
Bauer, Otto, 1936, *Zwischen zwei Weltkriegen?*, Bratislava: Eugen Prager Verlag.
Bermann, Richard A., (1928) 2006, "Editorial meetings of the *Oesterreichische Volkswirt*", in K. McRobbie and K. Polanyi-Levitt, eds., *Karl Polanyi in Vienna*, Montreal/New York/London: Black Rose Books, pp. 325–27. (First published in the *Ö. V.*, XXVI, n. 4).
Cole, G. D. H., 1920, *Guild Socialism Re-Stated*, London: Parsons.
Cole, G. D. H., 1935, *The Simple Case for Socialism*, London: Victor Gollancz.
Hobsbawm, Eric J., 1994, *Age of Extremes. The Short Twentieth Century*, London: Pantheon.
Laski, Harold J., 1933, *Democracy in Crisis*, London: G. Allen & Unwin.
Laski, Harold J., 1934, "Le tournant de la démocratie", *Archives de Philosophie du Droit et de Sociologie Juridique*, IV, n. 3–4, pp.156–168.
Macmillan, Harold, 1933, *Reconstruction: A Plea for National Policy*, London: Macmillan.
Mozetic, Gerald, Hg., 1983, *Austro-Marxistische Positionen*, Wien/Köln/Graz: Hermann Böhlaus.
Polanyi, Karl, 1922, "Sozialistische Rechnungslegung", *Archiv für Sozialwissenschaft und Sozialpolitik*, IL, n. 2, pp. 377–420. (Now in Polanyi, Karl, *Chronik der großen Transformation*, Band III, hg. von M. Cangiani, K. Polanyi-Levitt und C. Thomasberger, Marburg: Metropolis-Verlag, 2005).
Polanyi, Karl, 1924, "Die funktionelle Theorie der Gesellschaft und das Problem der sozialistischen Rechnungslegung (Eine Erwiderung an Prof. Mises und Dr. Felix Weil)", *Archiv für Sozialwissenschaft und Sozialpolitik*, LII, n. 1, pp. 218–28. (Now in Polanyi, Karl, *Ökonomie und Gesellschaft*, übersetzt von H. Jelinek, Frankfurt a. M.: Suhrkamp, 1979).
Polanyi, Karl, 1925, "Neue Erwägungen zu unserer Theorie und Praxis", *Der Kampf*, XVIII, n. 1, pp. 18–24. (Now in Polanyi, Karl, *Chronik der großen Transformation*, Band III, hg. von M. Cangiani, K. Polanyi-Levitt und C. Thomasberger, Marburg: Metropolis-Verlag, 2005).
Polanyi, Karl, 1933, "Austria and Germany", *International Affairs*, XII, n. 5, pp. 575–589.
Polanyi, Karl, 1934, "Fascism and Marxian Terminology", *New Britain*, June 20.
Polanyi, Karl, 1935, "The Essence of Fascism", in J. Lewis, K. Polanyi and D. K. Kitchin, eds., *Christianity and the Social Revolution*, London: Gollancz.
Polanyi, Karl, 1937, *Europe To-Day*, London: WETUC.
Polanyi, Karl, (1944) 2001, *The Great Transformation*, Boston: Beacon Press.
Polanyi, Karl, 1961, "Carl Menger's Two Meanings of 'Economic'", in *Studies in Economic Anthropology*, ed. by G. Dalton, Washington: American Anthropological Association.
Polanyi, Karl, 2002, *Chronik der großen Transformation*, Band I, hg. von M. Cangiani und C. Thomasberger, Marburg: Metropolis-Verlag.
Polanyi, Karl, 2003, *Chronik der großen Transformation*, Band II, hg. von M. Cangiani und C. Thomasberger, Marburg: Metropolis-Verlag.
Polanyi-Levitt, Kari and Mendell, Marguerite, 1987, "Karl Polanyi: His Life and Times", *Studies in Political Economy*, n. 22, pp. 7–39.
Schumpeter, Joseph A., 1950, "The March into Socialism", *American Economic Review*, XL, n. 2, May, pp. 446–456.

Chapter 2
Polanyi on Markets, Democracy and the Crisis of Liberalism

Alexander Ebner

2.1 Introduction

Karl Polanyi, who was born in 1886 in Vienna and died in 1964 in Pickering, Ontario remains a most influential theoretical figure in the social sciences, in particular stimulating both analytical and policy-related concerns that are related with the new institutionalism in economics, sociology and political science. Polanyian insights on the political economy of economic development from an institutional perspective have persistently shaped a variety of discourses that range from the theory of the welfare state to research in comparative economic systems and economic anthropology. Polanyi's "Great Transformation" may be singled out as a key contribution to both the domains of economic sociology and political economy, as it addresses basic tensions between the developmental dynamics of the market economy and the institutional substance of political democracy (Block 2001). Indeed, the main thesis of Polanyi's "Great Transformation", originally published in 1944, proposes that the institutional separation and material connectedness of market system and democratic polity contributes to a destabilisation of both spheres, implicitly paving the way of illiberal world-views and authoritarian regimes. In this context, Polanyi highlights the normative requirement of embedding the market system in social communities as a means for sustaining societal coherence. This line of reasoning runs through all of Polanyi's major works – yet its intellectual roots in the crisis of liberalism during the 1920s has been mostly overlooked. Indeed, as the present paper illustrates, the main arguments of Polanyi's notion of the "great transformation" date back to these debates and have been made public in the various essays

A. Ebner (✉)
Institut für Gesellschafts-und Politikanalyse,
Fachbereich Gesellschaftswissenschaften, Johann Wolfgang Goethe-Universität,
Robert-Mayer-Straße 1, 60054 Frankfurt am Main, Germany
e-mail: a.ebner@soz.uni-frankfurt.de

Polanyi contributed to the Austrian economic weekly "Der Österreichische Volkswirt". He was employed by this journal as a joint-editor from 1924 to 1933 in Vienna and continued to provide essays from his London exile until 1938. These essays may be rightfully portrayed as pioneering representations of Polanyi's evolving socio-economic thinking.

The paper proceeds as follows. First, the Polanyian perspective on the institutional evolution of the market society is taken to the fore with an emphasis on the notion of "the economy as instituted process", which addresses diverse patterns of social integration. Second, Polanyi's concept of the "double movement" of market expansion and social protection is discussed in relation with the problem of policy interventions that may destabilise the market system – with far reaching political implications. Third, Polanyi's reasoning on the "great transformation" of economy and polity is taken to the fore – with a special consideration of Polanyi's essays in "Der Österreichische Volkswirt" during the late 1920s and early 1930s, bearing witness to the fact that Polanyi had already developed his basic conceptual schemes in these early German writings as he applied them to the crisis of liberalism and the rise of authoritarianism in Europe. Concluding remarks then outline the relevance of these ideas for current debates on the relationship between market and democracy.

2.2 Market, State and Liberal Ideology

Polanyi's comparative institutional analysis of economic systems is well represented by the notion of "the economy as instituted process", which serves as a leitmotif of his research programme. It means that an analysis of the institutional substance of economic processes is indispensable for understanding their social coherence and historical dynamism, which is derived from both economic and non-economic institutions that constitute a specific mode of social integration (Polanyi 1957b: 249–250). Polanyi contrasts this substantive perspective from the considerations of neoclassical economic theory, which is said to refer exclusively to the logic of choices on means-ends relationships that are marked by resource scarcity. In the Polanyian perspective of a substantive perception of economic life, interchanges with the natural and social environment for the means of material want satisfaction are taken to the fore, basically referring to subsistence constellations (Polanyi 1957b: 243–244). Only this substantive perspective approaches the economy in adequate terms as an instituted process of coherent interactions between society and natural environment (Polanyi 1957b: 248–250).

All historically recorded types of economies are integrated through historically specific support structures that institutionalise the movement of goods and services as well as rights of disposal in the economic process. These institutional structures are denoted as reciprocity, redistribution and exchange, highlighting integrative patterns of interaction that are relatively independent from deliberate interventions of government or the variable ideals of cultural frameworks (Polanyi 1944/2001: 50–51, 1977: 36–37). At this point, the matter of embeddedness emerges as a major analytical device, for Polanyi claims that all historically recorded economic systems except of the market system submerge the economy in social relationships, framed by non-economic institutions. Production and distribution would not follow economic interests shaped by acquisitive motives, but rather resemble social interests, based on collectively shared norms and conventions. These may differ in diverse economic systems over time and space, yet in all of these cases the economic systems were driven by non-economic motives (Polanyi 1944/2001: 48). According to this logic of embeddedness, the economic system was historically set to be a function of social organisation – a pattern that remained intact until the rise of the market economy in the nineteenth century, which reversed relationships between economy and society as economic requirements would come to determine social structures. This would actually imply a disembedding of the economic sphere.

With intellectual reference to the approaches of Maine and Tönnies, this disembedding dynamism resembles a move from status to contract in terms of Maine, and from community to society in terms of Tönnies. Economic system are no more embedded in social relationships, as these are now embedded in the economic system, that is, they come to follow the commodity logic of the market (Polanyi 1947/1968: 70). Contract serves as the decisive feature of this disembedded economic sphere, in which legal aspects of exchange provide the institutional order of the market process. Status, in contrast to that, reflects the predominance of norms of reciprocity and redistribution which shape the embeddedness of production and consumption in societal institutions like family and kinship. The disembeddedness of the economic sphere is therefore analogous to the institutional separation of the market from social relationships apart form contractual exchange (Polanyi 1957a: 70–71). Accordingly, as the market becomes an institution in its own right that shapes the modern exchange economy, it coincides with legal concepts like the rule of law, which imply a reduction of social relations to the regulation of property and contract (Polanyi 1966: xvii).

The resulting type of market economy resembles a self-regulating system of markets. It is historically unique in its character as an economic system that is exclusively directed by market prices (Polanyi 1944/2001: 45). Yet self-regulation through market prices also implies that all production factors, goods and services – decisively involving labour, land and money – are turned into commodities, bought and sold at market prices while generating a market income (Polanyi 1944/2001: 72). Subjecting labour to the self-regulation of markets and thus separating it from other societal domains, however, tends to annihilate the organic interdependencies of the social whole. The underlying freedom of contract eliminates non-contractual organisations such as kinship. Indeed, the contractual exchange mode of the labour market, ideologically legitimised through the notion of non-interference in the spontaneous order of the market process, radically interferes with social relationships that are based on non-contractual interactions (Polanyi 1944/2001: 171). This tendency drives the formation of market society as an extended format of market principles beyond the economic domain. Consequently, the differentiation of economic and political spheres becomes a historically unique trend in the evolution of market economies. While in preceding formations the economic order served as a function of the social order now these relationships are redefined, as the separate economic system of a market economy promotes the formation of a market society as a supporting device. The unfolding of the market pattern as the dominant system in the economy leads to the relegation of society as a mere adjunct to the market. The market society is thus adapted to the institutional pattern of the market economy (Polanyi 1944/2001: 60).

However, this extension of the market sphere all over society breeds a basic structural contradiction. The essence of society is subordinated to the market mechanism, for labour and land as representations of the human substance and natural environment of society also become commodities. Together with money as a mere representation of purchasing power promoted by the state and the banking system, they share the characteristic that they are actually not produced for sale. Their existence is not to be derived from a commercial rationale. Thus their characterisation as marketable commodities is fictitious. This commodity fiction becomes the organising principle of the market society (Polanyi 1944/2001: 75–76). Indeed, the rise of the market society is necessarily based on this commodity fiction involving labour, land and money (Polanyi 1977: 9–10). This implies that changes in the institutional status of labour as a substantial resource of economic activity actually suffice for differentiating economic systems in their historical evolution (Polanyi 1977: 43).

Indeed, Polanyi outlines the actual historical process that leads to the formation of market economy and market society by highlighting two distinct settings, that is, the establishment of national markets in the mercantilist age of Western European development since the fifteenth century, followed by the social and technological disruptions commonly associated with the Industrial Revolution in Western Europe – and here primarily in England – since the early nineteenth century (Polanyi 1944/2001: 5–7). Decisively, the formation of the market system is not a spontaneous process as liberal theory may have it, but the politically administered result of artificial stimuli based on socio-economic constellations shaped by the likewise artificial phenomenon of the machine as a representation of disruptive technological change (Polanyi 1944/2001: 39, 60). However, in contrast to early modern constellations, both the industrial dimension of the "machine age" and the commodity dimension of the market system characterised the socio-economic disruptions of the nineteenth century. The self-regulating market system served as an institutional adaptation induced by the factory system of the machine age and its industrial civilisation – which was soon accompanied by a counter-movement for social self-protection that would give birth to the welfare state (Polanyi 1977: xlviii-l). The historical break of the Industrial Revolution thus combined technological and ideological factors.

Also economic motives needed to change, basically turning from subsistence to gain. Polanyi proposes that economic liberalism promoted the "utopian endeavour" of a self-regulating market system with a motivational emphasis on material gain, allowing for an institutional dominance that paralleled the homogenising intolerance of religious fanaticism (Polanyi 1944/2001: 31). Utilitarianism provided the backbone for market ideology as a sectarian creed that aimed at solving human problems through the provision of an unlimited amount of material commodities (Polanyi 1944/2001: 42). However, in liberal ideology, the ensuing "separateness" of economic and political spheres was well reflected by policy demands for a retreat of the state from economic regulation (Polanyi 1977: 47). Accordingly, the formation of market society implies a reassessment of the state as an institutional subordinate that should comply with the self-regulation of the market system (Polanyi 1977: 12).

Historically, the heyday of liberalism hit England in the 1830s, carried by an ideology which rejected any political-administrative measure that could obstruct the unimpeded flow of marketable resources and their self-regulation by market prices (Polanyi 1944/2001: 72). Yet this ideological coverage tended to hide the fact that the evolution of the market system and persistent interventionism were not mutually exclusive. Instead, it should become obvious that the formation and maintenance of market institutions requires persistent interventions, involving antitrust regulations as well as union laws – and at times even violent means (Polanyi 1944/2001: 155–156). The establishment of markets is thus not the result of spontaneous institutional change. Rather it is the outcome of conscious and often violent interventions on the part of the government (Polanyi 1944/2001: 258). Indeed, when viewed as a historical sequence, the institutional design of the market system in England during the first half the nineteenth century advanced primarily through legal instruments. The Poor Law reform of 1834 promoted a deregulated labour market and the commodification of labour, followed by the Bank Act in 1844 that established the gold standard for the self-regulation of the monetary sphere, whereas the repeal of the Corn Law in 1846 allowed for free trade in grain, thus promoting the transformation of land into a marketable commodity (Polanyi 1947/1968: 67–68). Yet the corresponding reign of an unhampered market regime was short-lived, if ever realised in history, for society was soon endangered in its totality. In particular, the institutional status of labour as a commodity included real humans that would become socially exposed and dislocated objects of market volatility. Thus, for society at large, the need of protection arose as a condition in safeguarding the reproduction of its substantial components (Polanyi 1944/2001: 76–77). Thus, both economic and political regime become subject to the conflict-ridden dynamics of a historical scheme that is denoted as "double movement".

2.3 The Double Movement and the "Great Transformation"

The extension of markets was historically paralleled by efforts in the self-protection of society, amounting to a "double movement" of market forces and social regulation (Polanyi 1944/2001: 79). In particular, a double movement of distinct organisational principles in society could be observed, namely economic liberalism promoting self-regulating markets, socially based in the trading classes vs. social protectionism as an effort to shield human and natural resources from the grip of the market forces through interventionist measures in legislation, administration and associative self-organisation, socially based primarily in the working and landed classes (Polanyi 1944/2001: 138–139). This interventionist countermovement against the expansion of markets and its underlying commodity fiction was incompatible with the working mechanism of the market itself, leading to a further intensification of institutional tensions (Polanyi 1944/2001: 136–137). Measures of social protectionism that lay the foundations for the welfare state since the 1860s in Western Europe obstructed price-based adjustments of labour markets by stabilising earnings beyond volatile market incomes as well as by regulating institutional features such as professional standards, thus reconstituting the human character of labour beyond the commodity fiction (Polanyi 1944/2001: 185–186). As the counter-movement and its protectionist stance came to disturb the self-regulation of the market system ever severely since the 1880s all over Western Europe, the national domain became the decisive terrain for political identity – implying a drive for national rivalry. Economic and political crises then culminated in World War I, followed by a prolonged period of instability afterwards that would pave the way for totalitarian solutions to the crisis of the market system (Polanyi 1944/2001: 210–212).

During the same period of liberal restructuring, the contradiction between the formation of markets and political democratisation became apparent. While the Chartists demanded universal suffrage, which could potentially empower those strata of society that were to be turned to wage labourers, the separation between economic and political sphere became decisive for upholding the market system under democratic conditions. Liberal ideas of constitutionalism, which were originally directed against the danger of the confiscation of private property through despotic rulers, were now reinterpreted for safeguarding private property against the impoverished masses. In particular, the US-American constitution represents such a type of "legally grounded market society" with its separation of powers that could hold voters relatively powerless against the interests of the owners of private property (Polanyi 1944/2001: 233–234). The double movement of market liberalisation and social protectionism is thus accompanied by increasing difficulties with the effective implementation and democratic legitimisation of related policy interventions. In consequence, the institutional stability of the market system is at stake.

Summarising these tendencies, Polanyi outlines two paradoxical aspects in the co-evolution of market and state that contradict liberal ideologies of the market system. First, as the English example illustrates, laissez faire principles were historically enforced by the state and did not evolve spontaneously in a natural market order. Indeed, even utilitarian liberalism of the Benthamite creed would favour strong government as the most indispensable agency of knowledge and power needed to make markets work (Polanyi 1944/2001: 145–146). In practice, as the expansion of markets required a massive restructuring of social affairs, particularly relevant regarding the public treatment of poverty, it was paralleled by an extension of interventions and regulations that eventually fuelled a bureaucratisation of government, endowed with extended powers for social control (Polanyi 1944/2001: 146). Second, while the establishment of the laissez faire economy was the product of deliberate state action, the political counter-movement that organised its resistance in England since the 1860s resulted from spontaneous activities scattered all over society, pragmatically assembling diverse social interests and political ideologies ranging from socialism to conservatism (Polanyi 1944/2001: 147). Obviously, this is a pointed counter-position to liberal worldviews, as represented most prominently in Hayekian liberal reasoning on the spontaneous order of the market.

Polanyi contradicts Hayek's notion of the rationalist utopia of planning by deliberate interventions as he claims that it is in fact the market system, which is the product of an utopian rationalism that manifests itself in coordinated government interventions to disembed the market sphere from non-market modes of social integration, whereas efforts in re-embedding regulation would proceed in the ad-hoc manner of diverse spontaneous moves for social protection (Holmwood 2000: 34–35).

This claim is rooted in Polanyi's thesis that the countermove against the expansion of markets resulted not from the impact of distinct social forces and ideologically fuelled political movements but from the cumulative increase of insights into the problems of socially disembedding market forces (Polanyi 1944/2001: 156). Accordingly, Polanyi rejects an analytical emphasis on the particular interests of social groups and classes in the political assessment of the counter-movement, for the latter would reflect a general interest that spans diverse social classes, based on insights on the required maintenance of the human and natural substance of society and thus highlighting broader social interests that are not to be defined in terms of narrow economic interests (Polanyi 1944/2001: 160–162). This rather idealistic depiction of the counter-move as a project of societal enlightenment against the market society resembles a Hegelian idealism that points to cumulative insights into the laws of motion of society – and indeed it has been criticised in these terms (Hejeebu and McCloskey 1999: 295). These problematic aspects of political considerations in Polanyi's approach imply that society is perceived as having a reality of its own, acting on its own behalf as an active, self-conscious entity (Burawoy 2003: 189–199).

Consequently, the double movement is best understood as a clash of social principles resulting from the contradiction between the market system and the persistence of modes of social integration beyond market exchange and commodification. A frictionless harmonisation of market system and policy interventions thus remains out of sight (Polanyi Levitt 2006: 162–163). Indeed, the notion of the double movement reflects a perception of the economy as a loosely coupled system, in which no pre-stabilising forces exist – although buffer components and backup mechanisms may provide temporary coherence (Block 2007: 7). Persistent friction may lead to a combined transformation of economic and political system in terms of a hollowing out of market and democracy – invoking the spectre of authoritarian or even totalitarian solutions to the imminent question of safeguarding the material and moral reproduction of society.

This societal divergence of political orientations regarding the transformation of the market system points already at the political and economic instability that resulted from protectionist disturbances, furthered by the counter-movement against the market system in Western Europe since the 1880s. Paralleling this advance of protectionism, the nation-state became the decisive terrain for political identity. Ensuing patterns of national rivalry together with prolonged economic and political crises culminated in World War I, followed by unsteadiness and reorientation afterwards (Polanyi 1944/2001: 210–212). Polanyi explains this permanence of instability by referring to the interconnectedness of the separated political, social and economic domains that would become subject to protectionist policies. As protectionism encouraged the monopolisation of market structures, interventions in support of a competitive order became ubiquitous, leading to an increasingly bureaucratic and corporatist setting that persistently distorted prices and prolonged recessions. The institutional separation of economic and political spheres intensified the disruptions emanating from destabilised markets. Thus, the transformation of the market system towards an authoritarian solution following World War I was not driven by new economic motives, but by new institutional mechanisms in coping with the market civilisation (Polanyi 1944/2001: 227–228). Because of the interconnectedness between the separated societal domains, market strains would affect other institutional zones such as national government and thus even affect international politics (Polanyi 1944/2001: 220).

Policy interventions into the market system therefore escalate a socio-economic destabilisation that leads to the "great transformation" of the market society with the option of an authoritarian solution. Underlying the controversial impact of these theses is Polanyi's belief in the socially disruptive yet economically equilibrating capacities of markets that are unhampered by policy interventions. Thus, in Polanyi's account, also business cycles are basically derived from policy interventions; a position which radically contradicts contemporary Keynesian ideas on the endogenous instability of markets (Dalton 1968: xxv). Indeed, with regard to the self-stabilisation of markets, Polanyi remains close to the positions of the Austrian School of Mises and Hayek with their monetary theory of the business cycle. Polanyi's positions thus remain paradoxically close to the Viennese milieu of their origin, in particular shaped by Mises's rejection of policy interventions into market processes. In other words, Polanyi is overdoing the case of market distortion by policy interventions, as he seemingly relies on a type of flawless market process that should become most prominent with general equilibrium theory (Hejeebu and McCloskey 1999: 302). Yet Polanyi's reconsideration of structural tensions arising from the separateness as well as connectedness of the diverse domains of economy, polity and other spheres of society which follow a distinct functional logic has also invited sympathetic interpretations in terms of systems theory. The market system is accordingly viewed as an autopoietic system, which exhibits a distinct logic that may conflict with the alien rationale of systems from which outside interventions emerge (Jessop 2001: 222–223).

From the consideration of policy interventions follows that the tensions, which arise from the protective regulation of the market system have consistently fuelled a transformation of the liberal bourgeois civilisation that had become prominent during the nineteenth century, leading to an upsurge of socialism and fascism as conflicting solutions to the turmoil of the 1920s. Socialism represents an inherent tendency of industrial civilisation towards a conscious subordination of the market to democratic principles by means of adequate public policies, basically confronting private efforts in achieving monetary gain as an exclusive motivation for productive activity, while abolishing private property of the means of production (Polanyi 1944/2001: 242). Fascism, however, as a non-socialist response to the failure of the market society resembles an interventionist reform of the market economy on the condition of eliminating democratic institutions in economy and polity (Polanyi 1944/2001: 245). The corresponding crisis of liberalism and the rise of authoritarian alternatives to the market system and the democratic order – to be termed as key components of a "great transformation" later on – has been a key issue in Polanyi's early German writings all the way through the 1920s, well before the Word Economic Crisis emerged. In particular, as outlined in the following section, most of Polanyi's ideas on the crisis of liberalism and the "great transformation" can be traced in his essays in "Der Österreichische Volkswirt".

2.4 The Crisis of Liberalism in Polanyi's Early German Writings

Reference to a mixed economy with democratic planning in a setting of industrial associations have been prevalent with Polanyi's thought ever since his first major publication addressed the socialist accounting debate in the theoretical discourse of the Austrian School, fuelled by Ludwig von Mises and his companions in response to the socialist advance after World War I (Mendell 1989: 577–578). While acknowledging the infeasibility of accounting in a socialist command economy, Polanyi proposes a decentralised model of guild socialism that should combine elements of market supply and demand with socio-political regulations, thus satisfying the diverse needs of society as articulated by industrial associations and consumers. According to Polanyi, the differentiation between capitalism and socialism should not be reduced to the dichotomy between market and plan, for it is rather to be associated with aspects of social productivity and the societal character of production and distribution at large, meant to benefit the common good (Polanyi 1922: 378–379). Polanyi's advocated type of guild socialism thus resembles a corporatist system of industrial democracy with communal property of the means of production that is governed by industrial associations and consumer organisations. Wages and prices are regulated in terms of social values, subject to democratic bargaining arrangements among the involved associations (Polanyi 1922: 403–405).

These normative positions on an associational type of socialist market economy that should be to be based on the democratic structuration of economic and social affairs have remained a cornerstone of Polanyi's assessments of contemporary political-economic development tendencies. Decisively, at the end of the 1920s, the crisis of liberalism and the decline of democracy became a major topic in a series of Polanyis's essays that were published in "Der Österreichische Volkswirt". These essays would lay the groundwork for Polanyi's concept of the "great transformation" of liberal market society. Of particular importance in this regard is a series of essays that was published in February 1928, highlighting the comprehensive reform proposals of the Liberal Party in the United Kingdom, which were debated well before the onset of the World Economic Crisis of 1929. In particular, Polanyi comments on the liberal reform movement within the Liberal Party as a political force that wanted to transcend the borderlines between individualism and socialism – and thus alienated itself from the world-views of classical liberalism. Indeed, the reform proposals are characterised as an illustration of the political-economic process that should be labelled subsequently as the "great transformation". The essay "Liberale Wirtschaftsreformen in England" points out that reform programme is based on safeguarding private property by making it subject to extended political regulations: Underlying attempts follow Keynesian recipes of a policy-related active role of the Central Bank, accompanied by an extension of the public sector (Polanyi 1928a). However, as outlined in the follow-up essay "Liberale Sozialreformer in England", the related proposals in the domain of social reform rather hint at a pattern of reform that provides solutions from the domain of political psychology to problems that originate from the sphere of political economy, that is, the matter of labour co-determination in large firms becomes more important than basic questions of wage formation and labour organisation. Yet this does not imply that the question of re-embedding de-commodification is ignored. Instead, quite to the opposite, Polanyi maintains that the reform programme of the Liberal Party addresses labour relations in a manner that transforms the character of wage relations – and wage labour in general – from a purely contractual relationship, as classical liberalism would define it, to a socially embedded and legally framed relationship among status groups. In other words, the commodity character of wage labour is transformed into a social relationship that accounts for distinct social values of labour without affecting the system of private property and market allocation (Polanyi 1928b).

Yet according to Polanyi the crisis of liberalism is also related to misconceptions in academic knowledge, and here in particular in the knowledge sphere of economic theory. Polanyi's essay "Schmalenbach und Liberalismus", also from 1928, takes issue with these misconceptions. As the title of the essay suggests itself, the key thrust of Polanyi's arguments is directed against Eugen Schmalenbach, a Professor at the Faculty of Economics and Social Sciences at the University of Cologne in Germany, who had claimed that the fix cost profile of large firms could promote the formation of industrial cartels – with disastrous consequences for market competition. In this context, Polanyi also discusses the Keynesian vision of the economic process, namely Keynes's stagnation thesis, which hinted at the relative decline of investment opportunities in the course of the process of economic development. This kind of argument actually implied a denial of the persistent relevance of technological innovation. In empirical reality, however, the 1920s have been a decade of major innovations and radical technological changes. Thus, the Keynesian stagnation scenario is at odds with the unfettered technological dynamics of the market system. The political importance of this assessment lies in the requirement of market regulation. While certain strands of liberalism tend to deny the need for monopoly control in the face of growth stagnation, it would be adequate to keep a focus on the issue of technologically driven monopoly power in a setting of regulated markets (Polanyi 1928c).

In exploring the underlying developmental tendencies, as examined in the essay "Wirtschaft und Demokratie" from 1932, Polanyi comes forward with the thesis that the World Economic Crisis has contributed to a long-standing rift between economy and polity. Both have become autonomous systems that remain almost unconnected, each following a distinct rationale. This separation of economic and political concerns leads to functional disturbances in the interaction between the systems.

Forces that originate from the terrain of political democracy persistently aim at interventions into the economy, arguing that the allocative and distributive results of the market mechanism require political adjustment. Economic interest groups, however, confront the democratic spectrum with arguments that highlight the lack of efficiency and responsibility in the political domain – putting a focus on issues such as increasing inflation, expanding subsidies, extended protectionism, mismanagement of currencies and the unimpeded growth of social expenditures and welfare benefits. Thus, both democracy and the market system have come under fire from opposing sides – as they are on the retreat all over Europe, while fascism and communism gain in intellectual relevance (Polanyi 1932).

Three essays from 1934, titled "Probleme der Demokratie in England", "Labour in Southport" and "Tory-Planwirtschaftler" shed further light on this issue, which is discussed in the context of political programmes for economic recovery in the United Kingdom – a debate that was most prominently influenced by the idea that economic planning would become the most effective way of organising the recovery process, thus heralding a foreseeable hegemony of socialist ideas. In this setting, the relationship between socialist planning and representative democracy is at stake. Accordingly, Polanyi identifies the danger of a hollowing out democracy, which could lead to its transformation to a politically neutral institutional form that would be compatible with both socialism and fascism – regardless of ethical content Polanyi (1934a). These dangers are also prevalent with regard to contemporary debates within the Labour Party, as exemplified by Labour's Southport Party Congress of 1934 – a controversial event that was identified as a representation of political strands of thought running parallel to fascist ideas. The proposal of a corporatist model in the management of socialised industries was indeed compatible with both socialist and fascist concepts of the corporate state. Thus, according to Polanyi, both the Labour Party and the Unions could be portrayed as promoters of a corporatist solution to the question of socialisation with potentially fascist leanings (Polanyi 1934b). Also the Conservatives would join this drive for economic planning, although with a distinct preference for industrial self-governance. As Polanyi points out with regard to proposals that were discussed at the Bristol Congress of the Conservative Party, a group of young conservatives led by Harold Macmillan – who would become Prime Minister from 1957 to 1963 – stood out with their idea that industrial planning should be enforced by government in order to promote the coordinated recovery of the British economy. In Polanyi's worlds, this would actually amount to a "bourgeois planned economy" – quite in line with the perception that market solutions to the matter of industrial growth and development had already lost much of their former appeal even within conservative intellectual circles (Polanyi 1934c).

In accordance with these statements, also Polanyi's comments on Roosevelt's New Deal, as published in the "Österreichische Volkswirt" during the mid-1930s highlight the tendency towards industrial coordination through governmental planning efforts. At the same time, the indispensability of participative and transparent democratic procedures is accentuated as a preventive measure against authoritarian tendencies (Polanyi 1935: 763–765). Indeed, Polanyi is persistently sensitive to the danger of an insulation of the state from society that would parallel the separation of market system and political sphere, resembling the evolution of a "self-regulating state" that combines the political power of a welfare bureaucracy with extended social control and undemocratic authoritarianism (Godbout 1991: 128–129). Preventing an authoritarian degeneration of the state and maintaining the democratic character of social protection and economic planning is of utmost importance to Polanyi, because the formation of the welfare state is decisive his policy approach as it directly affects the status of labour – the crucial characteristic for specifying the rationale of an economic system. Indeed, as Polanyi suggests, the formation of the welfare state represents a protective venture that could offer workers social status, secure income, teamwork, and a creative role in industry (Polanyi 1977: 1).

Historically, these endeavours are most positively associated with the experience of "Red Vienna", that is the socialist municipality of Vienna after World War I with its extended welfare programmes. It could be argued with some justification that the heyday of Viennese social democracy after World War I was a most affirmative point of reference for Polanyi's political beliefs. Interpreted as a major cultural achievement in European economic and social history, it was said to differ markedly from the reactionary Speenhamland system in nineteenth century England due to successful efforts of the Viennese social democrats in transcending the commodity production of capitalism while retaining the positive effects of the industrial system of labour and technology – including the aspect of regulated market allocation (Polanyi 1944/2001: 298–299). Crucially, in the Polanyian perspective, the distributive function of the welfare state is not to be separated from its impact on the democratisation of the labour process with all of its various political and social implications.

Yet Polanyi's policy proposals reach well beyond the domains of labour organisation and welfare state. Indeed, based on his theoretical positions on the primacy of technological requirements in the institutional evolution of the market system, Polanyi was keen to suggest that reform attempts would have to reach beyond the institutional grounds of capitalism with its primacy of material gain and rather challenge the set up of modern industrial civilisation at large, that is, the Machine Age in Polanyian terms (Polanyi 1947/1968: 59–60). Polanyi's normative position highlights the socialist option, yet amended in terms of safeguarding "freedom in a complex society" as a means for restoring the "habitation" of society through a democratically regulated industrial system (Polanyi 1944/2001: 257). Moral freedom and independence of mind would represent values of the market economy and its system of private enterprise that should be preserved, although set in a different institutional context that fosters the common good while confronting bureaucratisation (Polanyi 1944/2001: 263–264). Crucially, according to Polanyi, this deliberative way of confronting the problem of the technological civilisation is ignored by liberals like Hayek in their defence of the market system, for they do not acknowledge that democratically founded market interventions of producer and consumer associations hold the key to freedom in a complex society (Polanyi 1947/1968: 75–77). Again, this line of reasoning underlines Polaniy's normative concerns with a re-integration of economic and political spheres in the setting of a democratic type of polity.

2.5 Conclusion

In current discussions on globalisation, a specific "Polanyi problem" has been singled out, asking how the globalisation of the market system as a disembedding process is to be reconciled with re-embedding moves aiming at social security and cohesion (Munck 2004: 251–252). This problem corresponds with Polanyi's fear of a degeneration of the liberal project into political authoritarianism on a national scale, framed by economic pressures emanating from international rivalry (Harvey 2005: 70). As such a perception of the demise of liberal capitalism belongs to the set of ideas that are shared by both Karl Polanyi and Max Weber, it also highlights tendencies of a widespread underestimation of the reproductive capacity of the market system, in particular in its combination with a democratic polity (Roth 2003: 276–277). In this manner, globalisation represents a specific institutional constellation in the historical evolution of markets and democracy. Such an interpretation of the dialectics of movement and counter-movement in Polanyi's approach also allows for bringing back politics into the setup of the institutional evolution of states and markets. The insistence on the conflict-ridden potential of socio-economic change is a decisive analytical advantage of Polanyian reasoning in comparison with other institutionalist approaches to comparative capitalisms (Streeck 2009: 254–256). Actually, such a perception of Polanyi as an icon of socio-economic analysis with a normative drive for social reform is bound to have him replace Marx as a point of critical reference on economic and political affairs (Hart 2008: 1136, Hart and Hann 2009: 8–9).

Supposedly, a Polanyian diagnosis of globalisation would denounce global finance for undermining the coherence of national economies while spreading Polanyi's false utopia of self-regulating markets (Polanyi Levitt 2006: 152–153). Such a Polanyian view might consider financial deregulation as an economic trend that is cultivated by state action, meeting the counter-movement of efforts that aim at bringing global finance under social control, particularly in a transnational setting of rules and regulations (Helleiner 2000: 12–13). At this point, re-embedding efforts through state intervention provide the major terrain for future conflicts in the double movement. These efforts may be accompanied by the internationalisation of political initiatives for the de-commodification of labour (Munck 2002: 18). Polanyi's notion of the double movement then qualifies as a device for assessing the organised criticism of globalisation as a counter-move against the formation of a globalised commodity fiction (Birchfield 2005: 581–582). Policy implications that may be distilled from Polanyian considerations then highlight a reflexive, dialogical mode of governance as the solution to a sustained co-existence between market economy and the wider social and ecological system (Jessop 2001: 228–229). Such a reflexive mode of governance may also allow for those qualities of democracy, which were emphasised by Polanyi – and are currently contested by transformative political-economic pressures (Crouch 2004). Indeed, the evolution of markets and democracies remains undetermined in Polanyi's reasoning – thus adding to its enduring relevance beyond normative confines (Ebner 2010). Polanyi's essays in "Der Österreichische Volkswirt" provide most convincing evidence for this kind of assessment, as they actually laid the groundwork for Polanyi's subsequently formulated concept of the "great transformation" of liberal market society.

References

Birchfield, Vicki (2005), José Bové and the Globalisation Countermovement in France and Beyond: A Polanyian interpretation, *Review of International Studies*, Vol.31, No.4, pp. 581–598.

Block, Fred (2001), Introduction, in Karl Polanyi, *The Great Transformation: The Political and Economic Origins of Our Time*, Second Paperback Edition, Boston: Beacon, pp. xviii–xxxviii.

Block, Fred (2007), Understanding the Diverging Trajectories of the United States and Western Europe: A Neo-Polanyian Analysis, *Politics and Society*, Vol.35, No.1, pp. 3–33.

Burawoy, Michael (2003), For a Sociological Marxism: The Complementary Convergence of Antonio Gramsci and Karl Polanyi, *Politics and Society*, Vol.31, No.2, pp. 193–261.

Crouch, Colin (2004), *Post-Democracy*, Cambridge: Polity Press.

Dalton, George (1968), Introduction, in George Dalton (ed.), *Primitive, Archaic, and Modern Economies: Essays of Karl Polanyi*, New York: Anchor, pp. ix–liv.

Ebner, Alexander (2010), Transnational Markets and the Polanyi Problem, in Christian Joerges and Josef Falke (eds.), *Karl Polanyi, Globalisation and the Potential of Law in Transnational Markets*, Oxford: Hart, pp. 19–41.

Godbout, Jacques (1991), The Self-Regulating State, in Marguerite Mendell and Daniel Salée (eds.), *The Legacy of Karl Polanyi: Market, State and Society at the End of The Twentieth Century*, London: Macmillan, pp. 119–130.

Hart, Keith (2008), Karl Polanyi's Legacy, Development and Change, Vol.39, No.6, pp. 1135–1143.

Hart, Keith and Chris Hann (2009), Learning From Polanyi, in Hart, Keith and Chris Hann (eds.), Market and Society: The Great Transformation Today, Cambridge: Cambridge University Press, pp. 1–16.

Harvey, David (2005), *A Brief History of Neoliberalism*, Oxford and New York: Oxford University Press.

Hejeebu, Santhi and McCloskey, Deirdre (1999), The Reproving of Karl Polanyi, *Critical Review*, Vol.16, Nos.3–4, pp. 285–314.

Helleiner, Eric (2000), Globalization and Haute Finance – Déja Vu?, in Kenneth McRobbie and Kari Polanyi Levitt (eds.), *Karl Polanyi in Vienna: The Contemporary Significance of The Great Transformation*, Montréal and New York: Black Rose, pp. 12–31.

Holmwood, John (2000), Three Pillars of Welfare State Theory: T.H. Marshall, Karl Polanyi and Alva Myrdal in Defence of the National Welfare State, *European Journal of Social Theory*, Vol.3, No.1, pp. 23–50.

Jessop, Bob (2001), Regulationist and Autopoieticist Reflections on Polanyi's Account of Market Economies and Market Society, *New Political Economy*, Vol.6, No.2, pp. 213–232.

Mendell, Marguerite (1989), Market Reforms and Market Failures: Karl Polanyi and the Paradox of Convergence, *Journal of Economic Issues*, Vol.XXIII, No2, pp. 473–481.

Munck, Ronaldo (2002), Globalization and Democracy: A New Great Transformation?, *Annals of the American Academy of Political and Social Science*, Vol.581, No.1, pp. 10–21.

Munck, Ronaldo (2004), Globalization, Labor and the 'Polanyi Problem', *Labor History*, Vol.45, No.3, pp. 251–269.

Polanyi, Karl (1922), Sozialistische Rechnungslegung, *Archiv für Sozialwissenschaft und Sozialpolitik*, Vol.49, pp. 377–420.

Polanyi, Karl (1928a), Liberale Wirtschaftsreformen in England, *Der Österreichische Volkswirt*, February, Vol. XX, No.20, pp. 544–545.

Polanyi, Karl (1928b), Liberale Sozialreformer in England, *Der Österreichische Volkswirt*, February, Vol. XX, No.22, pp. 597–600.
Polanyi, Karl (1928c), Schmalenbach und Liberalismus, *Der Österreichische Volkswirt*, June, Vol. XX, No.40, pp. 1116–1117.
Polanyi, Karl (1932), Wirtschaft und Demokratie, *Der Österreichische Volkswirt*, December, Vol. XXV, No.13–14, pp. 301–303.
Polanyi, Karl (1934a), Probleme der Demokratie in England, *Der Österreichische Volkswirt*, May, Vol. XXVI, No.35, p.751.
Polanyi, Karl (1934b), Labour in Southport, *Der Österreichische Volkswirt*, November, Vol. XXVII, No.2, pp. 26–27.
Polanyi, Karl (1934c), "Tory-Planwirtschaftler", *Der Österreichische Volkswirt*, November, Vol. XXVII, No.3, pp. 47–48.
Polanyi, Karl (1935), Amerika im Schmelztiegel, *Der Österreichische Volkswirt*, Juni 1935, Vol. XXVII, No.39, pp. 763–765.
Polanyi, Karl (1944/2001), *The Great Transformation: The Political and Economic Origins of Our Time*, Second Paperback Edition, Boston: Beacon.
Polanyi, Karl (1947/1968), Our Obsolete Market Mentality, Commentary, Vol.3, repr. in George Dalton (ed.), *Primitive, Archaic, and Modern Economies: Essays of Karl Polanyi*, New York: Anchor, pp. 59–77.
Polanyi, Karl (1957a), Aristotle Discovers the Economy, in Karl Polanyi, Conrad M. Arensberg, and Harry W. Pearson (eds.), *Trade and Market in the Early Empires: Economies in History and Theory*, Glencoe: Free Press, pp. 64–94.
Polanyi, Karl (1957b), The Economy as Instituted Process, in Karl Polanyi, Conrad M. Arensberg, and Harry W. Pearson (eds.), *Trade and Market in the Early Empires: Economies in History and Theory*, Glencoe: Free Press, pp. 243–270.
Polanyi, Karl (1966), *Dahomey and the Slave Trade: An Analysis of an Archaic Economy*, Seattle: University of Washington Press.
Polanyi, Karl (1977), *The Livelihood of Man*, ed. by H.W. Pearson, New York: Academic Press.
Polanyi Levitt, Karl (2006), Keynes and Polanyi: The 1920s and the 1990s, *Review of International Political Economy*, Vol.13, No.1, pp. 152–177.
Roth, Guenther (2003), The Near-Death of Liberal Capitalism: Perceptions from the Weber to the Polanyi Brothers, *Politics and Society*, Vol.31, No.2, pp. 263–282.
Streeck, Wolfgang (2009), *Re-Forming Capitalism: Institutional Change in the German Political Economy*, Oxford: Oxford University Press.

Chapter 3
What Would the Emperors Have Done Differently in 1914 if One of Their Advisors Had Carefully Followed the *Österreichische Volkswirt*? *

Jürgen Backhaus

The "Emperors" we are now talking about are of course the German Emperor [that was his title, he was not Emperor of Germany, but his title was German Emperor], and the Emperor and King of Hungary. [That is why you have k + k, the first one stands for "kaiserlich", and the second one for "königlich".] The focus is on the Emperor of Austria and the King of Hungary. A point to be developed later, because it plays a role in Stolper's argument. Again, it is Gustav Stolper[1] himself who writes the central argument. So I first should like to tell you, what is the purpose[2] of the question, and then I should like to tell you what I found, then I will develop the main argument of the central article that I found, then I want to come to the answer.

At the time in 1914, economics was still taught by economists who were interested in the economy and for that reason I thought that a journal, which is calling itself "The Austrian Economist", would not do "Austrian economics", but would do economics from Austria and in this sense actually provides something useful in terms of information. The current situation is, of course, that economics is often done in a way that provides little insight to the economy. This remark is not intended as criticism as such. Economics has developed from cameralism to a method, there is no reason to be upset about the economics of crime, the economics of law, the economics of prostitution, these are all recent topics in the *European Journal of Law and Economics*; but also the economics of building nations and the economics of democracy in order to give you examples of recent really exciting developments in economics.

---

*This paper was first presented at the 20th Heilbronn Symposium in Economics and the Social Sciences, June 21–24, 2007, Heilbronn, Germany.

[1] Stolper, Gustav 1914. Article on the assassination in *Der Österreichische Volkswirt*.

[2] The third Emperor involved is the Tsar of Russia. He was the first to loose his throne (and life) in the events unfolding in 1914.

J. Backhaus (✉)
Universität Erfurt, Nordhäuser Strasse 63, 99089 Erfurt, Germany
e-mail: juergen.backhaus@unierfurt.de

On the one hand, economics is not necessarily only about the economy, because even as Mandeville[3] pointed out, the bees are behaving in a very economical manner, although they are not behaving in the sense economists tend to assume, at least they do not decide, they follow innate instincts. On the other hand, a recent development in economics, experimental economics, is actually going back to the assumptions of Mandeville and does not take opportunity costs[4] into account. To be sure, costs and choices are known to experimental economists today. From the modern point of view, it is not a problem as such if economists deal with other things than economics or, to be more precise, other things than those we find in the economy. As a matter of fact, the economy is full of phenomena that are not readily explained in an economic way. Take the example of fiscal sociology; take the example of Bücher. He is certain and emphasizes it that gift exchange is important in a *modern* economy and gifts are exchanged for reasons that are beyond economic considerations pure and simple. Titimus was of the opinion that the whole area of health can only be organized in non-economic ways and that is why the gift relationship was then discussed at his instigation. So it is quite possible that other people than economists have important things to say about economic affairs and so this simple notion – "economists talk about the economy" and "sociologists about the society" – that does not hold anymore. Sociologists have a way to analyze problems as Dahrendorf[5] has said in his Inaugural Lecture in Konstanz. That is the model of the *homo sociologicus*, and the economists of course have the *homo economicus*, these are competing approaches. The question is, of course, which one explains more with respect to a particular question and that requires that there is actually a question.

This is interesting, as we now get to the date, 1914, and the attempt at Sarajevo, the successful assassination of the k + k Crown Prince and his wife. The first question is: what is the question and what are the questions that this prompts? What kind of questions does an economist ask in Homo sociologicus? When we say 1914, we think of the beginning of the First World War, into which in 1917 the Americans stepped and tipped the balance. But was this the perception in July 1914? A relevant piece of information I learned from a Hungarian colleague, at the Hungarian Academy of Sciences, has prompted me to pose this question I shall now develop. A little bit of this background is actually discussed in *Der Österreichische Volkswirt*.

Germany was a confederated empire and it had as an empire hardly any tax base. They had primarily seignorage, after they had gotten so far as to launch an own currency. Germany started out with not only two dozen different currencies, but also even two different currency standards, and only in 1873, at the instigation of the Prussian Chancellor, who had a shrewd advisor, a Jewish banker by the name of Bleichenröder, he came up with the notion, the seignorage only in mind, to launch an imperial currency, and all that was minted was just one coin. They took as the standard the pure accounting currencies that the Hanseatic cities had used,

---

[3] The Fable of the Bees (Mandeville).
[4] James M. Buchanan, *Cost and Choice*. Chicago: University of Chicago Press, 1969.
[5] Dahrendorf, Inaugural Lecture in Konstanz.

Marcobanco, which had no real-world equivalent, and they just minted originally gold coins, and thereby quietly and very carefully introduced a common currency in the country that had two currency standards, gold and silver. This country, a confederated country consisting of 25 states, among them four kingdoms, nevertheless had a clear constitution. The exception was the 25th state, which was Alsace-Lorraine under the direct administration of the Imperial Chancellor. This feature had the interesting side effect that the Empire always had one legislative ground, where the Empire could push a legislative initiative and show that it worked by introducing it in Alsace-Lorraine. Actually, Moritz Julius Bonn[6] points to this and criticizes the Imperial Administration for its lack of effort to use this experimental ground. Today, federal legislation in Germany often has an experimental clause; one of the 16 states may just try something out and another state does something else. The federal act then sets a date by which time the parliament will decide on a common model based on this experience. So the criticism of Julius Moritz Bonn, which he also uses in terms of explaining the events of 1914 has to do with what he conceives of as a lack of reform effort on the part of the Imperial Prussian Administration – Prussia was the leading kingdom in the union and so had the chairmanship – what one considers a lack of vigour in reform effort on the part of that necessarily leading state. That is in July 1914 all we know is the *date* and the *event*, the k + k Crown Prince and his wife are assassinated by the student of an academic high school in Serbia.

The Empire since it had barely any tax base had as a consequence of introducing the currency an imperial central account but not a central bank; for want of another institution they just took the Prussian central bank. The bank could underwrite the issue of debt. This is indeed what the Empire did. When there was an effort on the part of the Empire and not on the part of the Member States, e.g. the Navy, the Empire could issue debt, and the debt had a special legal advantage. For instance, custodial management, be it in the private sector or in the public sector, had to be done as far as the preservation of assets was concerned in terms of imperial debt. The term in German is "mündelsicher". This was a special signal of approval. According to German law, any foundation has to have a sufficient capital base so as to be able in a sustainable way to achieve its legal purposes. These can be very substantial amounts of money. The Empire saw indeed a lot of gift-giving in the sense of setting up large foundations. These assets had to be held in imperial bonds. This arrangement later became very important.

The possibility of controlling the central bank also included the possibility of issuing bonds and there was an additional legal privilege or imperial bonds. After the assassination something very important happened. A large portion of these imperial German bonds insofar as they were not held by foundations but by French investors was suddenly sold at the Berlin exchange. This fact was picked up by *Der Österreichische Volkswirt* and explained with two arguments:

Argument one is the structural argument. The French banking system essentially is an oligopoly, and you can essentially take decisions at one coffee table because

---

[6] In his book *Elsässer Erinnerungen* (*Memoirs from the Alsace*), he was a professor at Strassburg.

only a handful of decision makers hold the entire bank. The other fact that needs to be mentioned is that apparently the cut that you always offer the launching bank when you launch a public bond issue that the German Imperial Bank was willing to offer was larger than what the French Central Bank was willing to offer. This is why the banking cartel in France proffered the German bonds on its public when it was perfectly normal for French people to save in bonds for early retirement.

Now the fact that I have only mentioned, but not yet explained, is that between the declaration of war and the assassination attempt what must have amounted to the entire outstanding German debt in France was unloaded on the German market. I got this information, because of the following thought. Albert O. Hirshman, a German émigré scholar of great repute, distinguished fellow of the *American Economic Association* and author of the book *The Passions and Interests: Political Arguments for Capitalism before Its Triumph*[7] has written this book in order to remind us of all those books and articles and ideas in the history of economic thought (Mandeville, Smith, and others) of the following argument forthright: Countries that trade with each other do not engage in wars against each other.

So my thought was if a very large portion of the German imperial debt was owned by French citizens, it was totally impossible for these two nations to fight a war, and in particular such a bloody war against each other. And since we know that the war of 1914–1918 was an extremely bloody one, totally new was the strategy of field Marshall von Falkenhain to fight a war of attrition which cost at Verdun more than half a million lives, and that scenario would have been impossible if the soldiers that were asked to fight actually fought the debtor whose bonds they needed for their retirement. My Hungarian colleague explained to me that indeed was pretty much unloaded on the Berlin market. Such a large operation could not have gone unnoticed. I carefully looked in *Der Österreichische Volkswirt* for an account of this operation and I looked in vain.

So what could the avid reader of *Der Österreichische Volkswirt* have told the Emperors? There is a very extensive article on the assassination in Sarajevo, which goes in a deep analysis of the constitutional situation of the Austro-Hungarian Empire. It is actually an interesting attempt in constitutional public finance. Because as the author, Gustav Stolper, points out the Empire has a poor structure,[8] he writes, there is a streak of potential dangers, one adding to the other. And it is the danger of a conflict between the Croats and the Serbs, who distinguish each other only by one characteristic, not their language, but their belief. In fact, he writes, the Catholic clergy, on the Croat side, is constantly fanning the flames of that conflict and the Serbian Kingdom is always happy to be engaged.

Now, the question of whether the academic high school student, the perpetrator was readily found, was actually essentially directed from Belgrade was a question that was indeed discussed at the time, and although the Serbian government came up with a rather lukewarm note of regret, they never said anything to the extent that

---

[7] Princeton, N.J.: Princeton University Press, Dahrendorf 2001, 2006; Hirschmann 1977.
[8] He is not talking about the k + k Empire as I had explained it before, from Istria to Bosnia.

they anything to do with it, the press which was carefully looked at by the crew at *Der Österreichische Volkswirt* and clearly by the crew in the Austrian diplomacy, could not fail to notice that the Serbian press almost competed to write articles about how important it was to finally kill this Crown Prince. So, in a way what the clergy did in Croatia, the press did in Belgrade and this is the first part of the focus of this article by Gustav Stolper.

Gustav Stolper then draws a most peculiar conclusion. Since from Istria to Bosnia-Herzegovina, Bosnia and Herzegovina had been annexed by Austria-Hungary in a totally bloodless effort; this is unbelievable. We know of very bloody conflicts in Bosnia-Herzegovina, but Eugen Freiherr von Philippovich[9] and Philipbergs father received this beautiful title because he commanded the campaign in Bosnia-Herzegovina to annex the province, and that was a conflict, of course, between Austria and Turkey; now, as in the case of Albania, where they have installed the Prince of Wied as a King, who really did not have much to enjoy there, the case of Bosnia-Herzegovina, although it was bloodless, did not bring anything to be happy about. As a matter of fact, the article goes into long discussions about the reports that the administrator sends to Vienna, the administrator by the way was a doctor juris, and the article says the reports are always talking about progress, but the only thing we know about Bosnia-Herzegovina is that first we had the annexation and now it is costing endlessly. The country is not really making much in the way of progress. There is no infrastructure, we have to pour money into it, but there are no tax receipts. The article continues to say that the political discussion in Vienna first of course always focused on the conflict between the demands of the Hungarians and what the Viennese government could accommodate, and that is why you have the k plus k, and then on the demands of the Czechs, which were continuously the focus of political concern, and the Chancellor Graf Bechthold, being sidetracked by the Czech problem, could not focus on the Balkan issue.

The peculiar construction of Czechoslovakia of 1918, an American idea, included the Czechs, the Slovaks, originally five million Germans, and of course a very large Jewish community. That peculiar construction seemed to assume that Czechs and Slovaks are basically the same and so one people of one nation, and that the Germans and the Jews did not exist. As a matter of fact, Wilson is reported to have been asked on the ship that brought him to the peace negotiations in Versailles, when he was coached. The coach asked him, "Mr. President, what do you plan to do with the five million Germans?" and he is reported to have said, "Professor Mazaryk, I was not told there were any Germans there". So, there was already a longstanding conflict with the so-called Czech-question, but the Slovaks were part of the Hungarian Kingdom. So, this was for this reason only a Czech-question, and it was a Czech-question because the Czechs requested independence. On the other hand, what would you have done then with this request and then how would the Czechs have dealt with the Jews who also had certain privileges? There were large Jewish communities in Bohemia and Moravia with a large extent of autonomy.

---

[9] Philippovich, Eugen Freiherr von. *Die Entwicklung der wirtschaftspolitischen Ideen im 19. Jahrhundert*. Tübingen: J. C. B. Mohr, 1910.

So, that was his focus, and Stolper in his article says it should not have been our only concern, because this "stretch of land from Istria to Bosnia", this is his formulation, was poor, in decay, and a costly proposition anyway, in need of "a well trained civil service and local autonomy in this stretch of land from Istria to Bosnia-Herzegovina". Then, the article continues, the assassination presents a very good opportunity to do just that because, in fact, the Crown Prince was not a mover of reform. He was very impatient and used up a lot of political and administrative talent, and that is why, in the present situation, there is hardly an able and courageous civil servant left who is willing to take responsibility. One should change that and introduce a constitutional reform so as also to get away from the single focus on the Czech problem. Austria has more than one nationality problem and they should be dealt with similarly and once and for all. Each province should have certain autonomy and a well-trained responsible, absolutely incorruptible civil service. Then economic development will occur and, the article continues, the time is excellent for this to be done because the Serbs are so clearly in the wrong at this moment that neither Britain, nor France, nor their continuous mentor, the Russian Empire, will dare come to their side and so we can peacefully enact this reform.

It did not take long, on 5 August, the declaration of war was issued. What could the Emperors have learned? The German Emperor could have learned that his Austrian ally had a deep problem, which he himself did not have and did not much care about either. They could have learned that there was a latent danger of war with Turkey. That was the war they were concerned with. The German Emperor could have learned that his major concern should be to keep the Austrian ally from engaging in such a war with Turkey. He would not have learned anything about a war with either France, or Britain, or Russia, because the article explicitly said that compared with earlier times that war would be totally improbable at this point of time. On 1 August 1914 the Austrian Emperor would have learned from the article that he should be careful not to overdo it with Turkey. Turkey is always referred to as a deep "Pforte" (gate), which means the opening where the ships could go through from the Mediterranean to the Black Sea, and they kept, of course, the gate. The Austrian Emperor could have learned that he could use the opportunity for imperial reform, in particular in the stretch of land between Istria and Bosnia. Interestingly enough, he could not have learned about the imminent war that was about to start, of course, in Eastern Prussia, and with the attempted landing of the Russian navy in Pommerania. On that issue, there is no information to be found in *Der Österreichische Volkswirt* in 1914.

In sum, Stolper's concern was not about Serbia which he considered isolated. His only concern was a war with Turkey.

References

Dahrendorf, Ralf, *Homo Sociologicus. Ein Versuch zur Geschichte, Bedeutung und Kritik der Kategorie der sozialen Rolle*, 16. Aufl., Wiesbaden: VS Verlag für Sozialwissenschaften 2006.

Dahrendorf, *Inaugural Lecture in Konstanz – Is this the same?*: Dahrendorf, Ralf, 2001: *Über die Machbarkeit der guten Ordnung* in: Allmendinger (Hrsg.), 2001, 1330–1337.

Albert O. Hirschmann, 1977. *The Passions and the Interests*: *Political Arguments for Capitalism Before Its Triumph*. Princeton, NJ: Princeton University Press.

Philippovich, Eugen Freiherr von. 1910. *Die Entwicklung der wirtschaftspolitischen Ideen im 19. Jahrhundert*. Tübingen: J. C. B. Mohr.

Gustav Stolper, 1914. Article on the assassination in: *Der Österreichische Volkswirt*.

Chapter 4
Demography in Germany at the Beginning of the Twentieth Century in the Light of *Der Deutsche Volkswirt* *

Gerhard Scheuerer

4.1 Introduction

In Germany, at the beginning of the twentieth century, scientific demography was based on classical political-economic theory, as it was in other countries. German academics and representatives of governmental statistic authorities postulated the use of statistical data in economic and social sciences. They established the Association for Social Policy in 1872 and the German Society for Sociology in 1909. Also in 1909, the German political sociologist (Kathedersozialist) and welfare scientist, Lujo Brentano, formulated his theory regarding the competition of pleasures (Genüsse) in relation to a population's fertility behaviour. Using Gossen's Second Law, Brentano can be considered a promoter of The Theory of the Family. In 1928, the German sociologist, Julius Wolff, criticised Brentano and introduced a sociological treatment of demography and fertility, which he named the new sexual morality.

---

*This paper was first presented at the 20th Heilbronn Symposium in Economics and the Social Sciences, June 21–24, 2007, Heilbronn, Germany.

G. Scheuerer (✉)
University of Erfurt,
Nordhäuser Strasse 63, 99089 Erfurt, Germany
e-mail: gerhard.scheuerer@t-online.de

"Der Deutsche Volkswirt" dealt with demographic issues at the turn end of twenties and beginning of thirties of the twentieth century. Ernst Kahn[1] published an essay on population retrogression in which he mainly followed Brentano's economic view and combined it with some sociological views of Julius Wolff. Kahn, as a Jewish person, names himself an "outsider",[2] arguing against the Nazi-ideology: he produced a different description of a fact which focused a "foreign body" (Fremdkörper) in a widespread national political ideology at that time in Germany.

4.2 Scientific Status of Demography in Germany at the Turn to the Twentieth Century

It is a commonly known fact that declining fertility in European countries started at the end of the nineteenth/beginning of the twentieth century.[3] During that time, demography was obviously not an independent science. Up until that time, demographic discussions were based on the classical political economics of Adam Smith, who argued that population growth has positive effects on society because it leads to economic growth. The theoretical views on demography go back to Malthus's theorems, which he published the first time at the end of the eighteenth century. Malthus held the belief that a population grows when its economic supply, measured as individual income, grows.[4] Malthus's theorems contradict empirical results, which prove fertility declines when income grows. Therefore, Malthus's theorems have been criticised continuously from the very beginning. Scientific discussions on population development and fertility considering the criticism of Malthus's theorems started at the end of the nineteenth century in Germany. At first (around 1870), the criticisms were rather mild, but they became stronger about 1900. Scientific discussions about demography arose essentially from governmental population statistics, which continuously improved statistical methods and presented more detailed arrangements of statistical data in the first decades of the twentieth century.

---

[1] Dr. phil.h.c. Ernst Kahn (1884–1959) was a relative of a distinguished and influential Jewish family in Frankfurt/Main. Today a street in Frankfurt's Nordweststadt is named after him. Kahn was co-partner of Lazard Speyer-Ellissen Bank from 1921 to 1933 and Chairman of the supervisory board of Colour Leather Factory Bonames AG, of the Frankfurter Baukasse AG, and many other boards. He was honorary town councillor (as a Social Democrat) and head of local ground-planning department, and lecturer on housing, the national economy, and statistics at Johann Wolfgang Goethe University Frankfurt/Main. He was a sociologist, committed to social policy, founded the Research Institute for Housing in Frankfurt/Main (Forschungsstelle für Wohnungswesen in Frankfurt am Main) and the Association Open Kitchen for the Unemployed (Verein für Erwerbslosenküche). Kahn emigrated in 1933 via England and the USA to Palestine (Frankfurter Biographie (1994)).
[2] Kahn (1930 II), p 212.
[3] Notestein (1945).
[4] Malthus (1798, 1872).

4.3 Attempts to Introduce Consistent Statistical Data in Scientific Research

Academics and members of governmental statistics established the Association for Social Policy ("Verein für Socialpolitik") in Germany in the year 1872. The association persecuted two main reasons:

1. To postulate the use of statistical data in the science
2. To spread independent statistical science

Members of the Association discussed a lot of practical and theoretical topics regarding the industrialisation of society. Of course, there were different opinions and they were discussed in the assemblies; some differences were unconquerable. In 1909, the German Society for Sociology ("Deutsche Gesellschaft für Soziologie") was established; consequently, as separation from the Association for Social Policy. As a result, sociology began developing as an independent academic science in German universities. At the beginning, this was primarily theoretical in nature and lacking in extensive empirical research. Social research, including the use of empirical statistical data, focused more and more attention on this when the Research Institute for Social Sciences at the University Cologne ("Forschungsinstitut für Sozialwissenschaft an der Universität zu Köln") was founded in the year 1919 (with internationally renowned sociologists e.g. Lindemann, Scheler, von Wiese, Brauer) and the Institute for Social Research at the University Frankfurt/Main ("Institut für Sozialforschung an der Universität Frankfurt/Main") was founded in the year 1924 (with internationally renowned sociologists e.g. Grünberg, Horkheimer, Marcuse, Adorno). Both Institutes stopped their activities at the beginning of the Nazi dictatorship and started their activities again after World War II. Therefore, German sociologists did not take part in developments in the use of empirical data in social research, which had advanced greatly in the 1930s, especially in the United States.

4.4 Political Economics

Welfare economics had already started to be developed as sociology became more and more meaningful in Germany at the beginning of the twentieth century. Pareto proved already in 1909 that economic optimum is possible without the population factor. Malthus's theorems were considered to be impractical in an industrial economy. The German political sociologist (Kathedersozialist) and welfare scientist Lujo Brentano published economic views in 1909. Concerning a population's fertility behaviour, he formulated a theory of competition among the different pleasures (Genüsse).[5] He argued that increasing consumption and striving for higher social class influences sexual desire and fondness for children, based on Gossen's Second Law.

---

[5] Brentano (1909).

Brentano takes into account benefits and therefore can be considered a precursor of current theories regarding the Economics of The Family, which takes into consideration opportunity costs as a scale of maximising benefit.

In 1928, the German sociologist Julius Wolf published his book entitled "The New Morality Regarding Sex and the Current Birth Problem" ("Die neue Sexualmoral und das Geburtenproblem unserer Tage").[6] He criticises Brentano's argument that capitalism changes feelings and customs, resulting from economisation. The main point in Wolff's argumentation is the change of morality as a social view.

It must be stated that the obvious scientific status of demography in the wide sense of scientific explanation of population development, however, was not established until after the 1930s.

4.5 "Der Deutsche Volkswirt" and Demography

The editor Gustav Stolpe strengthened the programme of "Der Deutsche Volkswirt" in its first issue by describing "the mutual interaction of policy and the economy".[7] News and results of the government's demographic statistics have been published regularly from the beginning. Population retrogression and economies were discussed in three essays in 1929. A fourth essay on this topic was written by Ernst Kahn and published in 1930[8] when Kahn presented parts of his book "The International Birth Strike"[9] (Der internationale Geburtenstreik).

Kahn bases his considerations on statistical data and according to the aims of the German Society for Sociology ("Deutsche Gesellschaft für Soziologie"), which was founded in 1909. He describes the following topics:

- Hidden realities, misleading statistics
- Population in foreign countries
- Economic future

Kahn criticises some methods and definitions used in governmental population statistics. He describes in detail actual situations of employment, production, consumption, housing, public finance, etc. Kahn takes into account what he considers three important causes of population retrogression, which combine both economic and social variables regarding fertility:

- Contraception, abortion
- Overestimation of economic motivation
- Infidelity and rationalism

---

[6] Wolf, Julius (1928).
[7] Der Deutsche Volkswirt (1926).
[8] Kahn (1930 I).
[9] Kahn (1930 II).

Kahn picks up on the considerations of Brentano; he studied the relationship between benefits and opportunity costs and can therefore also be considered a further precursor of the Theory of the Family developed by Gary S. Becker in the 1950s. But at the same time, Kahn pointed out an overestimation of economic motivation and he anticipated to a certain extent criticism of economic imperialism as we know it today. Furthermore, besides economic considerations, Kahn also included social considerations to a certain extent such as infidelity and abortion. The latter is not discussed in actual scientific and political discussions on fertility in Germany. Kahn formulates his own model of future population development in Germany, discussing and calculating structural changes in different economic fields, which will be provoked by changing age structure for example food, rents, clothing, luxury goods, etc. and their effects on other economic sectors. He demonstrates with his calculations that German Jews will age and their number will diminish up to 1970s.[10]

Kahn's explanations follow mainly Lujo Brentano's economic views and only to a small extent the social views of Julius Wolff concerning the new sexual morality.

In the year 1931, half a year after Kahn's essay, a fifth essay on population in "Der Deutsche Volkswirt" is titled "Population Retrogression". Kahn is praised as being a practitioner and splendid academic outsider who analyses the reality of population.[11] The essay tries to find a closer connection between sociological and economic considerations. It also describes, among other things, the following topics, saying that

1. Economic theory is based mostly on ceteris paribus assumption and treats many variables to be steady
2. Population is an external factor and explains a sometimes pessimistic view (overpopulation accompanies capitalism)
3. Industrialisation
   - Creates welfare
   - Influences human psyche

Kahn is praised for his 1930 essay in which he produced a theory opposite to the widespread opinion at the time and in which he discussed several future structural changes in different economic fields. The essay concludes that the strength of the economic reality gives politicians no chance to change the strength of the birth reality. They can only adjust laws effecting practice of having children and, however, the moralist will have his chance sooner or later.[12]

---

[10] Der Deutsche Volkswirt (1931), p 857.
[11] Der Deutsche Volkswirt (1931), p 855.
[12] Der Deutsche Volkswirt (1931), p 857.

4.6 The Nazi Time

After the Nazi's drove away the founding editor, Gustav Stolpe, in 1933, in the following years the Minister of the Interior, the Secretary of the Interior, some presidents of state statistical offices and of other state agencies published essays on demography and described at great length the criminal Nazi population policy in "Der Deutsche Volkswirt". Academics and experts of Nazi ideology were praised for doing so. "Der Deutsche Volkswirt" was brought into line (Gleichschaltung) and "Der Deutsche Volkswirt" streamlined to make it consistent with the Nazi's political ideology.

References

Brentano, Ludwig Josef: Die Malthussche Lehre und die Bevölkerungsbewegung der letzten Dezennien; Abhandlungen der Historischen Klasse der Königlich Bayerischen Akademie der Wissenschaften, 24, Band III, München 1909
Der Deutsche Volkswirt. Zeitschrift für Politik und Wirtschaft. 1. Jahrgang, Nr. 1 1926, p 11–13
Der Deutsche Volkswirt. Zeitschrift für Politik und Wirtschaft. 5. Jahrgang, Nr. 26 1931, pp 854–857 (abbreviation for author: T. St.)
Frankfurter Biographie: Personengeschichtliches Lexikon, herausgegeben von Wolfgang Klötzer, Band 1, Kramer Frankfurt Main 1994, p 382
Kahn, Ernst (1930 I): Bevölkerungsrückgang und Wirtschaft. In: Der Deutsche Volkswirt, Zeitschrift für Politik und Wirtschaft. 5. Jahrgang Nr. 5 1930, pp 142–148
Kahn, Ernst (1930 II): Der internationale Gebrutenstreik: Umfang, Wirkungen, Gegenmaßnahmen? Frankfurter Societäts-Verlag Frankfurt 1930
Malthus, Thomas R.: An Essay on the Principle of Population as it Affects the Future of Society; Murray London 1798
Malthus, Thomas R.: An Essay on the Principle of Population, or, a view of its past and present effects on human happiness; with an inquiry into our prospects respecting the future removal or mitigation of the evils which it occasions; Reeves and Turner London 8. Edition 1872
Notestein, Frank W.: Population – the long view. In: Schulz, Theodore (Ed.): Food for the World, University of Chicago Press, Chicago 1945, pp 36–57
Wolf, Julius: Die neue Sexualmoral und das Geburtenproblem unserer Tage. Fischer Jena 1928

Chapter 5
Issues of Economic Policy in Germany in the Interbellum

Gerrit Meijer

5.1 Introduction

In the issues of the Austrian and the German Economist, articles are published in which it is tried to explain theoretically what happens and to find a solution for the practical problems of the day on which the journal reports. In this paper, this will be illustrated with regard to the following topics. In the first section, this is monetary theory, in particular the discussion on the nature and value of money in the OVW (Austrian Economist) of 1912. The second section is on the business cycle theory which was elaborated on the basis of the Austrian monetary theory and capital theory: the monetary overinvestment theory and proposals with regard to the problems of the so-called Great Depression. The third section is on the constitution of the state. This concerns discussions on and proposals for political and financial reforms during the second half of the Weimar Republic. The fourth section is on some important aspects of the economic constitution: agriculture, economic power, and future of capitalism. The fifth section is on the attitude of the DVW (the German Economist) to national socialism before and after 1933, and also pays attention to the relation of the journal to neo-liberalism, its roots, and development. Finally, the paper gives some conclusions.

G. Meijer (✉)
University of Maastricht, Larixlaan 3, 1231 BL Nieuw-Loosdrecht,
The Netherlands
e-mail: g.meijer@hetnet.nl

5.2 Monetary Theory

5.2.1 The Nature and Value of Money: Menger and Knapp

Around the First World War, one of the problems in Germany and Austria is the problem of (hyper)inflation and monetary policy. This discussion is related to the discussions on money. In monetary theory of about 1900, the nature and value of money are the main topics. In this respect, we mention the names and theories of Carl Menger (1840–1921) and Georg Friedrich Knapp (1842–1926). To answer the questions "What is money?" and "What is the relation between money and the state?," we will pay attention to the discussion between these two authors.

Menger is well-known as the founder of the Austrian School of Economics. His article on the origins of money (1892) was written as a contribution to the discussions on the Austro-Hungarian monetary constitution. Knapp is a member of the German Historical School who published his book *Die staatliche Theorie des Geldes* in 1905.

The answer to the first question: "What is money?" depends according to Menger on what people accept and use as money. This differs according to circumstances of time and place. Although in most cases the fiat of the state comes after the introduction, sometimes it comes before. Then it is artificial, constructivist money. In this way, the spontaneous order is corrupted. The future of this money unit depends on the acceptance of it as legal tender. Most important in this respect is trust. In the long run, forced money cannot work.

With regard to the other question, it can be concluded that the difference of opinion between Knapp (1905) and Menger (1892), in which the first stated that money was a creation of the state and the latter that money had its origin in convention, was not an absolute one. Menger was aware of the fact that the state defines in modern times what the money unit is. Knapp knew from history that money as an institution was a result of human action, not of human design. According to Howard S. Ellis (1934), who extensively wrote on the Menger-Knapp discussion, Knapp did not write and contend that the state determined the value but only the validity of money (the acceptance as legal tender). The state can mismanage money as well as reform the monetary system. Examples are the German hyperinflation after World War I and the German monetary reform (1948) after World War II. Although the state not always defined what money is at all times and places (especially not in prehistory) and later on not for all kinds of money (due to the problem of defining what money is), it usually did. However, it were always people that in the end decided what money is, in spite of what the state had decided. The state is providing a service: seigniorage. People can refuse the money. In the short run, the state can dispose. In the long run, the people disposes (Meijer et al. 2006: 70).

5.2.2 Federn on Knapp and Mises

This discussion resounds in the *Oesterreichische Volkswirt* (Austrian Economist), referred to as OVW. Knapp is supported and followed by W.F. (Federn), the editor at that time (1912a). Federn (1869–1949) is of the opinion that Knapp's book has been of so great influence for two reasons. First, because of "the crystal clear construction of the theory, the common sense character of the doctrines, which could be summarized in a few propositions which were clear also for those who were not able or willing to study the book themselves."[1] Second, because of the actuality of the questions "which Knapp raised and for the first time completely answered."[2]

There was, Federn notices, a gap in Knapp's theory, filled up by Bendixen: the theory of the value of money (Federn 1912a: 1017). According to Federn, many metallists (especially Helfferich) have "moderated their demands."[3] However: "It are in particular the adherents to the School of Vienna, the marginal value theorists, to whom the lack of discussion of the problem of value gives rise to complete rejection of his doctrine. This has happened in particular in a recently published book of Ludwig von Mises."[4] According to Federn (1912a: 1017), the American economist Fisher, however, although an adherent of the marginal theory, connects Knapp's theory with his Quantity Theory of Money.

Federn disagrees with Mises (1881–1993), whose book on The Theory of Money and Credit (original in German *Theorie des Geldes und der Umlaufsmittel, 1912; second edition 1924*), on which he habilitated in 1913 at the University of Vienna, was fiercely criticized (Federn 1912b–e). Later on, the book was translated in English (1934), second edition in 1953 and the third edition 1981. The review of Mises's book by Federn (1912b–e) is a curious one and a good example of refusing discussion (Voegelin 1959: 367–368). The following list of observations by Federn can support this: The review starts with a few defamatory remarks. Then it gives an inaccurate exposition of the marginal value theory. Last but not least, without proof, Mises is disqualified as a bad/weak theorist, and a stranger in the world of financial affairs. One can understand that Mises was not amused of this kind of treatment of his scientific work, and this attack *ad personam* (Mises 1978: 30f.). In the second edition, Mises criticizes the President of the Reichsbank Havenstein and the Minister of Finance Hilferding for their depreciation policy of the mark in the relation to gold in 1923 as inflationary (Mises 1981: 230).

---

[1] "krystallklare Aufbau der Theorie, die Gemeinverständlichkeit der aufgestellten Lehrsätze, die in wenigen Sätzen zusammenfaszbar auch für jene einleuchtend waren, die nicht im Stande oder willens (sic G.M.), das Werk selbst durch zu arbeiten."

[2] "der Knapp Aufwarf und zum ersten Mal restlos beantwortete."

[3] "Wasser in dem Alten Wein getan" vor allem Helfferich.

[4] "Es sind besonders die Anhänger der Wiener Schule, die Grenzwerttheoretiker, denen die mangelnde Auseinandersetzung Knapps mit der Wertfrage Anlasz zur vollständigen Verwerfung seiner Lehre bietet. Dies ist insbesonders in einem kürzlich erschienenen Buche von Ludwig von Mises Geschehen."

5.3 Business Cycle Theory

At the end of the twenties and in the early thirties, the discussion in the *Deutsche Volkswirt* (the German Economist), referred to as DVW, switches to the theory of the business cycle in relation to business cycle policy. The forerunners in business cycle theory (the monetary overinvestment theory) were Wicksell (1898) and Mises (1912). In DVW, there are contributions related to this subject by G. Haberler, L.A. Hahn, F.A. Hayek, C. Landauer, H. Neisser, W. Röpke, A. Rüstow, H. Schacht, G. Schmölders, J.A. Schumpeter, G. Stolper, and Adolf Weber.

Carl Landauer (1891–1983) was a regular contributor to the journal from 1926 to 1933. On business cycle theory and policy, he wrote the following articles: Capital and Business Cycle (*Kapital und Konjunktur* 1927a), The German business cycle (*Die deutsche Konjunktur* 1927b), and under the title Free Banking (*Bankfreiheit* 1928e), an extensive and critical review of the book of Mises on *Geldwertstabilisierung und Konjunkturpolitik* (1928). Later on, he published again a series of three articles on business cycle theory: Secular crisis or business cycle (*Dauerkrise oder Konjunkturwelle* 1930); Causes of Crises (*Ursachen der Krisen* 1931a); and Scarcity of Capital as Cause of Crises (*Kapitalknappheit als Krisenursache* 1931b). *Mises* (1881–1973) sees the action of commercial banks as the origin of the business cycle. The objective of policy has to be to avoid all actions to artificially lower the interest rate and in this way to foster prosperity by credit. This can be done by introducing the free banking principle and to stop all intervention in banking by the state. Another less far going proposal is to maintain a fixed amount of credit, like in the Peel Act (compare Ellis 1934: 338). Landauer thinks these policy advices are too strict and/or unrealistic. His position with regard to credit policy is closer to Hayek. Hayek is more flexible in his policy advice: he proposes credit policy with neutral money as a norm.

Wilhelm Röpke (1899–1966) published articles on Eternal Prosperity (*Ewige Prosperität 1931a), reprinted in Röpke (1962); Monetary Theory and World Crisis (Geldtheorie und Weltkrise 1932*); and Autarky – a worn out slogan (*Autarkie- ein abgenutztes Schlagwort* 1933). He was one of the members of the *Brauns-Kommission* (1931c). For his contribution to business cycle theory and policy, see some of his publications (1931, 1932, 1936) and the publications on this subject by Allgoewer (2009, 2010, 2), Backhaus (1997), and Meijer (1988, 75–79, 99–100).

Alexander Rüstow (1885–1963) contributed with an article that became classic. In 1932, it was published under the title: *Interessenpolitik oder Staatspolitik in DVW* (Bd 7, nr 6, 169–172). This article was his contribution to the discussion within the *Verein für Socialpolitik* in Dresden 1932: *Freie Wirtschaft –Starker Staat (Die staatspolitischen Voraussetzungen des wirtschaftspolitischen Liberalismus), Schriften des Vereins für Socialpolitik,* Bd 187, 62–69. He pleads for a strong state, that means a state above the pressure groups. State intervention has to go in the direction the market works, not against the laws of the market. This also has to be the criterion for subsidies. This is the basis for the distinction between adaptation and maintenance interventions (subsidies). The state has to resist (counterbalance) the power of the pressure groups.

Röpke and Rüstow were directly influenced by F.Oppenheimer (1864–1943), who in 1933 published a book: *Weder so noch so. Der dritte Weg*. His program of reform differs from that of Röpke and Rüstow in the economic-political respect. Leading neo-liberals like Erhard and Preiser are his pupils (Erhard 1966; Preiser 1964; Röpke 1959 (2), 344–348). Oppenheimer sees the source of much social distress in the existence of the feudal landed property. In this system, agricultural workers are exploited and he sees almost no possibility for them to settle as independent farmers. This explains the migration from the country to the industrial towns. The agricultural proletariat is transformed into an industrial proletariat. They are the industrial reserve army and press wages downwards. To remedy this situation, Oppenheimer proposes to cut up feudal landed property. He advocates producer cooperatives with joint ownership and profit sharing. His aim is to preserve the peasantry and the crafts. In this way, urbanization and industrialization can be restricted. The mentioned neo-liberal authors reject the (economic side of the) theory of Oppenheimer. Nevertheless, similar proposals of reform can be found in their writings (Meijer 1987, 585–586).

Most of these writers (with the exception of Landauer, Neisser, Schacht, Schumpeter, and Stolper) we find after World War II in the Mont Pélèrin Society and/or contributing to ORDO-*Jahrbuch für die Ordnung von Wirtschaft und Gesellschaft*, that was published since 1948 in Germany, edited by Eucken and Böhm. Most of them emigra ted, due to the political situation in Germany, about 1933 to the U.S.A, some to England, Switzerland, and Turkey. Some other went in the "inner emigration" and were, as Röpke (1946, 2: 84) remarks, able to go on with their research and sometimes even to publish (see Sect. 5.5).

From authors from outside Germany who contribute to and/or are discussed in the *Deutsche Volkswirt* in relation to the subject of this section, we mention the Americans B.M. Anderson (1886–1949) and the Englishman T.E. Gregory (1890–1970). They contributed in particular on the topic of central bank policy (Anderson 1932; Gregory 1928). Special attention is paid to the Macmillan Report in a review by T.E. Gregory (1931), who was himself a (dissenting) member of the Committee. The Macmillan Committee was called after the chairman Hugh Pattison Macmillan. Other members of the Committee were Bevin, Bradbury, Brand, Gregory, Keynes, and McKenna. The Macmillan Report/Report of Committee on Finance and Industry was published in 1931. Moreover, special attention is given to the functioning of the international monetary system: the gold standard, in particular by Hayek (1932, 1965).

5.4 The Constitution of the State: State Reform and Finance Reform

In addition to these monetary and business cycle problems, a regular topic was the constitution of the state. The Weimar Republic had a constitution that was thought to be weak and one can find an impressive set of articles on and in favor of a unitary state, and against federalism by Landauer (1927c, d, e) and W.Schall (1882–1928) (1927a, b;

1928a–e). The 1928 articles of Schall were published separately in *Schriftenreihe der Deutsche Volkswirt 4: Probleme der deutschen Staatsreform* (1928f). H. Luther (1879–1962) who was *Reichskanzler* and Minister of Finance in 1925–1926, and president of the *Reichsbank* from 1930 to 1933, contributed to these subjects as president of the *Bund zur Erneuerung des Reiches*. Special attention is paid to the relation between reform of the constitution of the state and finance reform in the direction of centralization (Landauer (1928f); Luther (1929); Schall (1927a, b, 1928f); Schumpeter (1928); and Stolper (1927a, b, 1929a)). There is affinity with the ideas of Popitz (1884–1945) (1932). J.A. Schumpeter (1883–1950) contributed meanwhile classical articles on financial policy (1926, 1927a–d). These articles were published separately in the *Schriftenreihe der Deutsche Volkswirt 2: Das deutsche Finanzproblem. Reich, Länder und Gemeinden* (1928) and reprinted in Seidl and Stolper (1985). Moreover, *Gustav Stolper* was involved in this discussion and elaborated a stabilization plan for Germany (1927b, 1929b, *Stabilisation 1929, Das deutsche Wirtschaftsproblem, Schriftenreihe der Deutsche Volkswirt 1, 1927). Ein Finanzplan. Vorschläge zur deutschen Finanzreform* in the *Schriftenreihe der Deutsche Volkswirt 8,* 1929c.

Stolper (1888–1947) was in favor of a close relationship between Germany and Austria (1917a, b, 1921). In 1925, he moved from Vienna to Berlin. In party politics, he was involved in the *Deutsche Demokratische Partei,* since 1930 the *Deutsche Staatspartei*. Several contributors to and founders of the *Deutsche Volkswirt* were also related to (or even members and representatives) this party. Among them was Theodor Heuss (1884–1963) who became later the first president of the German Federal Republic (1949–1959). He was a regular contributor (e.g., on reform of the voting system) to the *Deutsche Volkswirt* (1928a, b), and a member of the *Deutsche Reichstag* (1924–1928 and 1930–1933).

Schacht (1877–1970) was long time (from 1919 to 1926) a political companion of Stolper in the *Deutsche Demokratische Partei*. In 1926, Schacht left the party. Their political cooperation came to an end and their personal relationship was finished. They never came to reconciliation (T. Stolper 1960: 326). From 1923 to 1930, Schacht was president of the Reichsbank. Schacht was in opposition to the Young-plan. On this subject, Stolper in 1930 came in open conflict with Schacht. Schacht resigns in 1930 as president of the Reichsbank. As Toni Stolper (1960: 207) writes: He fought a hard public battle with his friend Schacht, when Schacht after the signing of the Young-plan lost his way.[5]

5.5 Some Aspects of the Economic Constitution

Agriculture is an ever-returning subject of discussion. The main author is F.Baade (1893–1974). He wrote two series of articles. The first (1927a–c) on European agriculture was again published under the title *Entwicklungsmöglichkeiten der*

---

[5] "Er kämpfte mit seinem Freund Schacht eine harte öffentliche Fehde aus, als dieser nach der Unterzeichnung des Young-Planes Haltung und Richtung verlor."

europäischen Landwirtschaft, in the *Schriftenreihe der Deutsche Volkswirt 3* (1928). The second, on rye policy (1930), was reprinted in the *Schriftenreihe der Deutsche Volkswirt 10*: *Deutsche Roggenpolitik* (1931). Moreover, Dietze (1935, 1942), Gothein, Klepper, and Koehler have to be mentioned among others.

In the interbellum, another important topic is economic power. Landauer wrote on Power and Economy (*Macht und Wirtschaft* 1928b); Economic Law and Economic Constitution (*Wirtschaftsgesetz und Wirtschaftsverfassung* 1928c); and The Play Margin of Wage Policy (*Der Spielraum der Lohnpolitik* 1928d).

The problem of cartels and trusts is discussed in a series of articles on reform of the company law (Koehler, Mossler, Vogelstein 1931) and on competition policy by Vogelstein (1927, 1928a–d), published also as *Probleme der Monopolpolitik* of the *Schriftenreihe der Deutsche Volkswirt 5* (1928e).

Related is a discussion which took place on the ideas of Schmalenbach (1873–1955). This discussion is between Schmalenbach on the one side and Landauer (1928a) and Stolper (1928a, b, c) on the other side. The thesis of Schmalenbach is that technical development leads to big firms, in particular in the coal and steel industry, because of high fixed costs. For this reason, firms loose their adaptability and therefore injure the flexibility of the market process. This would result in the end of the free economy (Schmalenbach 1928, 1958, 3).

5.6 The Attitude of DVW Towards National Socialism and Neo-Liberalism

5.6.1 Attitude of the DVW to National Socialism Before and After 1933

Browsing over most of the volumes of DVW this journal until 1933 clearly was opposed to National Socialism. For that reason it was forbidden and it forced Stolper to leave for the U.S.A. The same is the case for most of the contributors. After 1933 the journal takes another course, because "it came in more compliant hands" (T. Stolper, 317).[6] In these volumes some writers look at the work of the Freiburg School c.q. ORDO-school. Some publications of the neo- or ORDO-liberals (published in 1936 and following years in the series *Ordnung der Wirtschaft*) are used as source for a so-called national socialist economic policy e.g., by H.J. Schneider (1943a, b). It concerns especially the work of Miksch (1937) and Böhm (1933, 1937) on competition policy, and a book published by Schmölders (1942) with contributions of e.g., Böhm, Eucken, Jessen, and Miksch, also on competition policy, which is very favorable reviewed in the same publication (1943: 949). Goerdeler and Schacht were both pro free market. During the economic crisis of 1935–1936 Schacht together with Goerdeler (*Preiskommissar*) helped lead the "free market"

---

[6] "weil es in fügsamere Hände" (Toni Stolper, 317) überging.

faction in the German government. They lost this struggle on the direction of the economy. Schacht who was in 1933 again appointed president of the Reichsbank 1933–1939 and in 1934 Minister of Economic Affairs, was put aside and became Minister without Portfolio in 1939.

5.6.2 The Roots of Neo-Liberalism

Looking backward, one sees the roots of neo- or ORDO liberalism in the contributions of the aforementioned authors. In earlier publications (Meijer 1987, 1988, Chap. III) I already made remarks on the beginnings of neo-liberalism, and on the relationship between neo-liberalism and national socialism during the Hitler regime. The School of Freiburg has been rather isolated in this period. The German neo-liberals despised national socialism; however, they did not openly resist in their scientific work. During the war, meetings were organized by a number of scholars under the guidance of Erwin von Beckerath (Hauenstein 1964; Salzwedel and Kloten 1966). Their reports were given and discussions were held about the problems related to the reconstruction, the transition from war economy to peace economy, and the new economic order that had to be built after the fall of Hitler. This group had connections with Goerdeler who organized the resistance in Germany against Hitler. The activities cover the period from 1941 to 1944. The meetings were mostly held at Freiburg. It is therefore that it is called the *Freiburger Kreis* (Freiburg Circle). To this group belonged Von Dietze, Eucken and Lampe from Freiburg; Böhm and Preiser from Jena; Albrecht from Marburg; Wessels and Hauenstein from Cologne; and Erwin van Beckerath and Von Stackelberg from Bonn. The latter participated only till the autumn of 1943, when he left for Madrid. This group was clearly anti-national socialist. The activities of this group have been very important for the economic policy in Germany after 1945 (see on this Lampe-Blumenberg 1986).

After the Second World War, the School of Freiburg started to publish ORDO-*Jahrbuch fur die Ordnung von Wirtschaft und Gesellschaft*, annually from 1948.

5.7 Conclusion

After the Hitler regime and the Second World War, the German economic policy meets similar problems as before. Insights have deepened and broadened during this period. The *Deutsche Volkswirt* made during the interwar period under the guidance of Stolper valuable contributions to the thinking about economic and political reforms for Germany after the war. In this paper, this was illustrated first with regard to monetary and financial policy. However, also with regard to problems of agriculture and economic power and competition, there is continuity in issues of economic policy and proposals for their solution.

References

Allgoewer, E., 2009, 2010, 2, Wilhelm Röpkes Beitrag zur modernen Konjunkturtheorie. In Rieter, H. and J. Zweynert, Hrg., Wort und Wirkung. Wilhelm Röpkes Bedeutung für die Gegenwart, Metropolis, Marburg

Anderson, B.M., 1932, Notenbanken und Warenpreise, VI.2: 1252–1256

Baade, F., 1927a, Europas Industriewirtschaft und ihre Agrarische Basis, II.1: 15–19

Baade, F., 1927b, Entwicklungsmöglichkeiten der europäischen Landwirtschaft, II.1: 49–52

Baade, F., 1927c, Bodenqualität und Bodenertrag, II.1: 80–83

Baade, F., 1928, Entwicklungsmöglichkeiten der europäischen Landwirtschaft. Schriftenreihe der Deutsche Volkswirt 3, Verlag des "Deutschen Volkswirt", Berlin

Baade, F., 1930, Deutsche Roggenpolitik, V.1: 171–177; 211–216; 244–248; 272–276; 307–311

Baade, F., 1931, Deutsche Roggenpolitik. Schriftenreihe der Deutsche Volkswirt 10, Verlag des "Deutschen Volkswirt", Berlin

Backhaus, J.G., 1997, Keynes's German Contenders 1932–1944: On the Sociology of Multiple Discoveries in Economics, History of Economic Ideas, Volume V, 69–84

Böhm, F., 1933, Wettbewerb und Monopolkampf, Heymann, Berlijn

Böhm, F., 1937, Ordnung der Wirtschaft als geschichtliche Aufgabe und rechtsschöpferische Leistung, W. Kohlhammer, Stuttgart

Ellis, H.S., 1934, German Monetary Theory 1905–1933, Harvard University Press, Cambridge, Massachusetts

Erhard, L., 1966, Wirken und Reden, Hoch, Ludwigsburg

Federn, W., 1912a, Die Staatliche Theorie des Geldes, OVW, 4.52: 1015–1017

Federn, W., 1912b, Zum Geldproblem: Das Geld und die Werttheorie, OVW, 5.6: 101–104

Federn, W., 1912c, Zum Geldproblem: Grenzwert- und staatliche Theorie des Geldes, OVW, 5.7, 121–122

Federn, W., 1912d, Zum Geldproblem: Geld und Umlaufsmittel, OVW, 5.8: 141–143

Federn, W., 1912e, Zum Geldproblem: Veränderungen des Geldwertes, OVW, 5.9: 161–164

Gregory, T.E., 1928, Das englische Notenbankproblem, II.2: 1155–1158

Gregory, T.E., 1931, Macmillan Bericht, V.2: 1523–1527

Hauenstein, F., 1964, Die Arbeitsgemeinschaft E. von Beckerath, in N. Kloten (Hrg.), Systeme und Methoden in den Wirtschafts- und Staatswissenschaften. Festschrift für E. von Beckerath, Mohr/Siebeck, Tübingen

Hayek, F.A.,1932, Was der Goldwährung geschehen ist, VI: 642–645; 667–681

Hayek, F.A., 1965, Was der Goldwährung geschehen ist. Ein Bericht aus dem Jahre 1932 mit zwei Ergänzungen. Walter Eucken Institut: Vorträge und Aufsätze, 12, Tübingen: Mohr

Heuss, Th., 1929a, Wahlrechtspolitik I: Geschichtliche und theoretische Grundlegung, IV.1: 17–20

Heuss, Th., 1929b, Wahlrechtspolitik II: Möglichkeiten der Wahlreform, IV.1: 49–52

Knapp, G.F., 1905, 1918(2), 1923(3), Die staatliche Theorie des Geldes, Leipzig: Duncker and Humblot

Knapp, G.F., 1924, The State Theory of Money, London: MacMillan, abridged translation of G.F. Knapp, 1923(3), Die Staatliche Theorie des Geldes

Lampe-Blumenberg, C., 1986, Der Weg in die Soziale Marktwirtschaft. Referate, Protokolle, Gutachten der Arbeitsgemeinschaft Erwin von Beckerath 1943–1947, Stuttgart: Klett-Cotta

Landauer, C., 1927a, Kapital und Konjunktur, I.2: 1443–1445

Landauer, C., 1927b, Die deutsche Konjunktur, I.2: 1443–1445

Landauer, C., 1927c, Die deutsche Einheitsstaat, II.1: 267–269

Landauer, C., 1927d, Wie soll der Einheitsstaat aussehen, II.1: 302–305

Landauer, C., 1927e, Wie kommen wir zum Einheitsstaat, II.1: 332–335

Landauer, C., 1928a, Konzern oder Syndikat. Zum Schmalenbach Gutachten, II.1: 851–854 8

Landauer, C., 1928b, Macht und Wirtschaft, II.2: 1003–1006

Landauer, C., 1928c, Wirtschaftsgesetz und Wirtschaftsverfassung, II.2: 1044–1046

Landauer, C., 1928d, Der Spielraum der Lohnpolitik, II.2: 1079–1081

Landauer, C., 1928e, Bankfreiheit (review of Mises 1928), II.2: 1670–1673
Landauer, C., 1928f, Oeffentlicher Aufwand und Verwendung des Volkseinkommens, II.2: 1733–1736
Landauer, C., 1930, Dauerkrise oder Konjunkturwelle, V.1: 370–374
Landauer, C., 1931a, Ursprung der Krisen, V.1: 635–637
Landauer, C., 1931b, Kapitalknappheit als Krisenursache, V.1: 670–673
Luther, H., 1929, Finanzreform und Staatsreform, IV.1: 171–174
Meijer, G., 1987, The History of Neoliberalism: A General View and Developments in Several Countries, Rivista Internazionale di Scienze Economiche e Commerciali (International Review of Economics and Business), Vol. 34: 557–591
Meijer, G., 1988, Neoliberalen over economische orde en economische theorie, Van Gorcum/Van der Vegt, Assen/Maastricht (Neoliberalism. Neoliberals on Economic Order and Economic Theory)
Meijer, G., et al., 2006, Heterodox Views on Economics and the Economy of the Global Society, Wageningen Academic Publishers, Wageningen
Menger, C., 1892, On the Origins of Money, Economic Journal 2: 239–255
Miksch, 1937, Wettbewerb als Aufgabe, Kohlhammer, Stuttgart
Mises, L., 1912, 1924(2), Theorie des Geldes und der Umlaufsmittel, Duncker und Humblot, München and Leipzig; translated The Theory of Money and Credit, 1934, Jonathan Cape, London; 1953, Yale University Press, New Haven; 1981, Liberty Fund Press, Indianapolis
Mises, L., 1928, Geldwertstabilisierung und Konjunkturpolitik, Gustav Fischer, Jena
Mises, L., 1978, Erinnerungen von …., Gustav Fischer Verlag, Stuttgart
Oppenheimer, F., 1933, Weder so noch so. Der dritte Weg, A. Protte, Potsdam
Popitz, J., 1932, Der künftige Finanzausgleich zwischen Reich, Landern und Gemeinden: Gutachten erstattet der Studiengesellschaft für den Finanzausgleich, Berlin
Preiser, E., 1964, Gedenkrede, in E. Preiser, Franz Oppenheimer zum Gedächtnis, Vittorio Klostermann, Frankfurt am Main
Röpke, W., 1931, Ewige Prosperität, V.1: 608–612. Reprinted in Röpke, W., 1962, Wirrnis und Wahrheit, Eugen Rentsch Verlag, Erlenbach-Zürich/ Stuttgart, 59–70
Röpke, W., 1931, Geldtheorie und Weltkrise, V.2: 1742–1747
Röpke, W., 1931, Praktische Konjunkturpolitik, die Arbeit der Brauns-Kommission, Weltwirtschaftliche Archiv, Bd 34: 423f
Röpke, W., 1932, Krise und Konjunktur, Quelle und Meyer, Leipzig
Röpke, W., 1933, Autarkie - Ein abgenutztes Schlagwort, VII.1: 437–439
Röpke, W., 1936, Crises and Cycles, Hodge, London
Röpke, W., 1946, 2, Die deutsche Frage, Eugen Rentsch Verlag, Erlenbach-Zürich
Röpke, W., 1959, 2, Franz Oppenheimer, in W. Röpke, Gegen die Brandung, Eugen Rentsch Verlag, Erlenbach-Zürich
Rüstow, A., 1932, Freie Wirtschaft – starker Staat (Die staatspolitischen Voraussetzungen des Wirtschaftspolitischen Liberalismus) in Schriften des Vereins für Sozialpolitik, Bd. 187: 62–69. Reprinted in A. Rüstow, 1963, Rede und Antwort, Hoch, Ludwigsburg, 249–258
Rüstow, A., 1932, Interessenpolitik oder Staatspolitik, VII.6: 169–172
Salzwedel, J. and Kloten, N., 1966, In Memoriam E. von Beckerath, Hanstein Verlag, Bonn
Schall, W., 1927a, Finanzausgleich und Wirtschaft, I.1: 441–444
Schall, W., 1927b, Finanzreform und Verwaltungsreform, I.1: 474–477
Schall, W., 1928a, Probleme der Staatsreform in Deutschland, II.2: 1471–1474
Schall, W., 1928b, Ersparnisse durch Staatsvereinfachung, II.2: 1503–1506
Schall, W., 1928c, Reich und Länder. Bundesstaat oder Einheitsstaat, II.2: 1535–1538
Schall, W., 1928d, Reich und Länder. Das preussisch-deutsche Problem, II.2: 1567–1570
Schall, W., 1928e, Zentralismus und Selbstverwaltung, II.2: 1599–1602
Schall, W., 1928f, Probleme der deutschen Staatsreform, Schriftenreihe der Deutsche Volkswirt 4, Verlag des "Deutschen Volkswirt", Berlin
Schmalenbach, E., 1928, Die Betriebswirtschaftslehre an der Schwelle der neuen Wirtschaftsverfassung, Zeitschrift für handelswissenschaftliche Forschung, Jg. 22

Schmalenbach, E., 1958, 3, Der freien Wirtschaft zum Gedächtnis, Westdeutscher Verlag, Köln. Originally 1949
Schmölders, G., Hrg., 1942, Der Wettbewerb als Mittel volkswirtschaftlicher Leistungssteigerung und Leistungsauslese, Schriften der Akademie für Deutsches Recht, Heft 6. Gruppe Wirtschaftswissenschaften, Berlin
Schneider, H.J., 1943a, Der Grundsatz des Leistungswettbewerbs, in Die Deutsche Volkswirtschaft in Kriegsgemeinschaft mit Der Deutsche Volkswirt und Wirtschaftsdienst, 769–772, 801–804
Schneider, H.J., 1943b, Verwirklichung des Leistungswettbewerbs, in Die Deutsche Volkswirtschaft in Kriegsgemeinschaft mit Der Deutsche Volkswirt und Wirtschaftsdienst, 865–868, 897–901
Schumpeter, J.A., 1926, Steuerkraft und nationale Zukunft, I.1: 13–16
Schumpeter, J.A., 1927a, Die Arbeitslosigkeit , I.1: 729–732
Schumpeter, J.A., 1927b, Finanzpolitik, I.2: 827–830
Schumpeter, J.A., 1927c, Finanzpolitik und Kabinettsystem, I.2: 865–869
Schumpeter, J.A., 1927d, Finanzausgleich, I.2: 1123–1126, 1156–1159
Schumpeter, J.A., 1928, Das deutsche Finanzproblem. Reich, Länder und Gemeinden, Schriftenreihe der Deutsche Volkswirt 2, Verlag des "Deutschen Volkswirt", Berlin
Seidl, C. and Stolper, W.F., 1985, Aufsätze zur Wirtschaftspolitik, Mohr and Siebeck, Tübingen
Stolper, G., 1917a, Das Mitteleuropäische Wirtschaftsproblem, Deuticke-Verlag, Vienna
Stolper, G., 1917b, Wir und Deutschland, Deuticke-Verlag, Vienna
Stolper, G., 1921, Deutsch-Osterreich als Sozial- und Wirtschaftsproblem, Drei Masken Verlag, Munich
Stolper, G., 1927, Das deutsche Wirtschaftsproblem, II.1: 11–13, 43–45, 75–77, 107–108, 141–143, 235–240, 397–401
Stolper, G., 1927, Das deutsche Wirtschaftsproblem. Schriftenreihe der Deutsche Volkswirt 1, Verlag des "Deutschen Volkswirt", Berlin
Stolper, G.,1928a, Gefesseltes Kapitalismus, II.2: 1115–1117
Stolper, G., 1928b, Betriebswirtschaft oder Philosophie, II.2: 1223–1226
Stolper, G., 1928c, Zwischen freier und gebundener Wirtschaft, II.2: 1295–1297
Stolper, G., 1929a, Ein Finanzplan, Vorschläge zur deutschen Finanzreform. Schriftenreihe der Deutsche Volkswirt 8, Verlag des "Deutschen Volkswirt", Berlin
Stolper, G., 1929b, Stabilisation 1929, Das deutsche Wirtschaftsproblem, Schriften der Deutsche Volkswirt 1, 1927
Stolper, G., 1929c, Die wirtschaftlich-soziale Weltanschauung der Demokratie, in T. Stolper (1960), Anhang: Schluszwort Programmrede für die Deutsche Demokratische Partei, Mannheim: Verlag Stilke; Berlin: Neuer Staat
Stolper, T., 1960, Gustav Stolper 1888–1947. Ein Leben in Brennpunkten unserer Zeit: Wien, Berlin, New York, Rainer Wunderlich Verlag Herrmann Leins', Tübingen
Voegelin, E., 1959, Diskussionsbereitschaft, in A. Hunold, ed., Erziehung zur Freiheit, Eugen Rentsch Verlag, Erlenbach-Zürich, 355–372
Vogelstein, Th.,1927, Kartellgericht und Wirtschaftspolitik, I.2: 830–832
Vogelstein, Th., 1928a, Das Kartellproblem, II.2: 1664–1668
Vogelstein, Th., 1928b, Monopol und Individualrecht, II.2: 1700–1704
Vogelstein, Th., 1928c, Monopolpolitik und Monopolrecht, II.2: 1730–1733
Vogelstein, Th., 1928d, Monopolpolitik des Staates, II.2: 1761–1764
Vogelstein, Th., 1928, Probleme der Monopolpolitik, Schriftenreihe der Deutsche Volkswirt 5, Verlag des "Deutschen Volkswirt", Berlin
Vogelstein, Th., 1931, Die Aktiengesellschaft in Recht und Wirtschaft, V.1: 701–704, 741–743, 777–781, 811–2, 852–854
Wicksell, K., 1898, Geldzins und Güterpreise, Gustav Fischer, Jena

Chapter 6
On "The Europeanization of Persia" by N. Basseches

Ursula Backhaus

6.1 Introduction

In the *Deutscher Volkswirt* (1928), Nikolaus Basseches has described in four parts, how Persia developed from an ancient state to a modern market economy.[1] Next to the developments in trade, industry, and banking, Basseches has analyzed the development of the agricultural sector. He has observed that in Persia, the developmental process was reversed, from a beginning industrialized stage back to the stage of handicraft and agriculture. In his articles, he looks for the reasons and finds them in the political environment, property structure, and legal infrastructure of the country. For instance, through concessions in banking and infrastructure, the English and Russians gain influence on the economic development in Persia, leaving little room for own Iranian impulses of development. What remains puzzling is the choice of the title of the five essays: "Europeanization," a term, which requires an explanation.

---

[1] 1928. "Die Europäisierung der persischen Volkswirtschaft. Die Landwirtschaft", (Europeanization of the Persian Economy. On Agriculture), *Der Deutsche Volkswirt*, Nr. 25, pp. 822–824. 1928a. "Die Europäisierung der persischen Volkswirtschaft. Handel, Industrie und Kapital", (Europeanization of the Persian Economy. On Trade, Industry, and Capital), Part 2, *Der Deutsche Volkswirt*, Nr. 28, pp. 937–939. 1928b. "Die Europäisierung der persischen Volkswirtschaft. Zwischen Russland und England", (Europeanization of the Persian Economy. In between Russia and England). Part 3, *Der Deutsche Volkswirt*, Nr. 30, pp. 1012–1014. 1928c. "Die Europäisierung der persischen Volkswirtschaft. Der Kampf um den persischen Markt", (Europeanization of the Persian Economy. The Struggle for the Persian Market). Part 4, *Der Deutsche Volkswirt*, Nr. 31, pp. 1052–1054. Basseches articles on Iran appeared in 1928d. In 1935, upon the request of the government, the name of Persia was changed to Iran.

U. Backhaus (✉)
IssF, Institute for Social Sciences and Forethought,
Magdeburger Allee 55, 99086 Erfurt, Germany
e-mail: ursula_backhaus@yahoo.de

Basseches has followed the historic method, but was obviously aware of the writings of Schumpeter more than a decade earlier.[2] With respect to economic development, Schumpeter has issued a warning: "The totality of changes in the economic relationships of nations, as described by economic history, consists of very complicated phenomena. Our insights into their nature and their mutual effects is only very limited" (1912, p. 94). According to Schumpeter, the term "development" does not automatically mean "a general *progress*," but could as well include a regress.

Schumpeter, who was up to delineate the general underlying characteristics of the process of development, further distinguished between the descriptive and the theoretical problem. The first relates to economic development as "a problem of economic history and economic geography," (1912, p. 95) and the second relates to the following two additional questions:

> First, how and by what process do concrete changes occur? Second, is it possible to recognize regularities in the way that everything new arises? And if so, can these regularities be formulated in a general way? Both problems are based on the same set of facts. But the first relates to the concrete, individual content of the economic development of nations. The other is more concerned with the form that national economic developments take. For the first problem it is important to know what happens. For the second problem it is important to know how things happen and the circumstances under which they happen. (1912, p. 95)

In his treatment of the Persian development, Basseches treated both the descriptive and the theoretical question as outlined by Schumpeter. Therefore, he not only distinguished between "a particular development, as well as the concrete content of that development" (Schumpeter 1912, p. 95), but also between "the manner and circumstances of the course of events as well as its mechanism" (Schumpeter 1912, p. 95). This is expressed by his concern for the causes of change in development. In particular, he has tried to identify why "new combinations" did not succeed and under what circumstances they could have gotten "driven through" (Schumpeter 1912, p. 96). Actually, what is referred to as "Europeanization" is understood here as part of this latter process. Basseches thought that economic developments such as the industrialization eventually will take place in Persia. Unlike Schumpeter, he does not bother with making his definitions explicit at the outset. Consequently, he does not critically discuss the term "Europeanization" which he uses synonymously to an improvement in economic development.[3]

---

[2] Compare, for instance, Schumpeter, Joseph A. 1912. "Das Gesamtbild der Volkswirtschaft." (The Economy as a Whole). *Theorie der wirtschaftlichen Entwicklung*. (The Theory of Economic Development). Leipzig: Duncker & Humblot, pp. 463–546. English translation by Ursula Backhaus. 2002. *"The Economy as a Whole. Seventh Chapter of Schumpeter's The Theory of Economic Development.* Joseph A. Schumpeter." *Industry and Innovation.* Vol. 9, nrs. 1/2, pp. 93–145.

[3] "Europeanization" was a phenomenon Basseches witnessed in his time. For instance, in 1925, Ataturk changed the alphabet of the Turkish language from Arabic to Latin characters as part of the "Europeanization" movement. Today, similar demands meet the opposition of Iranian linguists, who fear a loss in culture. "A global community should be one in which differences are accepted, not shunned. For instance, was Japan unable to develop economically while maintaining its national language and alphabet?" Saba Ghadrboland, "No Thanks. Changing Persian Script Would be Harmful." *The Iranian*, January 15, 1999.

The main aspects of his analysis of the Persian agricultural sector are presented in the first part of this paper; his analysis of Persian banking, industry, and trade is discussed in the second part. The paper ends with a summary and conclusions.

6.2 Agriculture

In the beginning of the nineteenth century, a new backward development, i.e., retrogression, with regard to industrial development and its consequences for trade could be observed in Persia. Due to innerpolitical processes, as well as in response to the world market and actions of world policy, Persia turned away from further developing its handicraft sector and manufacturing back to agriculture. The economic historian N. Basseches cannot interpret whether the latter was an agrarian revolution or counterrevolution, or whether the development of the agricultural sector had to be looked upon as progress or regress (1928a, p. 823). He provides the following background information for the reader to make a judgement:

During the time of the nomads, Canonical Law in Persia as an Islamic country did not allow full private property in land and soil.[4] When the nomads settled in villages, land and soil was divided up. The Shah received the land, and he asked 1/10 of the harvest and crop receipts for the lease, but in the early nineteenth century, in particular, high-standing individuals received the right to take advantage of the entire income of villages. This was accompanied by a system of selling civil servants positions. The so-established governors of provinces had to make large presents and additional tributes of the crop receipts to the Shah. The governors sold themselves the lower positions of government. Under this system, land and soil was not heavily demanded, but this changed when it became possible to sell crop on the world market. This led to the division of land among the ruling class and a system of feudal ownership of large landed estates emerged. The farming population became dependent on the feudal owners, and instability prevailed. The principle was retained that the Shah remained the final owner, and therefore, he was in a position to exchange the entire class of feudal owners. As the new owners of large landed estates, those civil servants emerged who made a fortune in the Persian state administrative system and who profited from systematic corruption. In addition, independent private bankers of Asia (the so-called "Saraffen"), the first "Saraffen" can be dated back to the Middle Ages, made a fortune by usury and tax lease (Steuerpacht), which they then invested in large landed estates. Both groups combined trading on the beginning world market with the ownership of large landed estates.

---

[4] Full private property includes uses, abusus, and usus fructus, which is the right of residual claimancy. In Islamic law, the Shari'a, abusus is critical. Compare Alchian, Armen A., and Harold Demsetz. 1972. "Production, Information Costs, and Economic Organization." American Economic Review, 62, no. 5: 777–795.

In modern times, Basseches has distinguished between five types of property ownership: state property, community property, land owned by the church, small property ownership by farmers themselves, and large landed estates. By far the largest part of the farming population works on large landed estates.

There are large local differences of the tribute a farmer has to pay to the lord of the manor. Traditionally, five elements of Persian agriculture are distinguished: soil, water, cattle, labour, and seeds. The owner of each of these elements receives one fifth of the harvest, but this rule knows many exceptions. Accordingly, a farmer who provides only his labour receives one fifth of the harvest proceeds.[5] In addition to these tributes, taxes such as the military tax have to be paid to the state.

Under such a system of heavy tributes (instead of lease fees), why is it still an advantage for a farmer to remain working on a large landed estate? Basseches identified as the main reason the security a farmer receives by the lord of the manor. Due to the lack of a legal system, the farmer would be subject to the arbitrariness and corruption of the civil service.

> Wäre der Bauer beim Fehlen eines Rechtssystems materiell unabhängig, so wäre er der Willkür eines jeden Beamten ausgeliefert. Unter dem Schutz des Großgrundbesitzers weiß er, daß wenigstens ein Fünftel der Ernte, seine Frau und sein Hemd ihm gesichert sind. Im Falle einer Missernte kann er hoffen, vom Großgrundbesitzer, wenn auch gegen wucherische Zinsen, ein Darlehn zu erhalten. Begibt er sich des mächtigen Schutzes seines Herrn, so ist nicht einmal sein physisches, nacktes Leben gesichert. (N. Basseches 1928a, p. 824)

Not all farmers remained at the estates. It could be observed that entire villages started to wander and became nomads again, while others settled down.[6]

Basseches has reported that the new political system tries to make the farmers more independent. Under Reza Shah's regime, an administrative reform and tax reforms according to the European model are proposed.[7] The purpose of the administrative reform is to establish a legal system and a central administration, where civil servants are paid by the state and where corruption is no longer part of the system. This would give farmers a position where they would be less dependent on the security provided by the owners of large landed estates.

Central to the tax reform is the introduction of the progressive income tax system with a large minimum of tax free income. This means that the farmer with a low income would not be taxed by the state, but that the lord of the manor would have to pay a higher tax than before. Basseches predicts two possible effects of the new tax system. The owner of the large landed estate could start selling part of his estate to the farmers and thereby reduce the amount of his tax payment; or the owner could

---

[5] In order to determine the amount of labour supplied, the farmer equals marginal revenue and marginal costs. If he receives only one-fifth, he will work less than if he would receive the full amount of the harvest proceeds.

[6] The problems resulting from the coexistence between nomads and settled farmers have been analyzed by Douglass C. North. 1981. *Structure and Change in Economic History*. W. W. Norton & Company.

[7] Reza Shah was the father of the deposed Emperor on the peacocks' throne.

adjust to the higher tax payment by a change in technology. Under the old tax (and administrative) system, only the most primitive agricultural technology is used, such as the wooden plough. Under the new tax system, landowners have an incentive to introduce more efficient agricultural implements. This would mean that they drive the more marginal farmers off the land.

Despite the structural shortcomings of the agricultural sector, Persian agricultural products could be sold at the emerging world market. Basseches has noted that this was not unrelated to the decline in other sectors such as industry, trade of manufactured products, and banking. Economic and political factors played a role in the decline.

6.3 Trade, Industry, and Capital

Due to the rapid development of an encompassing road and railroad system in Europe, as well as its fast process of industrialization, Persia's famous route of traffic connecting Europe and Asia lost in importance. While European industrial products flooded the Persian market, raw materials for the European industrial production and Persian foodstuffs and agricultural products were in demand. This structure of the import and export streams not only contributed to the decline of the development of the Persian handicraft and manufacturing sector, but also diminished the role of the Persian merchant who traditionally held the position of a middleman between orient and occident.

Indian, Armenian, and Caucasian merchants became the new middlemen. The British Empire Bank and the Russian-Persian Bank started to replace the traditional banking system[8] of independent private bankers, the "Saraffen," and gained influence on the bazaar, the heart of the Persian economy. The bazaar is an organizational form, where the distribution of goods takes place according to the rules of supply and demand.

The political influence of Great Britain and Russia declined during the *First World War*, and the Persian handicraft and industrial sector started to recover. Guilds were formed within the handicraft sector, and the already existing guilds of the Persian merchants at the bazaar gained in political importance by their unification. Eventually, the diminished possibilities for export through the world market due to the war as well as a lack of financial means slowed down the Persian economic recovery. In addition, the agricultural problem has not yet been solved. Both dependency of farmers from the owners of large landed estates and corrupt civil servants dominating the state administration prevented the development of an inner market. Persia tried to introduce custom duties for its industry to develop,[9] but Basseches predicted only a small chance of success, as long as the foreign political and economic influence mainly by Great Britain and Russia was strong.

---

[8] Compare Mahmoud A. El-Gamal. 2006. *Islamic Finance. Law, Economics, and Practice.* Cambridge: Cambridge University Press.

[9] Friedrich List held that an industry must be protected before it can be established.

His third and fourth articles were devoted to analyzing those foreign influences and their effects on the Persian economy. He described the Shah's political maneuvrings between the two nations. This strategy provided the Shah regime with substantial financial means, which allowed importing luxury products. As a developmental strategy for the country, the Shah agreed that both England and Russia acquired concessions to build telegraph lines in Persia. He agreed to other concessions as well, for instance in the area of natural resources, thereby giving England and Russia even more political and economic influence on Persia. Concessions are a controversial method in developing a country. On the one hand, they provide the development desired, such as telegraph lines, on the other hand, the foreign country holding a concession gains substantial political and economic influence on the country to be developed.

In his articles on the English and Russian influence on Persia, Basseches has also described how other nations such as the Germans,[10] French, or Americans had been restricted in their endeavors in Iran. They try to gain a foothold in the Persian market by forming trade organizations, where Persians participate themselves. In the early nineteen twenties, a change took place in the political climate of Persia, namely an opposition formed to political and economic influences of foreign nations. Therefore, Basseches considered the participation strategy as a promising route in order to develop an infrastructure, and based on it, to further industry and trade in Persia.

6.4 Summary and Conclusions

Basseches has described the development of Persia from an ancient state to a market economy. The development of an inner Persian market is prevented by structural deficits in the organization of the agricultural sector, but tax and administrative reforms are underway in order to remedy the situation. Even worse is the British and Russian influence on the development of Persian trade, industry, and banking. While the Shah regime profited from the rivalry of the two nations by gaining advantages from both of them, he agreed to a controversial type of development, to concessions. According to Basseches, the strong British and Russian political and economic influence prevented that own impulses for development of a Persian industry could enforce the economic recovery from within; in his own words, that "Europeanization" could take place.

---

[10] Since transit through Russia was prohibited, Germans used parcel post for its trade with Persia. In 1912/1913, the value of German exports to Persia by way of parcels was roughly one million; in 1914, it was about 1.5 million US$ (compare Basseches, 4. 5. 1928, p. 1054).

References

Alchian, Armen A. and Demsetz, Harold. 1972. "Production, Information Costs, and Economic Organization." *American Economic Review*. 62, (5), pp. 777–95.

Nikolaus Basseches, 1928a. "Die Europäisierung der persischen Volkswirtschaft. Die Landwirtschaft", (Europeanization of the Persian Economy. On Agriculture), *Der Deutsche Volkswirt*, Nr. 25, pp. 822–824.

Nikolaus Basseches, 1928b. "Die Europäisierung der persischen Volkswirtschaft. Handel, Industrie und Kapital", (Europeanization of the Persian Economy. On Trade, Industry, and Capital), Part 2, *Der Deutsche Volkswirt*, Nr. 28, pp. 937–939.

Nikolaus Basseches, 1928c. "Die Europäisierung der persischen Volkswirtschaft. Zwischen Russland und England", (Europeanization of the Persian Economy. In between Russia and England). Part 3, *Der Deutsche Volkswirt*, Nr. 30, pp. 1012–1014.

Nikolaus Basseches, 1928d. "Die Europäisierung der persischen Volkswirtschaft. Der Kampf um den persischen Markt", (Europeanization of the Persian Economy. The Struggle for the Persian Market). Part 4, *Der Deutsche Volkswirt*, Nr. 31, pp. 1052–1054.

El-Gamal, Mahmoud A. 2006. *Islamic Finance. Law, Economics, and Practice*. Cambridge: Cambridge University Press.

Ghadrboland, Saba. 1999. "No Thanks. Changing Persian Script Would be Harmful." *The Iranian*, 1-15-1999.

North, Douglass C. 1981. *Structure and Change in Economic History*. W. W. Norton & Company.

Schumpeter, Joseph A. 1912. "Das Gesamtbild der Volkswirtschaft." (The Economy as a Whole). *Theorie der wirtschaftlichen Entwicklung*. (The Theory of Economic Development). Leipzig: Duncker & Humblot, pp. 463–546. English translation by Ursula Backhaus. 2002. "*The Economy as a Whole*. Seventh Chapter of Schumpeter's *The Theory of Economic Development*. Joseph A. Schumpeter." *Industry and Innovation*. Vol. 9, nrs. 1/2, pp. 93–145.

Chapter 7
The Austrian and German "Economist" in the Interwar Period: International Aspects

Marcel van Meerhaeghe

7.1 Introduction

The *OV* delivers not only weekly comments on economic and social-political events, but also publishes studies on the same subjects. In 1915, for example, Fr. H. devotes an article on Bismarck as an economist. Its main conclusions, which are to be found again in later publications, are worth reproducing:

> Bismarck is an empiricist, who despises all theory …and has often shown his sarcastic contempt. He was for a long time an enthusiastic free-trader and later a promoter of rigorous customs protection. He claims a brake on industrialisation that produces the industrial proletariat, and later recognises industry as a pillar of national welfare. Colonial policy is first looked at suspiciously, later included in his programme. Similar changes occur in the financial, transport and social policies …. Not the maximum increase of productivity is the supreme purpose, but the always stronger consolidation of the national idea …(*OV,* March 27, 1915, p. 406)[1]

Another example is a paper published by F. Waldmann on June 5, 1909 on the financial significance of the Belgian Congo (F. Waldmann 1909). At that time, reliable statistics were not available and the author could only give an approximate picture. But it concludes rightly that the Belgian colony yields much more than the relatively poor German colonies (Ibid., p. 4).

---

[1] Bismarck ist ein Empiriker, der alle Theorie … verachtet und dieser Geringschätzung oft genug beissenden Ausdruck verliehen hat. Er vertrat lange den entschiedensten Freihandel, um später das Prinzip des lückenlosen Zollschutzes zu verwirklichen. Er forderte die Hemmung des Industrialismus, der das revolutionäre Proletariat hervorbringe und hat später die Industrie als einen Grundpfeiler des nationalen Wohlstandes anerkennt. Die Kolonialpolitik wurde von ihm zuerst mit Misstrauen betrachtet und später in sein Programm aufgenommen. Auch die Finanz-, Verkehrs- und Sozialpolitik weisen ähnliche Wandlungen auf.

M. van Meerhaeghe (✉)
University of Ghent, Kriekenbergdreef 21, 9831 Deurle, Belgium
e-mail: hvm@klaproos.be

The *OV* occasionally devotes his attention to an important publication. On September 11, 1915, for example, Dr. Schwoner writes a review of a book on the economic repercussions of the war on America (edited by the American Academy of Political and Social Science in July 1915). The war is considered "... a never returning chance to conquer a leading position at the expense of British and German competition" (Schwoner 1915, p. 833).

7.2 Versailles

Keynes' publication on *The economic consequences of the peace* (1919) had a great impact. The fact that Keynes had been a member of the British delegation to the Paris conference increased the influence of his book. First, the book remembers that Germany had accepted to lay down his arms

> in reliance on a solemn compact as to the general character of the peace, the terms of which seemed to assure a settlement of justice and magnanimity and a fair hope for a restoration of the broken current of life (Keynes 1919, p. 23–24).

The compact included, in addition to the Fourteen points of January 6, 1918, several addresses of the President of the United States of America of which the first of 11 February declares that "(t)here shall be no annexations, *no contributions, no punitive damages*! Self-determination ... is an imperative principle. But ... the surrender of Alsace-Lorraine was not incompatible with the self-determination principle!"

Nonetheless, the Treaty of Versailles was "in many particulars ... not consistent with these (American) assurances" (Keynes 1919, p. 34). Keynes explains how this was possible. The American President Wilson was a great disappointment

> he had no plan, no scheme, no constructive ideas whatever for clothing with the flesh of life the commandments which he had thundered from the White House; moreover his mind was slow and inadaptable (Keynes, ibid., p. 27).

and he was no match for the 15 years older French *Président du Conseil*, who knew what he wanted (and who alone among the Four could speak and understand both conference languages). In fact, Clémenceau managed to bring to success "what had seemed to be, a few months before, the extraordinary and impossible proposal that the Germans should not be heard" (Keynes, ibid., p. 34).

As to the bill of the financial transfers, it was beyond all possibility of Germany meeting it. Keynes speaks not without reason of a Carthaginian peace (Keynes, ibid., and, for example, p. 22 and 32).

Unfortunately, I did not find the slightest reference to Keynes' book in the *OV*. Only years after its publication, it is sometimes mentioned in a commentary (e.g., in W.F. 1923 p. 840). It would have been interesting to compare its views with those of other periodicals. But that does not mean lack of interest in the subject.

Several leaders in 1919 are devoted to the Treaty. On March 17, 1919, G. St(olper) declares its contents "so absurd that it ridicules each standard of political intelligence".[2] President Wilson has to pay for its "ignominious betrayal".[3] He was considered a great poet, but he is only a silly talker (seichter Schwätzer). He is a small mind (ein kleiner Geist), and "as all small minds in possession of power, becomes arrogant".[4] The loss of Alsace-Lorraine is not sanctioned by a referendum and the French hatred against the German nature (... deutschen Wesens, Ibid., p. 592) of these German-speaking provinces[5] finds already expression at that time.

Stolper cannot understand the attribution of German territories to Poland, once more in glaring contradiction to the famous Wilsonian principles of self-determination, but remains pessimistic as regard Poland:

> A Poland that kills his Jews and has Germany as mortal enemy, that is encircled, in the North by Russian, in the East by Ukrainian hate, has forfeited her life, before it can start as a new created state[6] (Stolper 1918, p. 594).

He rightly finds that the "... Treaty of Versailles does not yet show the spirit which will transform the chaos into a new order"[7] (St.; 1919, p. 787).

Stolper's conclusions are clear: Germany's future seems without hope[8] (Stolper 1919, p. 594). The fact that Wilson abandoned the noble principles he proclaimed and which induced Germany to accept the armistice is deeply resented. Of course, several articles are devoted to the peace with Austria. The first one is again evident: the "peace provisions are unacceptable, in the sense that they are impracticable" (W.F. 1919, p. 803). They imply the bankruptcy of Austria (Ibid, p. 804). The others illustrate this impracticality once more (G. St., September 6, 1919; Hoffmann 1919).

---

[2] So wahnwitzig, dass er jedes Massstabes der politischen Vernunft spottet, Der Weltfrieden, *OV*, May 17, 1919, p. 591.

[3] ... den schmählichsten Verrat ...(Ibid).

[4] ... wie alle kleinen Geister im Besitze der Macht der Überheblichkeit anheimfällt (Ibid).

[5] Of course, the patient but systematic and continuous frenchification has not been without results. A similar gallification occurred in Italian (Nizza) and Flemish-speaking regions conquered or acquired by France. Two hundred years ago, only Flemish was spoken in Dunkirk!

[6] Ein Polen, das seine Juden totschlägt und ein verarmtes Deutschland zum Todfeind hat, das im Norden von russischem, im Osten von ukrainischem Hass umbrandet ist, hat sein Leben verwirkt, bevor es noch als neu erstandener Staat seine Bahn antritt.

[7] Der Friede von Versailles ... zeigt noch nicht den Geist, der das Chaos zu neuer Ordnung formen wird.

[8] ... lässt die Situation, in der Deutschland heute schwebt, so hoffnungslos erscheinen.

7.3 The Reparations

The reparations and the Reparations Commission are dealt with in the Treaty that formally asserted Germany's war guilt,[9] but because of their specificity and for the sake of good order I consider them separately, as they are dealt with extensively in the *OV* and the *DV*. They are considered as compensation for material losses and suffering caused by the war. The US did not ratify the Treaty and waived all claims on reparations. The Commission consists of ten representatives (two each from Belgium, France, Britain, Italy, the United States). Some payments were to be made in kind (e.g., coal, steel, ships). Reparations were also claimed in treaties with German allies, but the amounts were never set and nothing was collected.

7.3.1 Reactions

Already on July 5, 1919, G. St(olper) complains that after the Treaty the competence of the Reparation Commission has been defined in such a way that "… it (the Commission) is, in fact, the dominating organ of the German economy and could abolish the sovereignty of the German government"[10] (St(olper) 1919, p. 740). He wonders whether

> the financial and commercial-political provisions of the Treaty are compatible with the festively announced purpose of the allies to contribute, at least indirectly, to the reconstruction of the German economy[11] (Ibid., p. 744).

A leader of June 12, 1919 refers to Austria: it is a reaction to a "credit note" of the Reparations Commission, which "reflects the despair of the allies in respect of the reconstruction of Europe"[12] (St. 1920, p. 695). Austria has become "an object without right of say and power of foreign political plans".[13] There is only one resource: "joining the German *Reich*[14]" (Ibid., p. 698).

The chaotic conditions in the German economy after the war made it difficult for the allies to collect the amounts fixed. A German request for a moratorium receives

---

[9] Though the responsibility for the war could not be attributed to a particular country.

[10] … dass sie tatsächlich zum beherrschenden Organ der deutschen Wirtschaft wird und die Souveränität der deutschen Regierung aufheben konnte.

[11] … soll noch geprüft werden, wie weit sich die finanziellen und handelspolitischen Bedingungen des Friedensvertrages mit der feierlich kundgegebenen Absicht der Alliierten, am Wiederaufbau der deutschen Wirtschaft wenigstens indirect mitzuwirken, vereinbaren lasse.

[12] spiegelt die …ratlosigkeit wieder, die unter den Alliierten in den Fragen des Wiederaufbaus Europas herrscht.

[13] … ein willen- und machtloses Objekt fremder politischer Pläne.

[14] … nur eine Rettung gibt: Den Anschluss an das Deutsche Reich.

a sharp answer, that "surprises more by its hateful tone of command than by its content"[15] (*O.V.* 1922, p. 641). The *O.V.* stresses that the policy required by the Commission means

> a budget deficit, printing of bank-notes, depreciation, capital destruction, over-consumption, social unrest, pauperism of the most valuable parts of the people … an ominous document by which the Reparations Commission has answered the German moratorium demand. Poincaré was once more the victor (Ibid., p. 641–42).

The Commission claims 60 billion marks new receipts to be paid within the time fixed; it also claims control of the expenditure which the *OV* finds even more humiliating (Ibid., p. 642).

France only overestimates the German capacity to pay. France and Belgium, at that time still France's military ally, do not shrink before violence and in 1923 even occupy the Ruhr district after Germany was declared in default (till 1925). The *OV* finds that everybody will understand

> … that it is difficult for Germany to negotiate with an adversary, who is assaulting you in full peace time, shooting down dozens of your citizens, confining hundreds, robbing housing and possessions of thousands of men, women, children and old people and expel them from the region (*OV,* W.F., May 12, 1923, p. 840).

7.3.2 Plans

The Reparations Commission and its American chairman Charles G. Dawes (1923–1924) had to find a solution for the collection of the German reparations debt of almost 20 billion marks. The so-called Dawes Plan (1924) is seen as a means of stabilising the German finances. Reparation payments should start at 1 billion marks for the first year and should rise over a period of 4 years to 2.5 billion per year. The plan provides a loan to Germany of 800 million gold mark, the reorganisation of the *Reichsbank*; the inclusion of transportation, excise, and customs duties in the reparation payments. It lays down that the Ruhr area be evacuated. The plan went into effect on September 1, 1924.

Reparations were made promptly, but it became soon obvious that Germany could not continue those huge payments. Hence, early reactions and efforts to find another settlement.

Meanwhile, Germany could pay mainly by means of foreign loans, though she was aware that it could be only a temporary solution. It insisted on a revision of the Dawes plan. The *OV* believes even that it will happen before the end of 1928 (W.F. 1928, p. 765).

But the discussions about composition and competence of the Reparations Commission dragged along (cf. Stolper 1928, p. 171). On April 5, 1929, the *OV* is still insisting on a quick decision (Stolper 1929a, p. 883), but finds that a solution

---

[15] … nur durch den gehässigen Befehlston, weniger durch ihren materiellen Inhalt (überraschen konnte).

depends on the American approval, since France and still more Britain hope to pay in this way their American debts. On April 19, 1929, Stolper regrets once more that the European allies use Germany as a buffer (Prellbock) in their efforts to reduce their own war loans towards the US (Stolper 1929b, p. 955).[16] W.F. and others complain bitterly that Germany bereft of her fleet and colonies, which paid already billions for 6 years, should still pay ten times the amount France had to pay Germany in 1870.

Finally, another American chairman, Owen Young, forwarded the Young Plan (1930), which made reparations a financial, rather than a political, matter. The Plan sets the total reparations at 26, 350 million dollars to be paid in 58.5 yearly reparations of on average 2 billion gold mark (473 million dollars) and a loan to Germany of 300 million dollars (awarded in 1930). The Plan was in operation until 1931. The Bank for International Settlements was to be the banker of all transactions.

Already on December 20, 1929, Stolper passes a annihilating judgment on the Young Plan: it is "hardly a tolerable document; it is a document of scepticism"[17] (Stolper 1929, p. 369). "Every difficulty that the signatories of the plan could not or did not want to regulate they pushed to the Bank for International Settlements"[18] (Ibid.). The "burden on Germany is outrageous, immoral, economically pernicious"[19] (Ibid.,p. 370). But the *DV* admits that the disappointment was induced by the exaggerated expectations during the discussions (*DV*, March 14, 1930, p. 767). And a few months later, W.F. finds that international public opinion considers the reparations as too high and writes these prophetic warning

> France could make this concession (the revision of the Young plan). ... because France is most threatened when social distress pushes the German people more and more into the arms of radical parties. But it will again talk about the sacredness of treaties[20] (W.F., Vol. 23, 1930–1931, p. 94).

Hitler recognises in *Mein Kampf* that a discussion of Versailles would be the condition of the success of his party in the future (Blasius, in Benz 1997, p. 781). In fact, the world economy began to deteriorate still more. In Germany, the crisis started in 1927/1929 in agriculture (falling prices) and in many industries (selling problems). The decrease of tax receipts led to less public investment.

---

[16] See other contributions by Stolper: Kapitalnot und Reparationen. Die Transferklausel, Probleme der Reparationspolitik IV, October 26, 1928, Der notwendige Weg. Probleme der Reparationspolitik V, November 2, 1928, Die Endregelung. Probleme der Reparatioinspolitik, VI, November 9, 1928, Wo stehen wir? December 21, 1928, Der Young –Plan, June 7, 1929, Der Young-Plan II, June 14, 1929.

[17] Der Young Plan ... ist kaum ein ertragliches Dokument. (Es) ist ein Dokument der Skepsis.

[18] Man hat alles, was man nicht regeln wollte oder konnte, der Internationalen Bank zugeschoben, ...

[19] Die Tributlast, die auf Deutschland liegt, ist ungeheuerlich, ist unmoralisch, ist wirtschaftlich verderblich.

[20] Frankreich könnte diesen Nachlass (eine Revision des Young-Planes) ... gewähren, ... weil Frankreich vor allem bedroht ist, wenn die soziale Not das deutsche Volk immer mehr in die Arme der radikalen Parteien treibt. Aber es wird wieder von der Heiligkeit der Verträge reden.

In 1931, a 1-year moratorium (the so-called Hoover moratorium) on all intergovernmental loans was announced. The Treaty of Lausanne of July 9, 1932 substituted a bond issue for the reparation debt and made a formal end to the German reparations (though the pact was never ratified).

The depression and the enormous number of unemployed (6 million in 1932) contributed to the rise of the nation-socialist party.

7.4 Conclusion

The discussions in the two German-language periodicals illustrate once more that the harshness of the Treaty of Versailles explains the rise of Hitler and the subsequent World War II.

In comparison with the German daily press, the opinions of the two weeklies are often sharper and less diplomatic: they had less to take into account the "instructions" or wishes of political parties, nor, more in particular, of the federal and local governments. Moreover, the interested reader will find more profound studies on, for example, all the technical questions related to the reparations problem (which I avoided as much as possible in my short survey, given their limited present interest), than in the daily press. The quality of the chief editors has to be mentioned here.

Though German was still an international language and much better known than nowadays, the international influence of the German periodic press remained limited and negligible in comparison with the mighty Anglo-Saxon, mostly anti-German press.

References

OV: Der Oesterreichische Volkswirt.
DV: Der Deutsche Volkswirt.
Blasius, article on 'Versailles' (Friedensvertrag) in *Encyklopädie des Nationalsozialismus*, ed. Benz W., Graml H., Weiss H., dtv, 4th ed., 2001 (1997).
H. F., 1915, Bismarck als Volkswirt, *OV*, 27 March.
Keynes, J., 1919, *The economic consequences of the peace,* London: Macmillan.
Schwoner A., 1915, Die Chancen des Weltkrieges für die Vereinigten Staaten, *OV*, 15 Sep.
St. G., 1919, Der Weltfrieden, *OV*, 17 May.
St. G., 1919, Der Friede von Versailles, II, *OV*, 5 July.
St. G., 1919, Der Friede von Versailles, III, *OV*, 12 July.
St. G., 1919, Der Friede von Versailles, IV, *OV*, 19 July.
St. G., 1920, Die Kreditnote der Reparationskommission, *OV*. 12 June.
St. G., 1928, Das Reparationsproblem, *DV*, 17 November.
Stolper, G., 1929, Vor der Entscheidung, *DV*, 5 April
Stolper, G., 1929, Das Ende einer Fiktion, *DV*. 19 April.
Stolper, G., 1929, Wo stehen wir? *DV*, 20 December.
W.F., Lösung der Reparationsfrage?, *DV*, 7 April.
W.F., Revision des Youngplanes?, *DV*, Vol. 23 (1 Oct.1930–31 March 1931).
Waldmann F., 1909, Der wirtschaftliche Wert der belgischen Kongokolonie, *OV*, 5 June.

Chapter 8
From Stabilization to Depression: Comments in the *Österreichische Volkswirt* on Economic Policy in Austria Between 1923 and 1929*

Günther Chaloupek

8.1 *Der Österreichische Volkswirt* (1908–1998)

The weekly periodical *Der Österreichische Volkswirt* (OVw) was founded in Vienna, then capital of the Habsburg monarchy, in 1908 by the economist Walther Federn, with financial support from banking circles.[1] The British *Economist* (established 1843) served as a model for the OVw's concept of "serious and independent periodical for economic policy", independent "of advertisers, authorities, parties, etc."; whose readers could always be sure that "what they read represents the conviction of the editors" (Federn 1918/19-1, p. 2).[2] Walther Federn was its chief editor from the beginning until 1934. He was joined in this function by Gustav Stolper between 1914 and 1925, when Stolper founded the *Deutsche Volkswirt* and moved to Berlin. To ensure independence, the editors followed the principle that proceeds from subscriptions and sales cover all costs of production, with advertisements as source of profits[3], which were considerable especially when circulation increased in the 1920s. During that period, the OVw was widely read not only in Austria, but also in the succession states of the Habsburg monarchy and to some extent also in Germany. In its comments and analyses, the OVw's orientation was truly international, with special focus on central Europe.

---

*This paper was first presented at the 20th Heilbronn Symposium in Economics and the Social Sciences, June 21–24, 2007, Heilbronn, Germany

[1] Mainly from Siegfried Rosenbaum, who was the president of the *Anglo-Österreichische Bank*.

[2] In the interest of brevity, for citations from the OVw (in the author's translation), this abbreviated form will be applied. Each volume of the OVw has two parts, running from October to March, and from April to September.

[3] According to T. Stolper 1960, p. 148f.

G. Chaloupek (✉)
Chamber of Labour Vienna, Prinz-Eugen-Straße 20-22, 1041 Vienna, Austria
e-mail: Guenther.CHALOUPEK@akwien.at

The OVw was able to entertain a sizeable editorial staff in its Vienna office at Porzellangasse 27,[4] a permanent bureau in Prague, and had permanent correspondents in Berlin, Budapest, Agram (Zagreb), Warsaw, and Bucharest. Some of the staff members and correspondents later became famous as academic economists or social scientists, e.g. Karl Polanyi[5] and George Katona.[6] Frequently, the OVw published contributions from outside authors,[7] among which one can find Joseph Schumpeter, Gottfried Haberler, Friedrich A. Hayek, Fritz Machlup, Oskar Morgenstern, Michael Hainisch,[8] Friedrich Hertz,[9] Hans Kelsen, Paul Lazarsfeld, Benedikt Kautsky,[10] Karl Pribram, Peter F. Drucker,[11] Hermann Neubacher,[12] even Arthur Seyss-Inquart,[13] Hans Neisser,[14] Günter Schmölders, Karel Englis[15] and Theodor Heuss – the latter was a close friend of Stolper and became the first president of the German Federal Republic.

The OVw always strictly opposed all forms of authoritarianism and fascism and, consequently, encountered difficulties when Chancellor Dollfuss established his authoritarian regime in Austria in February 1934. Under a new chief editor, it could not only continue publication, but also to comment on economic and political events from a certain critical perspective. A few weeks after the occupation of

---

[4] In his contribution to the "Almanch 1908–1918–1928" (p. 20f), Richard A. Berman draws a vivid picture of life and work in the editor's office of the Volkswirt.

[5] Karl Polanyi, 1886–1964, author of "The Great Transformation" (1944), was a member of the editorial staff between 1924 and 1933. In that year, he had to give up this position under pressure of the changing political climate in Austria and in Germany and moved to England.

[6] George Katona, 1901–1981, founder of the theory of psychological economics and of the economics of consumer behaviour, was on the editorial staff of the *Deutsche Volkswirt*. He emigrated to the USA in 1933.

[7] If not otherwise indicated, the main sources of information were Hagemann/Krohn 1999, The New Palgrave 1987 and Österreich-Lexikon 1995.

[8] Michael Hainisch, 1858–1940, Head of state of the Republic of Austria 1920–1928.

[9] Friedrich Hertz, 1878–1964, economist and statistician, worked for the Association of Austrian Industrialists and for the government. He emigrated to London in 1938.

[10] Benedikt Kautsky, 1894–1960, son of Karl Kautsky, was head of the statistical department of the Austrian Chamber of Labour.

[11] According to his autobiography, Peter F. Drucker (1909–2005) was invited as a guest author for the first time in 1927 (Drucker 1978, p. 123f). His occasional contributions to the OVw appeared in the 1930s.

[12] Hermann Neubacher, 1883–1960, was director general of the major housing company of the city of Vienna. He joined the NSDAP in 1933 and was appointed the mayor of Vienna after the *Anschluss* (until 1939).

[13] Arthur Seyss-Inquart, 1892–1946, Austrian lawyer, who had been appointed to minister of internal affairs under Hitler's pressure in February 1938, commissioner for the Netherlands during the period of German occupation, received a death sentence at the first Nürnberg trial.

[14] Hans Philipp Neisser, 1895–1975, deputy research director of the Institute of World Economics at Kiel, emigrated to the USA in 1933.

[15] Karel Englis, 1880–1961, Czech economist, minister of finance and governor of the national bank of the Czechoslovak Republic.

Austria by Nazi Germany in 1938, the OVw was closed down until the end of World War II. In December 1945, the first issue of the post-war relaunch appeared, but, as it became evident rather soon, the relaunch was not a continuation of previous years of success. Publication was finally terminated in 1998, 90 years after the journal's foundation.

The comments and analyses (longer articles) on economic developments in Austria were mostly written by Federn and, until his departure in 1925, Stolper, and after that by Franz Klein. Therefore, I will mainly refer to the longer articles of Stolper and Federn, and only occasionally to their shorter comments, or to contributions of other authors.

As founder of the OVw, Walther Federn (1869–1949)[16] was its editor in chief until 1934. He was characterized by one of his friends "as a liberal, but not in the sense of economic liberalism. For him, liberalism above all meant what the French revolution had called 'the rights of man'".[17] Federn's main orientation was that of a monetary economist.[18] He wrote extensively on matters of financial markets and banks, also on public budgets. From his numerous analyses of balance sheets of Austrian companies which were published in the regular supplement of the OVw, Federn gained deep insights into the structural problems of Austria's economy. After the German occupation of Austria, Federn emigrated to the USA. He died in New York in 1949.

Federn outlived Gustav Stolper (1888–1947),[19] who was 19 years younger. Stolper joined the editorial staff of the OVw in 1911, and he advanced to co-editor in chief in 1914. Stolper's contributions offer a comprehensive view of economic and political matters; his power of analytical thinking impressed many leading politicians and top company executives who also sought his private advice. Stolper was also highly appreciated as speaker at economic conferences. A proliferous writer, Stolper published several books during his period of editor in chief of the OVw.[20]

Neither Stolper nor Federn undertook any greater efforts to lay down the general framework that was underlying their thorough and penetrating analyses of economic events which they always tried to present in a more general context – either that of

---

[16] In contrast to Stolper, biographical information on Walther Federn is scarce. There is a short entry in the International Biographical Dictionary of Central European Emigrés 1933–1945. Karl Polanyi's farewell speech at Federn's funeral was published – together with a short, anonymous obituary by the OVw – in 1949.

[17] Quoted form the introduction to Polanyi 2002, p. 15. Drucker (1978, p. 124) described Federn as "a venerable, white-bearded, very deaf old gentleman".

[18] Among his scientific publications, mention should be made of his contributions in the *Jahrbuch für Gesetzgebung, Verwaltung und Volkswirtschaft im Deutschen Reich,* which lead to a controversy with Ludwig Mises (Federn 1910), and also in the *Schriften des Vereins für Sozialpolitik* (Federn 1925).

[19] On Stolper's life see the extensive biography of his second wife Toni Stolper (1960).

[20] Stolper 1917, 1921.

the national economy, of history, or of politics. Although often sympathetic with the positions of the Austrian Social Democratic party, they rejected Marxism as well as the extreme anti-interventionist approach of the Austrian School.

8.2 The Economic Problem of "Deutschösterreich" Between the World Wars

The breakdown of the Habsburg monarchy in 1918 left Austria in a position that was the most uncomfortable of all succession states. Unable to feed her population with own agricultural products, and also poorly endowed with natural resources, Austria's manufacturing sector was highly dependent on export markets for machinery and equipment, for locomotives and for various kinds of expensive luxury products. At a stroke, Vienna had lost a large part of its functions as administrative capital of an empire with 53 million inhabitants. Also, its service sector, above all its banks, the stock exchange, and its wholesale trade were faced with the necessity to reorient towards markets and clients in countries which had established themselves as independent states, and which were eager to ascertain their sovereignty by creating their own legal systems, putting up trade barriers in order to protect their industries and promote the development of new ones. According to the predominant view, Austria was suffering form "hydrocephalitis", since one third of the population (two out of six million) was concentrated in Vienna which also harboured much of Austria's manufacturing industry.

The predominant view among the Austrian population was that, by the unequal peace treaty of Saint Germain, statehood has been forced upon the country which as economic and political entity was unviable and incapable of living ("nicht lebensfähig").[21] The only solution to this fundamental problem of the Austrian state was accession ("Anschluss")[22] to the German Reich which had been adopted almost unanimously by the Austrian parliament, but which was fiercely opposed by France and Britain and strictly prohibited by the Saint Germain treaty. In the years following the war, there were only a few voices in public opinion that disagreed from this predominant view, among whom were the economists Joseph Schumpeter and Friedrich Hertz.

---

[21] This was also Gustav Stolpers' resumé of his own empirical analysis, whose findings resulted in the consistent conclusion of the unviability of the German-Austrian state. On the other hand, Stolper emphasizes that "possible ways of consolidation had to be discussed" (Stolper 1921, p. XI).

[22] Until the rise of the Nazi movement in Germany, the term "Anschluss" was lacking any fascist or authoritarian connotation. Accession to Germany was unanimously supported by the Social Democratic party of Austria (until Hitler's appointment in 1933), by the *Großdeutsche Partei* ("Greater Germany"), and also by the majority of the Christian Social Party. Austria would have preferred "Deutschösterreich" as its official name, but this was forbidden by the Saint Germain treaty.

Austria's economic development in the years following World War I was characterized by economic chaos, hyperinflation, extreme poverty and starvation. Inflation reached its climax between August 1921 and September 1922, when prices increased at a monthly rate of 36%.[23] When inflation was stabilized by the government headed by the clergyman Ignaz Seipel from the Christian Social party, the purchasing power of the Crown had dropped to 1/14,400 of the pre-war value. In 1925, the Austrian Crown was replaced by the *Schilling* (S), with 1 S equivalent to 10,000 Crowns. Immediately after stabilization, the country plunged into recession. There was a swift recovery after which Austria enjoyed 5 years of economic growth during which some improvement in living standards occurred. However, pre-war levels of GDP were only briefly surpassed in the years 1928/1929 after which Austria's economy fell into depression.[24]

8.3 The Stabilization of the Post-War Economy

Both Federn and Stolper had rejected the way the Seipel government had finally achieved financial stabilization. The stabilization plan rested fundamentally on help from outside, i.e. the issue of government bonds under the auspices of the League of Nations and guaranteed by the victorious powers of the World War. In exchange, Austria had to subject her public finances to control by the League of Nations which appointed a high commissioner who had to confirm all decisions related to the budget of the federal government. The OVw strongly opposed the plan, above all, for political reasons, since it amounted to nothing less than an abandonment of a major part of state sovereignty. As a consequence, parliamentary democracy which had been fully established only a few years before was hollowed out, while the terms of the loan of 625 million Crown in gold re-enforced the barriers against accession to Germany. In the economic context, the OVw argued that consolidation would have been possible without help from foreign powers with about half as much of foreign exchange raised from several domestic sources (Stolper 1922/23-1, p. 35ff).

In his book *Deutsch-Österreich als Sozial- und Wirtschaftsproblem,* Stolper had argued that economic policy would have to acknowledge the increased role of the state in the economy. In a rough calculation, he estimated the government's share in non-agricultural national income was about half. As a consequence, the state's responsibility for economic development and for income distribution was no more a matter of ideology. Hence, the alternative was not between bourgeois and socialist, but "between reasonable and unreasonable financial policies" (Stolper 1922/23-1, p. 410). If the OVw did by no means deny the urgent need for reduction and eventual elimination of the budget deficit, it criticized the government's approach that it did not sufficiently take into account the repercussions of a sudden reduction of the

---

[23] Kernbauer 1991, p. 46.

[24] For an overview of Austria's economic development in the twentieth century see Butschek 1985.

budget deficit on the economy as a whole. Stolper pointed to the risks of the sharp increase of excises, turnover taxes and tariffs through which the government wanted to eliminate the budget deficit within 2 years (1923/1924). Stolper's argument foreshadows a Keynesian demand-side approach when he warns that extreme restrictiveness could fail to achieve its aims and become self-destructive if the consequent "decline in economic activity exceeds the reduction of public expenditure".[25] In this context, Stolper pointed to the negative experience of other countries "which had initiated a reform of state finances with the primitive methods of pre-war times" (Stolper 1922/1923, p. 435). More specifically, in a previous article Federn had already argued that for all its austerity, the budget for 1923 was unrealistic with respect to revenues as well as expenditures, and that in the end the deficit would be higher than preliminated. Negative effects on national income and employment would be inevitable, but they should not be "coolly ignored", as was the attitude of the government, which did not make any efforts to soften the consequences. This could be done through "compensating the suppression of internal demand by promotion of exports" (Federn 1922/23-1, p. 91). As a principal alternative to the tax hikes enacted by the government which directly and indirectly lead to an increase in production costs also of exported goods, Stolper proposed a differentiated consumption tax imposed and collected by autonomous associations[26] which had the advantage of avoiding as far as possible cost increases for exports and thus provided for the necessary "elasticity of the tax system" (see Sect. 8.8 of this contribution) with respect to economic activity (Stolper 1922/23-1, p. 436f).

To the surprise of the OVw and the government, at the end of the year 1923 the effective budget deficit was considerably lower than preliminated. If in 1922 49% of expenditures had not been covered by revenues, in 1923 this percentage declined to 14.9%, and in 1924, balance was achieved. On the other hand, the unemployment rate went up sharply from 4.7% 1922 to more than 10% in 1923. The deficit in the balance of trade soared to almost 1.5 billion Schilling, which amounted to 16% of GNP in 1924.[27] Clearly, such a deficit would be unsustainable over a longer period.

After successful stabilization of the currency and consolidation of the federal budget, issues of tax reform figured less prominently on the OVw's economic policy agenda. Mainly in the context of reconstruction of the Austrian capital market (see next Sect. 8.4),

---

[25] "Jedenfalls bieten hier bereits die Ereignisse der letzten Monate mit drastischer Deutlichkeit eine Lehre: Erfolgreiche Finanzpolitik setzt einen Wirtschaftsapparat in vollem Gang voraus. Anderseits sehen wir, dass auch bei radikalster Sparsamkeit der wirtschaftliche Apparat rascher zusammenschrumpft, als eine Einschränkung der öffentlichen Ausgaben möglich ist" (Stolper 1922/23-1, p. 435).

[26] Stolper had made this proposal in his ambitious "Finanzplan" which he had published in August 1921. According to this plan, the necessary restriction of public and private expenditure should have been achieved through differentiated taxation of consumption. The responsibility for deciding on the details of this tax rested with associations in which entrepreneurs and workers of each economic branch would be organized. In this respect Stolper's plan echoes the concept of guild socialism which he had supported in his book "Deutsch-Österreich als Sozial- und Wirtschaftsproblem".

[27] Butschek 1985, pp. 42ff. One should bear in mind, however, that before 1945 no figures for national product and income were available to which the figure for the trade deficit could have been related.

Stolper and Federn supported reductions of the tax burden on companies which could help to improve their financial situation. With a smaller part of profits taken away by the corporate income tax, firms would be able to pay higher dividends, which would make shares more attractive and enable companies to issue new shares and raise capital in the stock exchange. The reduction of business taxes (including those imposed by the Social-democratic provincial government of Vienna) would not lead to a permanent reduction of public revenues, since more of what "state and province sacrifice for the moment could come back once businesses have recovered" (Federn 1927/28-1, p. 621).

On the whole, the OVw's proposals for tax reductions were moderate, and it did not join in the permanent complaints from the business associations which called for a substantial reduction of taxes and public expenditure as well as of wages and social costs. "We do not blame entrepreneurs if they find social burdens unbearable, but we will not get tired of supporting the claims of workers and employees for a minimum of social protection which enables them to reproduce their ability to work during the long period which this people must survive, until it can rise to a new life in the (German) *Reich*" (Federn 1927/28-2, p. 1467).

Excursus on rent control and housing policies of "Red Vienna"

The OVw's position on the issue of continuation of rent control introduced during the war illustrates its general orientation with respect to social policy. As a consequence of the combined effect of inflation and the general freeze of rents introduced during the war, rental income from urban dwellings had been eliminated. Furthermore, the portion of income which low income households had to spend on rent had been drastically reduced. Real standards of living of the working class as well as of the bourgeois upper middle class depended to a considerable extent on the continuation of low rents. On the other hand, it was obvious that, in the long run, existing rents would be insufficient to adequately maintain urban housing structures. From the early twenties onwards, the continuation of rent control became an increasingly controversial issue of social and economic policy. Social Democrats and trade unions defended the freeze, whereas the Christian Social party sided with the landlords.

In 1925, Stolper wrote a series of articles on the issue of rent control, which, according to his initial statement, had been narrowed down to the question of adequacy of amount, whereas protection against unwarranted eviction ("Kündigungsschutz") was no more questioned (Stolper 1924/25-1, p. 451). Despite the fact that there were no limits for rents for newly built dwellings, construction of new apartment buildings in Vienna was close to zero. In response, the Social-democratic administration of the city of Vienna had started an ambitious programme of new construction of municipal apartments ("Gemeindebauten") which was partly financed through a (progressive) tax on all dwellings in the city ("Wohnbausteuer"). Stolper defended both the city's investment programme and the special tax which provided the financial base. If private construction activity was not forthcoming, public housing construction programmes were the only method to ensure that at least part of the apartments worn out each year would be replaced by new ones. "Where private capitalism fails, society has to intervene. Even if one does not advocate municipal construction activity in principle … that activity on the part of the city of Vienna must be welcomed as necessary and beneficial" (ibidem, p. 459). With respect to the special tax, Stolper argued that those who call for a termination of rent controls should not criticize the tax. Whereas an increase in rents would by no means assure that the revenues would be used for the necessary construction of new apartment buildings, the housing tax constituted a modest burden on those who benefit from rent controls and could therefore be considered a suitable instrument for redistributing those gains to households in need of new apartments (ibidem, p. 482). At the same time, Stolper acknowledged that an adjustment of rents would be required in order to ensure adequate maintenance and repair of buildings in the long run. However, he also pointed to the serious risks which any major increase of rents would imply due to its impact on cost of living and also wages of the urban population. Compensation would inevitably entail an increase of wages and of salaries of civil servants, thus deteriorating competitiveness on export markets and increasing public expenditure. Hence, an abolition of rent control would be possible only after thorough improvement of general economic conditions in Austria (ibidem, p. 511).

Five years later, Federn confirmed Stolper's views on the economic policies of the city of Vienna: "Burdensome as the municipal taxes may be … an unbiased comparison with Berlin teaches one to appreciate the provident and effective financial policy of the municipal administration. This also holds for the city's housing policy" (Federn 1929/30-2, p. 369).

8.4 The Reconstruction of the Capital Market

Only a few months after stabilization of the currency, the inflow of foreign exchange into the Austrian monetary system triggered off an increase in share prices which developed into a boom at the Viennese stock exchange during the year 1923. At that time, a considerable part of the population owned shares which had served as instrument to protect income during the period of rapid inflation. Increased share prices provided easy gains for many people, but at the same time there was an uneasy feeling about this boom which occurred in an economy which had consumed a major part of its wealth accumulated before the war, and where the financial statements of companies were distorted or meaningless and could not serve as basis for making decisions on investment. Much of the exaggeration of the boom was due to speculative investments from abroad[28] and to abuses from insiders which were tolerated by the supervisory authorities.[29] In an unfounded mood of optimism, some interpreted the boom as recuperation of the Viennese stock market and return to pre-war heights. The OVw expressed a widespread unease when Federn warned against excessive exuberance which had led to interest rates for call money above 100%.

---

[28] "Wer im Sommer 1923 im Ausland war, hatte leicht Gelegenheit, noch mitten im Börsenwirbel, noch während die obskursten Aktien von Genfer und Brüsseler Liftboys und Friseurgehilfen gekauft wurden, den Stimmungswechsel wahrzunehmen" (Stolper 1923/24-2, p. 975).

[29] Such as purchase of shares without effective payment, "Bezugsrechtsraub", etc.

The consequences of a collapse would be overly serious for a country like Austria that is dependent on the inflow of foreign currency to pay for its import surplus (1923/24-2, p. 846f). But he could not offer a recipe how to bar such excesses.

Inevitably, the collapse came at the turn of the year 1923/1924, depressing Austria's capital market for decades. In the following years, the reconstruction of the capital market as precondition for an improvement of the economic situation of the country represented a main concern of the OVw. Essentially, confidence of investors would have to be regained by re-establishing clarity and transparency of financial statements of companies. Some healing effects could be expected from the crisis such as insolvency of dubious companies or withdrawal of their shares, and also of shares of companies which were too small to figure on the stock exchange. As a consequence, some financial assets would be reconverted into savings accounts, enabling banks to finance such companies through bank loans as the more appropriate form (Stolper 1923/24-2, p. 724). What was next required in the first place was a "Goldbilanzgesetz" in order to enable companies to reconstruct their accounts on the basis of a thoroughly new evaluation of their assets and liabilities under the conditions of the new currency. Federn criticized the draft of the *Goldbilanzgesetz* for its insufficient requirements to achieve true transparency and made several proposals for improvement. In particular, Federn emphasized that without mandatory regulations for a uniform scheme of positions in financial statements, for declaration of the principles which firms applied for valuation of various kinds of assets and liabilities, with the possibility to net different types of positions in financial statements, etc., even in their renewed form financial statements of companies would not provide sufficiently reliable information for the investor (Federn 1924/25-1, p. 394).

What is remarkable for a journal such as the OVw which had a major part of its readers among financial circles is that Stolper and Federn never left any doubt that financial markets did not exist for themselves, but that they were subordinated to serve the needs of industry. At the height of the crisis in early 1924, Stolper had deplored "the financial detachment of entrepreneurs from companies, of the parallel existence of rich industrialists and poor companies. If resistance of industry against the supremacy of banks is so weak that the antithesis between financial and industrial capital is resolved without difficulty, the reason is that the foreign exchange account or the stock market have become the main concern of the industrialist whose orientation is that o a financial capitalist" (Stolper 1923/24-1, p. 725)

Stolper criticized the hope that Vienna could again become a European financial centre without a solid industrial base in the country as dangerous illusion (see Sect. 8.5). Repeatedly, the OVw suggested that banks should reduce their overwhelming dominance as shareholders and also in the control of Austrian companies. Expectations that the capital market would recover once companies publish their Goldbilanzen were quickly disappointed. On average, share prices at the Vienna stock exchange remained below the value of share capital plus reserves as declared in financial statements.[30]

---

[30] Noell 1927, p. 207f.

For Walther Federn, this was just a reflection of unrealistic accounting practices. His pessimistic conclusion from the OVw's systematic analysis of financial statements of companies listed at the Vienna stock exchange was that "depreciation allowances are far below pre-war standards, whereas they ought to be higher due to technical obsolescence and increased cost of equipment". Capitalists were disappointed "by the way the managements present the financial statements for their companies that do not permit any judgement on their real situation" (Federn 1927/28-1, p. 567). As a consequence, the Vienna stock exchange remained unattractive for foreign investors for whom there was an urgent need in capital-poor Austria.

8.5 Structural Imbalances and *Lebensfähigkeit* (Viability) of the Austrian Economy

Ever since the publication of Gustav Stolper's book "Deutsch-Österreich als Sozial- und Wirtschaftsproblem" (1921), the OVw had upheld its position of unviability of Austria as an economic entity, and that political union with Germany would be the only solution of the Austrian problem. Among the few who challenged this position were the Austrian economist and social scientist Friedrich Hertz,[31] and the authors of a report commissioned by the League of Nations,[32] the British economist Walter T. Layton and the French economist Charles Rist.

The strongest evidence for the structural insufficiency of the Austrian economy was its deficit in the balance of commodity trade which amounted to 1.5 billion Schilling in 1924, with only minimal tendencies to decline. In the 1920s and 1930s, hardly any information – except for receipts from tourism – was available on the external account of capital and on the trade balance for invisibles. In 1925, Hertz published a pamphlet "Zahlungsbilanz und Lebensfähigkeit Österreichs", in which he argued on the basis of pre-war data that Austria still had a substantial surplus in the invisible account, compensating much of the trade deficit which would therefore give less reason to worry about than the supporters of union with Germany suggested. By this, he suggested that Vienna had been able to maintain or regain its leading position as international centre for international finance and trade in East-central Europe which could be the basis for continued recovery of Austria's economy. Some of the essential judgements of the League of Nations' official report were also based on Hertz's estimates.

In his review of Hertz's pamphlet, Walther Federn above all argued that, in the first place, "unviability" did not mean that Austria would be unable to survive at any level of economic activity, but rather that, given the structure of its economy and, in particular, of its manufacturing industry, she was unlikely to make use of its productive capabilities within a reasonable time span in an environment of newly formed

---

[31] The OVw occasionally published contributions by Friedrich Hertz.
[32] Layton and Rist 1925.

small states each of which were pursuing protectionist policies. Federn also showed in detail that Hertz conjectures on the surplus in trade of invisibles and on capital income of wealthy Austrians from abroad were unrealistic (1924/25-2, p. 1297ff). Federn also argued that the hopes Hertz entertained concerning the return of pre-war conditions once European economic recovery had made sufficient progress were misguided, and that for Austria "it would take too long" (ibidem, p. 1300).

In an extensive review of the Layton-Rist-report, Stolper re-emphasized Federn's argument against the statistical estimates of capital income flowing into Austria. In particular, Stolper criticized the report's optimism with respect to the role of Vienna as financial centre of East-central Europe. For a country as poor as Austria had become after the World War, it would be impossible to sustain a major financial centre, since it would never be able to generate the necessary volume of savings. If Viennese banks had succeeded to keep part of their function as financiers of companies in other East-central European states, these loans had to be refinanced from banks in Western Europe (1924/25-2, p. 1433ff). Six years later, Stolper's concerns about the "enormous risks" implied in such a role as intermediator were confirmed by the collapse of the *Creditanstalt* in 1931.

In the same year (1925), the OVw published a "Denkschrift der Österreichisch-Deutschen Arbeitsgemeinschaft" "Das österreichische Wirtschaftproblem" (memorandum on the Austrian economic problem), which was signed by prominent representatives of a variety of institutions of economic policy, among them there were Benedikt Kautsky and Edmund Palla from the Chamber of Labour, Max Tayenthal, retired secretary of the Chamber of Commerce, Hermann Neubacher, several Austrian industrialists, and Gustav Stolper, who was the main author of the memorandum. The arguments used there in support of the thesis of unviability are the same as referred to above. What is new and remarkable in the memorandum is the evaluation of unification with Germany and creation of a federation of Danubian states as alternatives for solution of Austria's economic problem. Disregarding the question whether such a federation could ever be considered a realistic project, the memorandum argues that it would in any case be inferior to reunification with Germany, because a federation of the envisaged type would not re-establish the internal market which had been constituted by the defunct Habsburg monarchy. What it had guaranteed was "not only more or less free trade in commodities", but also uniform conditions for economic activity in the whole area (1924/25-2, 9. 1158). With decentralized political authorities, the newly formed states would continue to put up impediments against trans-border economic activities and thus prevent Vienna to regain its previous role as economic capital of the region. In modern terms, the memorandum introduced the distinction between free trade area and internal market which became essential in the 1980s in the debate on the course of European economic integration. Only full unification with Germany could establish the conditions under which Austria would be fully embedded in a larger economic area.

When prospects for unification became vaguer during the 1920s, the OVw nonetheless constantly rejected any euphemistic descriptions of the state of the Austrian economy. If Hertz, in his aforementioned pamphlet, had denied contentions that, after the collapse of the monarchy, Austria lacked an industrial base, Federn held against that the problem was quite different, namely that Austria's traditional industrial base lacked unhampered access to markets that now had become external. In the second half of the 1920s, Federn never became tired of pointing to the signs of continued industrial weakness of the economy despite some progress in production and employment. Based on systematic, careful analysis of financial statements of industrial companies, Federn was able to substantiate his rather pessimistic evaluation in the absence of comprehensive statistics on industrial production. Repeatedly, he argued that allowances for depreciation were insufficient, that for several major industrial establishments indebtedness to banks was too high and increasing due to the inability to meet the requirements for current interest payments. In many cases, official published accounts of companies rendered a misleading picture of the financial situation that was already under great strain (1927/28-1, pp. 121ff, pp. 149ff). In 1928, Federn wrote that "there is not much time left to be lost. The crisis of the capital market that has been lasting for 4 years threatens to turn into a catastrophe for the whole economy" (1927/28-1, p. 623).

8.6 Banks

The few economists who disagreed with the pessimistic perspective on the newly formed state as an economic entity based their hopes and expectations on Vienna's position as international financial centre, in particular on the indispensability of the services of the large Viennese banks and of the stock exchange for the economies of the succession states. After the war, Joseph Schumpeter shared this view when he wrote that, even though "a financial and commercial centre does not have the indestructible vitality of an industrial centre .... and every day a bit of this position gets lost, the fundamental structure is still there. To preserve it ... is *the* principal task of Austria's politics, the only one that must be taken serious" (Schumpeter 1920/1921, p. 505).[33] Despite the unusual circumstances, under which the short boom of the Viennese stock market had developed in 1923, illusions had appeared that the good times of the monarchy could come back. "Based on the traditional connections of its banks and its commerce, during the year 1923 Vienna was well on its way to occupy a dominant position as central marketplace for money and trade of the Danubian states, and as mediator between these areas and the important centres of the West".[34] Fritz G. Steiner, director of the small *Kompassbank* and author of this pamphlet, still entertained the hope in 1925, that banks could take the lead in Austria's economic recovery if they succeeded in regaining their former position.

As I have already pointed out, the OVw never shared the view that Vienna could continue to function as financial centre without a strong industrial base. Its realistic assessment of the role of the banks under the new conditions put the OVw in an

---

[33] He may have changed his view later.
[34] Steiner 1925, p. 30f.

almost unique position to evaluate the weaknesses and possibilities of the Viennese banks on a realistic basis. The OVw had relentlessly criticized the hypertrophy of the banking sector during the period of rapid inflation. When most of the banks which had been newly established after 1918 went bankrupt after the collapse of the stock market boom, the OVw saw this as a necessary adjustment and objected to the endeavours of the government to cover up the failures of incompetent managements and corrupt supervisory authorities with unsparing criticism. Federn and Stolper did not hesitate to unveil the dubious and often fraudulent practices of owners and directors of the banks that came under pressure. Thus, the OVw had the leading role among the few independent newspapers vis á vis the government and the Christian Social party and their efforts to protect former ministers and functionaries who were involved in these scandals. "In order to obtain the licence for a bank ... admission to the stock exchange, or permission for dubious conditions for the issuance of new stock, one had to secure only the promotion of a member of parliament of the ruling parties or to use similar connections, and all concerns of the *Himmelpfortgasse* (i.e. the Ministry of Finance as supervisory authority) could be overcome" (Stolper 1923/24-2, p. 1043).

Although "most of the *nouveau riches* (had) vanished as a determining power of economic life in Austria" (ibidem) within a few months after the collapse of the stock market boom, information about malpractices and abuses and also about persons who had participated in these activities became available with considerable delay and remained a major issue of political debates[35] and public criticism for several years. Through Stolper's and Federn's superior knowledge and understanding of the functioning of banking business and financial markets, and also through information obtained from insiders, the OVw often played an active role in the process of clearing the swamp that the crisis of 1924 had left behind.[36]

In the OVw's view, the eradication of dubious banks was not only unavoidable, but also necessary for the banking sector to regain its credibility and to perform its functions in the process of recovery of the Austrian economy, and in particular, for the reconstruction of the capital market. The OVw attentively followed the development of the "big five" Viennese banks (*Creditanstalt, Bodencreditanstalt, Bankverein, Niederösterreichische Eskomptegesellschaft, Länderbank*) as soon as they resumed publishing meaningful annual financial statements in the new currency. In his analysis of the combined statements of these banks, Federn noted that in 1926 their total assets (2,557 million S) amounted to 42% of the pre-war level,

---

[35] In 1921, the Austrian parliament established an independent commission for the supervision of banks. The commission played a decisive role in this process (see Ausch 1968).

[36] The series of bank insolvencies started with the Depositenbank in 1924. The case with the greatest losses for which the government had to step in was the involvement of the state-owned Postsparkasse (Postal Savings Bank) which become known in 1926. The bank had financed Sigmund Bosel's speculations against the Franc which resulted in a loss for the bank of more than 200 million S. Several government ministers (e.g. finance minister Ahrer and foreign minister Mataja) were directly or indirectly involved in scandals or in attempts of camouflage. Karl Ausch's (1968) history often refers to reports and comments of the OVw.

whereas their equity was only 26% of its previous value. Even with the reduced volume of loans and other assets, the Viennese banks were still able "to exert considerable influence on the economies of neighbour states". This influence "is based on the confidence which the large banks of Vienna enjoy among western countries" which prefer to give loans to banks and industrial companies in Eastern Europe with endorsement of a Viennese bank. From the analysis of the balance sheets, Federn drew the conclusion that "altogether the Austrian banking system is sound and has adjusted to the requirements of the domestic economy. Expectations for prosperous development are justified, provided that general economic conditions do not get even more difficult" (Federn 1926/27-2, p. 847f). In the following year, Federn confirmed his positive overall assessment. At the same time, he emphasized that most of the profits of the banks came from foreign assets, whereas from the side of their domestic customers, banks were confronted with the problem of "frozen loans". To reduce the large volume of such loans would take time, depending "on the improvement of conditions in industry and on the scope for writing of losses" (Federn 1927/28-2, p. 824).

8.7 Portents of Crisis: The Collapse of the *Bodencreditanstalt*

Federn's warnings were proven right even before the outbreak of the Great Depression. On October 7, 1929, the government announced that negotiations for a merger between *Bodencreditanstalt* and *Creditanstalt* had been successfully concluded. In the preceding weeks and months, the *Bodencreditanstalt*, which was the second-largest of the Big Five, was under increasing pressure to meet its obligations. The immediate cause of the collapse was a withdrawal of deposits in reaction to threats of a "march upon Vienna" by the fascist *Heimwehr*-movement in September 1929. But – as Federn had pointed out earlier in his analyses of balance sheets of industrial companies, but without explicitly mentioning the *Bodencreditanstalt* – there were more fundamental causes for the breakdown. The *Bodencreditanstalt* had overextended its credit with its forward strategy of buying up the shares of troubled companies as well as its own shares in order to avoid the necessary downward revaluation of frozen loans and shares which formed a major part of the bank's assets. Federn also pilloried the strong involvement of the *Bodencreditanstalt* in party politics which had been initiated by Rudolf Sieghart, the bank's president with little competence in banking business proper. For that purpose, Sieghart had entertained his own group of news media ("Tagblatt-Verlag"). He also financed the *Heimwehr*-movement through various channels (Federn 1929/30, p. 41ff, ibidem, p. 70ff).

It appears that Federn tried to shy away his own doubts when he expressed the hope that in taking over the *Bodencreditanstalt*, the *Creditanstalt* "certainly has evaluated all the assets cautiously, that it has reduced the positions of frozen and dubious loans, while it has also realized that it can pay only a small quota to the former shareholders of *Bodencreditanstalt*" (p. 41). In this case, however, Federn was proven wrong 18 months later.

8.8 The OVw's General Views on Economic Policy

Except for the short period following World War I when Gustav Stolper in his contribution to the debate on socialization expressed strong sympathies for a model of "guild socialism" as an economic order,[37] the editors of the OVw accepted the market economy which implies that they rejected economic socialism. In the political reality of Austria between the world wars, things were more complicated than suggested by this simple alternative. According to its Marxist ideology, the Social Democratic party proclaimed socialism as long run goal. But in practice, its economic policies were designed to improve the condition of the working class within the market economy through extending the influence of government. The other extreme of the spectrum, economic liberalism was advocated by the economists of the Austrian School of economics, which enjoyed only little support among political parties. The economic policies of the Christian Social Party and its governments were clearly interventionist in their orientation to preserve the interests of the traditional middle classes (peasants, small shop owners, urban landlords).

For the editors of the OVw, a return to the pre-war laissez faire system was impossible "since close and deep-rooted connections between politics and the economy have been established during the war and thereafter" (Federn 1927/28-2, p. 1466). On the one hand, the OVw in many ways advocated policies to improve conditions under which business enterprises operate, e.g. as regards taxation, the functioning of the capital market, infrastructure, and political stability. The OVw "did not blame entrepreneurs if they found the burdens of social legislation too heavy", but, on the other hand, it would never become tired of supporting the claims of the working classes "for the minimum of social protection they need to sustaining their labour power and for raising a capable new generation" (ibidem, p. 1467). For Stolper, it was evident that, "where private capitalism fails, society has to intervene" (Stolper 1925/26-1, p. 453). With their plea for an interventionist approach in economic policy,[38] the OVw and its editors rejected the ideology of free market economy of the Austrian School, which did, however, not pre-empt publication of contributions of Hayek and other members of that school in the pages of the OVw.

Overall, the OVw in its views and positions aimed at solutions for economic problems that were sound under an overall perspective of the economy as well as with respect to a fair balance of conflicting interests. The editors of the OVw remained critical towards the Social Democrats for their ideological obligation to Marxism. On practical issues, however, the OVw often supported positions and proposals of the Social Democrats against the Christian Social governments' policies which were often obliged to questionable social interest, corrupted or, at worst, anti-democratic.

---

[37] Stolper 1921, esp. pp. 277ff.

[38] In the sense of the concept of "interventionism" as developed by Wilhelm Röpke (1929) – interventions introduced in a systematic context, as opposed to "ad hoc interventionism", which is a mere reaction to emerging problems and special interests.

The contributions of the editors and of the other members of the editorial staff very seldom refer to contemporary theoretical literature on economic issues. Likewise, one can only occasionally find explicit references to theoretical propositions underlying the arguments used in the debate of policy issues. As regard issues of the monetary system, in 1910 Federn had engaged in a controversial debate against Ludwig Mises about gold convertibility of the Crown, the currency of the Habsburg monarchy. Federn defended the position of the Austro-Hungarian Bank which had objected to demands from the Hungarian government to make gold convertibility a legal obligation. Federn argued that a managed gold currency had the advantage that during periods when the price of money increases abroad, the effects on the domestic interest rate are minimized or at least postponed, and also, that in times of political disturbance large outflows of gold could be forestalled (Federn 1910, p. 168f). Mises (1909a, b) had taken the opposite position of a pure gold standard, supporting the demand for full convertibility.[39]

In his proposals for tax reform, Stolper's main arguments are very similar to those Schumpeter used in his contributions to the Deutsche Volkswirt in the German debate of the later 1920s. In a country, where, according to Stolper's estimate, the state controlled more than half of non-agricultural national income, financial policy ("Finanzpolitik") had to accept responsibility for the functioning of the economy as a whole. If financial policy decides about the distribution of the social product between the public budget and the private sector, "the impact and the degree of effectiveness of financial policy are determined by the methods through which this distribution is effected. The measures can either be brutal-mechanical", or they can be "differentiated and elastic" (1922/23-1, p. 410). It is such an elastic design of financial policy through which the social product can be brought up to a level at which the overall burden of taxation becomes acceptable again. In view of Austria's enormous trade deficit, Stolper argued that taxation on consumption had to be increased, whereas taxes on production needed to be reduced. Stolper's specific proposals included a differentiated consumption tax with low tax rates on essentials and high tax rates for luxuries. High tariffs which were the method preferred by the government had the undesirable effect of increasing costs of production and exports. Stolper also proposed a refund of the cumulative turnover tax for exported goods (1922/23-1, p. 433f). Similar to Stolper, Schumpeter (1985a, b) also attributed strong effects to changes in the tax structure. A small initial reduction of the overall tax burden, if appropriately structured as just described, would be able to produce significant change. A skillful tax policy could enact tax increases without damaging economic performance. Schumpeter thought that the tax burden on enterprises was excessively high and constituted the main impediment to sustained recovery. He also favoured taxation of consumption.[40]

---

[39] Obviously, Mises was deeply irritated by Federn's critique. In his memoirs, written many decades later, he still tried to defame Federn and the OVw in an unfair way (Mises 1978, p. 30f).

[40] Chaloupek 2003, p. 251.

In the context of the debate about unification of Austria with Germany, Stolper's (and his co-authors') arguments anticipate the economics of the internal market, as opposed to a mere customs union. One might be tempted to dismiss the OVw's scepticism towards the "viability" of Austria as an economic entity and its firm support of accession in the light of the experience of increasing economic prosperity of Austria after World War II. However, one has to take into account that the evolution of the European and the international economy after 1945 towards free trade and economic integration was diametrically opposed to the protectionist environment which Austria faced after the dissolution of the Habsburg monarchy.

8.9 The OVw's Support for the Constitution and for Parliamentary Democracy

The OVw had taken a sharply critical position with respect to the programme by which Austria's currency was stabilized in 1922/1923 not only for economic reasons, but also because the editors were not prepared to accept that the country with its newly established parliamentary democracy had to surrender a major part of its sovereignty to foreign control. When Austria's economy moved forward on the path of consolidation and normalization during the 1920s, the OVw gave its support to political developments and forces from which a strengthening of parliamentary democracy, a peaceful resolution of political conflicts and a softening of the opposition between social classes could be expected.

The OVw therefore sharply opposed efforts of the leader of the Christian Social party Ignaz Seipel to use political threats and other forms of pressure exerted by the fascist Heimwehr-movement to reduce the rights of parliament and to change the constitution towards corporatist rule and authoritarian government. In a commentary of Seipel's withdrawal as federal chancellor in August 1929, Franz Klein[41] sharply attacked him for his deliberate manoeuvres "to shake the foundations of parliamentary democracy" in Austria which had become more and more firmly established during the course of the 1920's (1928/29-2, p. 733). In another article, Klein welcomed the appointment of the industrialist Ernst Streeruwitz for federal chancellor and praised him for his unconditional support of parliamentary democracy.

When a new government formed a few months later under chancellor Johannes Schober introduced a draft bill that called for fundamental "reform" in the Austrian constitution of 1920, Franz Klein dramatically warned against the changes which, in his view, amounted to nothing less than a "counter-revolution", which would open the road towards "dictatorship from the right" (1929/1930, p. 97).

---

[41] Franz Johann Klein, 1895–1964, changed his name to Robert Ingrim in 1946; member of the editorial staff 1926–1930. He moved to Switzerland in 1933, emigrated to Canada and USA, returned to Switzerland in 1947 (according to communication from Dr. Eckhart Früh, Vienna).

The OVw supported the installation of an economic conference composed of non-partisan experts and representatives of all interest groups by chancellor Schober in 1930 and expressed its hopes that it would help to preserve peace in internal politics (Federn 1929/30-1, p. 621).

When chancellor Dollfuss finally established his authoritarian dictatorship in 1934, this could not be without consequences. In issue No 49, dated September 1, 1934, the OVw published a formal statement that Walther Federn had resigned from the position of editor in chief. If the statement suggested that it had been Federn's free decision, this is hardly credible under the given circumstances. Editorship as well as ownership of the periodical was given into the hands of Maria L. Klausberger, member of the editorial staff since 1931. The last issue under her editorship appeared on March 12, 1938. In December 1945, Margarethe Klausberger-Fuchs, adoptive daughter of Maria Klausberger, started the relaunch of the journal. But the conditions for the success of the OVw between the world wars had disappeared. Its dispersed readership among the German speaking liberal intelligentsia in central and east-central Europe had disappeared with the take-over of communism after World War II.

References

Almanach 1908-1918-1928. 10 Jahre Nachfolgestaaten. Sonderausgabe zur Zwanzigjahrfeier des "Österreichischen Volkswirts", Wien 1928

Ausch, Karl, Als die Banken fielen. Europa-Verlag, Wien Frankfurt Zürich 1968

Bermann, Richard, *Die Redaktion,* in: Almanach 1908-1918-1928, p. 20f

Butschek, Felix, Die österreichische Wirtschaft im 20.Jahrhundert, Gustav Fischer-Verlag, Stuttgart 1985

Chaloupek, Günther, *The Second Cleavage of the Austrian School: Schumpeter's German Writings on Economic Systems and Economic Policy in Comparison with Mises/Hayek,* in: Jürgen Backhaus(ed.), Joseph Alois Schumpeter. Entrepreneurship, Style and Vision. Kluwer Academic Publishers, Boston-Dordrecht-London 2003, pp. 245–260.

Drucker, Peter F., Adventures of a Bystander, Harper Row, New York 1978

Federn, Walther, *Das Problem der gesetzlichen Aufnahme der Barzahlungen in Österreich-Ungarn,* in: Jahrbuch für Gesetzgebung, Verwaltung und Volkswirthschaft im Deutschen Reich, Vo. 34(1910), pp. 151–172

Federn, Walther, *Die Kreditpolitik der Wiener Banken,* in: Julius Bunzel (ed.), Geldentwertung und Stabilisierung in ihren Einflüssen auf die soziale Entwicklung in Österreich. Schriften des Vereins für Sozialpolitik Vol. 169, Duncker & Humblot, Munich and Leipzig 1925, pp. 54–74

Hagemann, Harald/C.-D. Krohn (eds.), Biographisches Handbuch der deutschsprachigen wirtschaftswissenschaftlichen Emigration nach 1933, K.G. Saur-Verlag, München 1999

Hertz, Friedrich, *Zahlungsbilanz und Lebensfähigkeit Österreichs,* in: Schriften des Vereins für Sozialpolitik Vol. 167(1925)

International Biographical Dictionary of Central European Emigrés 1933–1945, Vol. II, Verlag K.G. Saur, München 1983

Kernbauer, Hans, Währungspolitik in der Zwischenkriegszeit. Oesterreichische Nationalbank, Vienna 1991

Layton, W.T./Charles Rist, Die Wirtschaftslage Österreichs. Verlag des Verbandes österreichischer Banken und Bankiers, Wien 1925

Mises, Ludwig von, *Das Problem der gesetzlichen Aufnahme der Barzahlungen in Österreich-Ungarn,* in: Jahrbuch für Gesetzgebung, Verwaltung und Volkswirthschaft im Deutschen Reich, Vol. 33(1909a), pp. 985–1037

Mises, Ludwig von, *Zum Problem der gesetzlichen Aufnahme der Barzahlungen in Österreich-Ungarn,* in: Jahrbuch für Gesetzgebung, Verwaltung und Volkswirthschaft im Deutschen Reich, Vol. 33(1909b), pp. 1877–1884

Mises, Ludwig von, Erinnerungen von .., Gustav Fischer Verlag, Stuttgart 1978

Noell, Günter, Die Ergebnisse der Goldbilanzierung der Aktiengesellschaften in Oesterreich, Libau (Estonia) 1927

Österreich-Lexikon, ed. R. Bamberger et al., 2 Vol., Vienna 1995

The New Palgrave. A Dictionary of Economics, eds. John Eatwell, Murray Milgate, Peter Newman, Macmillan Press, London and Basingstoke 1987

Röpke, Wilhelm, *Staatsinterventionsimus,* in: Handwörterbuch der Staatswissenschaft, 4th edition, supplementary volume, Jena 1929, pp. 861–882

Polanyi, Karl, *Walther Federn als Mensch,* in: Der österreichische Volkswirt, Vol 35(1949), Nr.7, p. 3

Polanyi, Karl, Chronik der großen Transformation, Band 1: Wirtschaftliche Transformation, Gegenbewegungen und der Kampf um die Demokratie, eds. Michele Cangiani and Claus Thomasberger, Metropolis-Verlag, Marburg 2002

Schumpeter, Joseph.A., *Sozialistische Möglichkeiten von heute,* in: Archiv für Sozialwissenschaft und Sozialpolitik Vol. 48(1920/21), reprinted in: Aufsätze zur ökonomischen Theorie, Mohr Siebeck, Tübingen 1952, pp. 465–510

Schumpeter, Joseph.A., *Steuerkraft und nationale Zukunft,* in: Der deutsche Volkswirt Vol.1(1926/27), reprinted in: Aufsätze zur Wirtschaftspolitik, Mohr Siebeck, Tübingen 1985, pp. 55–63 (1985a)

Schumpeter, Joseph.A., *Finanzpolitik,* in: Der deutsche Volkswirt Vol.1(1926/27), reprinted in: Aufsätze zur Wirtschaftspolitik, op. cit., pp. 55–63 (1985b)

Steiner, Fritz Georg, Geldmarkt und Wirtschaftskrise, Manz-Verlag, Wien 1925

Stolper, Gustav, Das mitteleuropäische Wirtschaftsproblem, Deuticke-Verlag, Vienna 1917, 1918[2,3]

Stolper, Gustav, Deutsch-Österreich als Sozial- und Wirtschaftsproblem, Drei Masken-Verlag, Munich 1921

Stolper, Toni, Ein Leben in Brennpunkten unserer Zeit. Gustav Stolper 1888–1947, Rainer Wunderlich Verlag Hermann Leins, Tübingen 1960

Walther Federn zum Gedächtnis. In: Der österreichische Volkswirt, Vol 34(1949), Nr.7, p. 3f

Chapter 9
Gustav Stolper: Mentor of a Young German Democrat

Sabine Wenhold

Lilo Linke (1906–1963) – Gustav Stolper (1888–1947), "Der Deutsche Volkswirt" and its circle – From typist to journalist and "social reformer"[1]

This paper examines Lilo Linke, "ein demokratisch beschwingtes Berliner Kind"[2] on her life's journey from Weimar republican Berlin into exile via London to South America.

The main sources of the following portrait are letters, diaries, intimate, sometimes autobiographical, accounts of four people closely related to each other. Gustav Stolper and Lilo Linke were in close exchange as partners at work and as lovers. Their affair lasted from 1929 till Gustav Stolper's premature death in 1947, including his wife Toni in a triangle and as a close friend Margaret Storm Jameson (1897–1986), writer, political activist and first female president of the British PEN-Club in 1938.

A passage from her autobiography may introduce us to the stimulating intellectual sphere the Stolpers frequented in the Berlin of the Weimar period. Storm Jameson is a guest at a dinner-party in Stolper's Dahlem villa in early 1932:

"Gustav Stolper and his wife lived in a society where intelligence, good manners, tolerance, uncommon sense, wit, worldly knowledge, join to quicken a cell which can only exist in a capital city, and there only at certain times on certain conditions. Their house in a suburb of Berlin, among pine-trees, was an instance of the new moneyed simplicity: the interior walls of four living-rooms could be rolled back

---

[1] Toni Stolper on the cover of: Auszüge aus Briefen an eine Freundin [i.e., Lilo Linke, S. W.], Gustav Stolper, letters to Lilo Linke, 1933–1947, August 1961, Stolper papers, NL 186/000065, fol. 1, Bundesarchiv, Koblenz.
[2] Toni Stolper, Ein Leben in Brennpunkten unserer Zeit, Wien, Berlin, New York, Gustav Stolper 1888–1947, Tübingen 1960, p. 334.

S. Wenhold (✉)
Student, Department of History, University of Bremen,
Schwachhauser Heerstrasse 58, 28209 Bremen, Germany
e-mail: sabine.wenhold@web.de

to form a vast central square with immense windows and an invisible source of warmth: the nursery, which I saw when Mrs. Stolper took me with her to say goodnight to her two young children, was divided at night by a sliding wall. The furniture in all the rooms was light and strong; there were admirable modern paintings, and, lying about, weeklies and monthlies in three languages. Had you wanted an example of the Berlin farthest from the brawling in the streets, there it was, cultured, cosmopolitan-on the edge".[3] One of the dinner-guests, the American journalist Edgar Mowrer, a friend of Gustav and Toni Stolper, paints a gloomy, indeed prophetic picture of Germany's near future: "This country smells of trouble, as if somebody had buried a rat under the boards".[4] This scenario seems to be still far beyond the imagination of the German guests. The subject is changed, the conversation turns to literature. Chauvinism does not stand a chance with this group of cultured and cosmopolitan Europeans of German nationality: "Precisely that seems to have been their crime and the cause why their country had to rid itself of them"[5] is Storm Jameson's résumé only 2 years later. Further on, she will be using her influence to save hundreds of refugees from NS-concentration camps.[6] Being a founder-member of the 'Peace Pledge Union'[7], Storm Jameson realises the enormous threat National Socialism posed to peace in Europe. Events in Germany, her own experience in Berlin, and a visit to German occupied Vienna in 1938 including the moving account of her visit to Toni Stolper's sister Anna Jerusalem[8] made her dissociate herself from pacifism: "War which modern ingenuity has made the collective suicide of nations, the last triumph of the irrational, is accepted by Fascists as the highest activity of the human spirit".[9]

In February 1932, Storm Jameson visits a friend in Berlin, Lilo Linke, who introduces the English author to her friends Toni and Gustav Stolper. This is how Storm Jameson remembers Gustav Stolper from their first visit in Lilo Linke's apartment: "a fine intelligent head [...] an air of authority and success, of a man who knows he is better informed than anyone he is likely to meet",[10] an assessment well justified.

---

[3] Margaret Storm Jameson, Journey from the North, vol. 1, London 1969, p. 275.

[4] Ibid. p. 275f; Storm Jameson, Introduction to Lilo Linke, Tale Without End, New York 1934, p. XVII f, Mowrer was right in a very personal sense: in mortal danger he had to leave Berlin overnight on August 1, 1933, see: Gustav Stolper, letters to, August 31, 1933, NL Stolper 185/65, fol. 1.

[5] Ibid. p. XVIII.

[6] Catherine Clay, British Women Writers 1914–1945, Professional Work and Friendship, Aldershot 2006, p. 169.

[7] See Martin Ceadel, Pacifism in Britain 1914–1945 The Defining of a Faith, Oxford 1980; Paul Berry and Marc Bostridge, Vera Brittain, A Life, London 1995, p. 350, 353–354.

[8] Storm Jameson, journey, vol. I, p. 382f.

[9] Phyllis Lassner, A Cry for Life: Storm Jameson, Stevie Smith, and the Fate of Europe's Jews, in: Holsinger, Paul. M. and Schofield, A. M., ed.: Visions of War: World War II in Popular Literature and Culture, Bowling Green, Ohio 1992, p. 182.

[10] Storm Jameson, Journey, vol. I, p. 274.

Gustav Stolper, central figure of "Dienstag" – and "Stegerwald Kreis",[11] well connected in high places, politics and business circles alike, was among the best informed persons of Weimar Germany's public life. This get-together is the beginning of a lifelong friendship. They see each other frequently in London and 1947 in New York, when Storm Jameson recalls having met "Europe" again, in the living room "of a highly-cultivated and intellectually alert Austrian-Jewish household".[12]

At their farewell in Berlin, Toni Stolper takes Storm Jameson's hand: "I am glad that Lilo has made a good English friend, [...] perhaps she will need you",[13] which was about to come true only a year later.

Lilo Linke was born on October 31, 1906 in Berlin. Her father served as a minor official with the Berlin city council. The lower middle class environment where she grew up was characterised by want, narrow-mindedness and the growing anti-Semitism of Lilo's mother: "My Mother believed in the lampoon: 'The Protocols of the Elders of Zion', as in a bible",[14] Lilo Linke remembers in her autobiography years later, and she was horrified to see her mother and her brother became dedicated National Socialists. Her friendship with a well-educated Jewish girl made her aware of the existence of a different, highly cultivated world beyond her own nationalist milieu and had a crucial influence on her future life. Her mother was outraged: "She accuses the Jews of having led her child away from her".[15] Lilo Linke grows up against the background of mass poverty following World War I, hunger, inflation, death and bloody civil strife during the November Revolution.

Having finished secondary school, she worked as a trainee in a bookshop and joined the youth movement of the white-collar trade union, an activity stimulating her growing political awareness. She joined the "Reichsbund Demokratischer Jugend", the liberal left-wing youth organisation of the DDP, the German Democratic Party, and became a member in 1927. She started working as a typist in their youth organisation's central office in Berlin, much to the dismay of her uncompromising parents: – "In their opinion I would in all probability land before long in the arms of the communists".[16]

From within the youth organisation, she soon started her own political activities like giving minor election speeches and campaigning for the DDP. She learned how to promote with enthusiasm the liberal point of view on complex problems like the

---

[11] Dienstag-Kreis: see: Harro Mold, Hegemonialbestrebungen der deutschen Außenpolitik in den letzten Jahren der Weimarer Republik, Gustav Stolpers "Dienstag-Kreis", in: Jahrbuch des Instituts für Deutsche Geschichte, Walter Grab, ed. Tel Aviv 1976, p. 419–448; Toni Stolper, Ein Leben, p. 204; Stegerwald-Kreis: see ibid. p. 290.

[12] Storm Jameson, Journey, vol. II, p. 216.

[13] Storm Jameson Journey, vol. I, p. 276.

[14] Lilo Linke, Restless Days, A German Girl's Autobiography, New York 1935, p. 83; Lilo Linke, Restless Flags A German Girl's Autobiography, London 1935; Lilo Linke, Tage der Unrast. Von Berlin ins Exil: ein deutsches Mädchenleben 1914–1933. Mit einem Nachwort und herausgegeben von Karl Holl, Bremen 2005.

[15] Ibid. p. 100.

[16] Ibid. p. 285f.

expropriation of Germany's former ruling houses or the building of a naval cruiser. In 1928, she accompanied Georg Bernhard, editor of "Vossische Zeitung", campaigning in Eberswalde.[17]

She met the leading party figures like Theodor Heuss, Gertrud Bäumer, Marie-Elisabeth Lüders,[18] Willy Hellpach,[19] the DDP chairman Erich Koch-Weser and Gustav Stolper[20] who was co-opted onto the party executive in 1926. Since 1926, he was founder-editor and co-owner of "Der Deutsche Volkswirt", Germany's leading business paper, drafted on the concept of the British "Economist".

In January 1929, Lilo Linke started working as a typist in the Volkswirt office. Her close relationship to Gustav Stolper continued until his death despite long periods in exile. Decades later, Toni Stolper remembers: "Lilo war eine faszinierende Erscheinung, jung, schön, kühn, begabt, ihr kleinbürgerlich beschränktes, später nationalsozialistisches Familien-Milieu ohne Rücksicht weit hinter sich lassend…Sowohl in ihrer Jugend wie in ihren späteren Jahren neigte Lilo Linke stark nach links, gefühlsmäßig wie in ihrem Lebensstil. Sie hätte auch noch in eine spätere Generation deutscher Jugendbewegtheit gepaßt".[21]

The eminent economist Joseph A. Schumpeter, co-author of the Volkswirt and professor in Bonn, but after 1932, at Harvard, tells Gustav Stolper in May 1926: "Ihr Deutscher Volkswirt muß eine große Sache sein oder gar nicht".[22] Stolper answers Schumpeter, his close friend since days back in Vienna, explaining his ideas: He has in mind not a specialist magazine but a combination of "Economist" and "Nation": "es soll neben dem volks – und privatwirtschaftlichen auch den ganzen Komplex der Außenpolitik, der großen sozialen und weltanschaulichen Strömungen, soweit sie das politisch – soziale Leben berühren, erörtert werden;" Stolper plans the paper to present a synthesis of foreign policy and economy including cultural topics, thus to become a focal point "für alle geistigen Menschen, soweit sie in und für Deutschland etwas zu sagen haben".[23]

---

[17] Lilo Linke, Restless, p. 353ff; Modris Eksteins, The Limits of Reason, The German Democratic Press and the Collapse of Weimar Democracy, Oxford 1975, p. 120.

[18] Lilo Linke, Restless, p. 103.

[19] Willy Hellpach, see: Claudia-Anja Kaune, Willy Hellpach (1877–1955), Biographie eines liberalen Politikers in der Weimarer Republik, Frankfurt a. M. 2005; Christian Jansen, Antiliberalismus und Antiparlamentarismus in der bürgerlich-demokratischen Elite der Weimarer Republik, Willy Hellpach Publizist der Jahre 1925–1933, in: Zeitschrift für Geschichtswissenschaft 49, 2001.

[20] Minutes of the DDP executive meeting, January 23, 1926, in: Quellen zur Geschichte des Parlamentarismus und der politischen Parteien, vol, 5, Karl Dietrich Bracher, Erich Matthias und Rudolf Morsey, ed., Linksliberalismus in der Weimarer Republik, Die Führungsgremien der Deutschen Demokratischen Partei und der Deutschen Staatspartei 1918–1933, eingeleitet von Lothar Albertin, p. 361, Düsseldorf 1980.

[21] Toni Stolper to Karl Holl, in: Karl Holl, Lilo Linke (1906–1963) von der Weimarer Jungdemokratin zur Sozialreporterin in Lateinamerka, Materialien zu einer Biographie, in: Exilforschung, Ein internationales Jahrbuch, vol. 5, 1987, Fluchtpunkte des Exils und andere Themen, p. 70.

[22] Toni Stolper, Ein Leben, p. 189.

[23] Ibid. p. 190f.

9 Gustav Stolper: Mentor of a Young German Democrat

Gustav Stolper, born in Vienna from an educated Jewish background,[24] was, according to his contemporaries, a winning and brilliant personality. The economist Fritz Bade recalls him having: "Beweglichkeit des wirtschaftlichen Denkens[…], die von jedem, der mit ihm zusammenkam, als etwas Besonderes und Mitreißendes empfunden wurde".[25] Gustav Stolper had given public opinion a journalistic forum "auf dem sich die miteinander ringenden Auffassungen in der Wirtschaftspolitik unter eigener Verantwortung der Autoren auseinandersetzen konnten".[26] Despite the dramatic circumstances, Toni Stolper remembers those years as a period of enthusiastic reconstruction inspired with great hopes. According to his son Wolfgang[27], Gustav Stolper believes: "daß mit Vernunft und moralischem Mut die kleinsten Chancen genutzt werden mußten, um die Entwicklung in vernünftige Bahnen zu leiten". It is either optimism or: "Handlung eines tief moralischen Menschen, der das Richtige tut, auch wenn es hoffnungslos erscheint".[28] Way back in Vienna, Stolper had formed an Austrian-German network with excellent connections in Berlin where Hjalmar Schacht introduced him socially and put the Reichsbank statistics at the Volkswirt's disposal.[29] Stolper gathered some of the best brains into the Volkswirt circle. He frequently supported their careers and invited them to contribute to his paper, sometimes even without sharing their opinion, no matter if they have a leaning towards the Social Democrats or the unions. Next to Stolper and his wife, the editorial staff consisted of the Lujo Brentano disciple Carl Landauer, Social Democrat, Jew and professor at Berliner Handelshochschule, and after 1933, had a chair atBerkeley. He was in charge of general economics and social policy. The analysis of the financial markets was the responsibility of the psychologist Georg Katona, who will be teaching at New York's New School for Social Research and at the University of Michigan from 1933. Heuss, Schumpeter and other specialists of rank and file were regular contributors, as there were Hjalmar Schacht, Otto Braun, Wilhelm Röpke, Alexander Rüstow, Fritz Bade, Fritz Naphtali, Hans Luther, August von Hayek, Kurt Rietzler, Gertrud Bäumer, to name but a few.

---

[24] This goes specially for the Kassowitz family, i.e. Toni Stolper's family, Gustav Stolper's father migrated from Galicia to Vienna.

[25] Fritz Bade (economist at Kiel university, co-author of Der Deutsche Volkswirt), Gustav Stolper, in: Weltwirtschaftliches Archiv, vol. 62, Kiel (1949) I, p. 3.

[26] Ibid.

[27] Wolfgang Stolper, Staat und Wirtschaft, Die Tragödie von Weimar, in: Institut für Weltwirtschaft, no. 41, Kiel, October 3, 1968, p. 89.

[28] See a similar commentary of Gustav Stolper's lifelong friend Theodor Heuss, in: Heinz Rieter, Der Deutsche Volkswirt 1926–1933, Eine Fallstudie zur publizistischen Umsetzung wirtschaftspolitischer Konzeptionen, Sonderdruck aus: Studien zur Entwicklung der ökonomischen Theorie XVII, Die Umsetzung wirtschaftspolitischer Grundkonzeptionen in die kontinentaleuropäische Praxis des 19. Und 20. Jahrhunderts, part 2,.Erich W. Streissler, ed., Berlin, (1997) p. 121; close friendship of the Stolper and Heuss families, see: Theodor Heuss, Tagebuchbriefe 1955–1963, Eine Auswahl aus Briefen an Toni Stolper, Eberhard Pikart, ed., Tübingen and Stuttgart 1970.

[29] It could not be clarified if this was the official or the secret statistics.

This group of illustrious authors guaranteed the academic and stylistic quality of the Volkswirt.[30] It was the beginning of a journalistic success story. On the advisory council were members of the "Dienstag Kreis", among them Theodor Heuss, Bernhard von Bülow, Helmut James von Moltke and Kurt Rietzler. They also wrote for the Volkswirt, sometimes using a penname. The "Dienstag Kreis" was a private, highly confidential circle, a body of ideas whose main topic was the sphere of foreign politics. As a peaceful reconciliation with France seemed to be out of reach for the time being, the main focus of discussion was on the idea of Central Europe and subsequently on the implementation of a customs union project favoured by the late Friedrich Naumann.[31] From 1931/1932, the confidential forum for discussing domestic policies irrespective of all party – and class barriers – was the "Stegerwald Kreis", named after the minister of labour and "Zentrum" – party politician Adam Stegerwald. Members included influential industrialists and bankers and the Social Democratic union leader Fritz Tarnow[32]. Stolper sat in the Reichstag from 1930 to 1932 for a Hamburg constituency: "wollte Politik und Wirtschaft in ihrer gegenseitigen Durchdringung zeigen".[33] In addition, Stolper maintained good relations with a circle of German journalists working abroad as well as with foreign correspondents accredited in Berlin. Among them were Edgar Mowrer, already mentioned, Dorothy Thompson,[34] her husband Sinclair Lewis and the British journalist Harrison Brown whom Lilo Linke will meet again in exile in Britain. In 1934, Dorothy Thompson would be expelled from Germany overnight following a spectacular interview she had conducted with Hitler, unmasking the dictator. A host of friends and personal contacts helped Lilo to put down roots into this wide area.

Only a few month later, she worked as Stolper's private secretary: "Again a new field of experience opened to me, more intricate and confusing than even that of politics. I should have been lost in it if I had not found somebody to lead me", but Dr. Berger, this is how she calls Gustav Stolper in her autobiography, "was in every regard an outstanding personality.[...] generous enough to become my teacher, instead of being annoyed by my lack of knowledge,[...]he possessed the genial ability to explain a complicated economic process in its essential outline in such a way that I could understand what I was writing down for him".[35] According to Stolper's calculation, the party youth was a reservoir of young talents. For Lilo,

---

[30] Rieter, p. 111ff; Toni Stolper, Ein Leben, p, 196ff; Hans Jörg Klausinger, Gustav Stolper, Der Deutsche Volkswirt, and the Controversy on Economic Policy at the End of the Weimar Republic, in: History of Political Economy, 33:2, Duke University, 2001, p. 242f.

[31] See footnote 9.

[32] Toni Stolper, Ein Leben, p. 290f.

[33] Knut Hansen, Demokrat zwischen Wirtschaft und Politik – der Publizist Gustav Stolper (1888–1947), in: Liberal, Vierteljahreshefte für Politik und Kultur, vol. 1, Februar 1995, 37th year, p. 69.

[34] See: Peter Kurth, American Cassandra, The Life of Dorothy Thompson, Boston, Toronto, London 1990; Dorothy Thompson, Kassandra spricht, Antifaschistische Publizistik 1932–1942, Leipzig and Weimar 1988.

[35] Lilo Linke, Restless, p. 385.

9 Gustav Stolper: Mentor of a Young German Democrat

it was the chance of her life which she took up with courage, prudently supported by her mentor.[36] "Stolpers rege Sympathie für begabte Frauen, die mit sich etwas anzufangen wußten und redliche Arbeit nicht scheuten",[37] is Toni Stolper's comment, followed by a hint clearly referring to Lilo Linke: "Menschen der Berliner Nachkriegsgeneration in ihrer kühnen, beschwingten, zuweilen durch die frühe Not gehärteten Eigenart bewegen sich um die Arbeitstische der Redaktion [...] junge Frauen unter den Männern [...] diese und jene aufblühende Begabung erregt die Lust zur Gestaltung".[38] At one of these desks in the editorial office, she will soon be sitting opposite Toni Stolper and, under her guidance, she will be writing the "Chronik aus der Woche", her first journalistic attempts. In this chronicle past January 30, 1933, Lilo Linke will, for as long as possible, denounce the Nazis' terror, the daily infringement and that of the law, and of the constitution.

Political conditions in Weimar changed from bad to worse following the general elections of 1929, which proved to be disastrous for the DDP. The inability and the unwillingness of the non-socialist parties to save Germany from the approaching Nazi-threat pushed Lilo further to the left. After a short interlude with the still-born Radical Democratic Party – their paper "Radikaldemokratische Blätter" published her review of the movie "Kuhle Wampe",[39] – she joined the SPD, the Sozialdemokratische Partei Deutschlands, a step Gustav Stolper did not prevent her from doing.

Meantime, Stolper had become a successful editor and had risen to the position of the DDP's expert economist with a promising future. Crucial for him was the Mannheim Party Convention on October 5, 1929, where he gave an impressive programmatic speech,[40] which earned him standing ovations and the attention of the foreign press. His concept is a declared belief in parliamentary democracy as the only possible system where society is based on economic and social freedom of the individual. He disapproves of class struggle and considers private property to be a prerequisite of individual freedom. Only capitalism is able to create a maximum of material wealth and subsequently the greatest possible welfare for all and to be committed at the same time to the settlement of diverging economic and social interests and to fight mass poverty.

[41]"A great speech" Lilo remembered, "which I know by heart because I had typed it so carefully";[42] Toni Stolper comments on this event: "A high point in Lilo's

---

[36] Toni Stolper, personal notes, no date, property of Karl Holl, Bremen.
[37] Toni Stolper, Ein Leben, p. 430.
[38] Ibid. p. 238.
[39] Bertold Weinsberg, Erinnerungen an Lilo Linke, in: Informaciones Revista Israelita, Quito, June 15, 1963, p. 5.
[40] Die wirtschaftlich – soziale Weltanschauung der Demokratie, Programmrede von Dr. Gustav Stolper auf dem Mannheimer Parteitag der Deutschen Demokratischen Partei am 5. Oktober 1929, Berlin 1929.
[41] Ibid.; Hansen; Rieter; Toni Stolper, Ein Leben, p. 223; Lilo Linke, Restless, p. 388.
[42] Ibid. p. 387.

Berlin Volkswirt years lingers in memory when Gustav in long midsummer hours of 1930 [sic, S.W.] ambling according to his orator's style over the open terraces of our house, dictated to her into the typewriter the great concept and detailed clauses of his Mannheim Program for the D D P".[43]

The DDP shrank to insignificance. The merger with the right-wing "Jungdeutscher Orden" to "Deutsche Staatspartei" in 1930, the opportunism of her own party members, the considerable victory of the NSDAP in the September 1930 election, bloody street fighting and the banking crisis after the "Nordwolle"-crash had driven Lilo Linke to despair. From July to November, she travelled all over England, with only five pounds in her pocket. She stayed with factory workers, farmers, miners and trade union secretaries: "to find out what my English comrades were thinking and doing,[...]" finding friends and shelter everywhere. "In poor people's houses she shared a bed with the children, as contented as when she could be given a room to herself. In the morning her hosts sent her on her way with advice and another address".[44] In autumn 1931, she visited the Labour Party's annual conference in Scarborough where she met Margaret Storm Jameson, who remembered Lilo as: "the goose-girl of the German fairy-tales, tall and slender, with a flawless skin, pale rose on white, red unpainted mouth, hair like fine yellow silk, eyes of a clear blue, the shape and colour of a kitten's". Not only Lilo's appearance struck Storm Jameson. Lilo Linke was a freedom-loving person. Her fearlessness, her distinctive sense of social responsibility, her independent political judgement and her iron determination to carry through combined with a great kindness left a big impression on her new friend.[45] With a letter of recommendation she passed Lilo Linke on to the young Labour MP Aneurin Bevan, with whom she became friends.[46]

Back in Germany, Gustav Stolper helped Lilo Linke to win a scholarship[47] at Frankfurt's "Akademie der Arbeit", a joint foundation of Frankfurt University, the trade unions and the government administration to qualify young, already working adults at university level: "für die neu anfallenden Funktionen in Politik, Wirtschaft und Gesellschaft der Weimarer Republik".[48] University lecturers, administration officials and self-employed persons teach law, economics, trade, political science,

---

[43] Toni Stolper, personal notes.
[44] See: Storm Jameson, Journey, vol. 1, p. 270f; Storm Jameson, in : Lilo Linke, Tale, p. XIff; Lilo Linke, Restless, p. 299.
[45] A study of Lilo Linke's character, see: Storm Jameson, Journey, vol. I, p. 308–313.
[46] Storm Jameson, in: Lilo Linke, Tale, p. XII.
[47] Toni Stolper, personal notes.
[48] Hildegard Feidel-Merz, in: Christine Wittrock, Die Akademie für Arbeit in Frankfurt am Main und ihre Absolventen, Frankfurt a.M. 1991, p. 8, reference to Lilo's immatriculation for 1930/1931, p. 63; Die Akademie der Arbeit in der Universität Frankfurt am Main 1921–1931, zu ihrem zehnjährigen Bestehen im Auftrag des Dozenten-Kollegiums, Ernst Michel, ed., Frankfurt 1931; Otto Antrick, Die Akademie der Arbeit in der Universität Frankfurt A.M., Idee, Werden, Gestalt, Darmstadt 1966; Frankfurter Zeitung, May 3, 1931, 2nd morning edition, Ernst Michel, Zehn Jahre Akademie der Arbeit; Generalanzeiger der Stadt Frankfurt, May 2, 1931.

politics, sociology and social policy. Among them are eminent people like Walter Eucken, Eugen Rosenstock-Huessy, Willy Hellpach, Emil Lederer, Kurt Rietzler, and Hugo Sinzheimer. Lilo's stay in Frankfurt supplemented her practical experience in politics and journalism with sound theoretical knowledge. Politically very active in a group of like-minded young students, she saw one of her friends bleeding to death in street fighting following the Prussian coup d'état, when Otto Braun's minority government was removed from office by the Reichsregierung. Full of disgust, she describes in her autobiography Hitler's appearance at a mass rally, bursting with venom before an audience of 15,000 raging people.[49] Today this text is used as teaching material in the US-curriculum of history students. Unfortunately, there is only very little correspondence left from this period. Lilo writes to Toni: "Ich will alles daran setzen, in dieser Zeit reifer und reicher zu werden. Ich weiß, daß ich das mir aber auch Gustel und Dir schulde. Und so freut mich jeder kleine Erfolg, den ich erringe, dreifach".[50] Gustav Stolper watched Lilo's development with sympathy. On October 6, 1930, there is a short note in his diary: "Telephon mit Lilo, ihre Stimme ist frei und fest. Sie ist [...] glücklich, sehr tätig",[51] Back in Berlin, Gustav Stolper provided Lilo with her own apartment and made her a member of the editorial staff.[52] "I accepted with delight. It was interesting work: I had to read a great many German and foreign newspapers and afterwards to write a short weekly chronicle of political and economic events in the whole world".[53] Her joy was short-lived. On January 30, 1933, Gustav Stolper's nightmare came true: "What will the program [of the N S D A P] be if not dictatorship, inflation and autarky, three demands, each of which will mean the destruction of Germany?"[54] On February 24, 1933, the first column of the Volkswirt ends as follows[55]: "Es ist höchste Zeit, daß das Gefühl für Freiheit und Rechtssicherheit in Deutschland wieder hergestellt werde, wenn diejenigen, die im Namen der Nation Gewalt begehen, die Nation nicht zertrümmern wollen". On March 17th, the paper's front page carried merely Hindenburg's decree "zum Schutz von Volk und Staat" of February 4, 1933: "...Der Volkswirt ist bis zum 10. April 1933 verboten worden". Gustav Stolper had already decided to leave Germany: "Wir wandern aus. Dem Hitler tue ich nicht die Ehre an, unter ihm zu leben".[56] Stolper and his family emigrated to the USA. Lilo Linke followed Storm Jameson's invitation to come to England. She left Germany in June 1933. Under outrageous intimidation, the enforced sale of the Volkswirt produced

---

[49] Lilo Linke, Restless, p. 395.
[50] Lilo Linke to Toni Stolper, May 21, 1930, Toni Stolper Collection, box 5, general correspondence L – O, Leo Baeck Institute, New York.
[51] Stolper papers, NL 186/116, fol. 1.
[52] Toni Stolper, personal notes.
[53] Lilo Linke, Restless, p. 407.
[54] Gustav Stolper, Was nun? Der deutsche Volkswirt, 6, 45, quote: Klausinger, p. 259.
[55] Der Deutsche Volkswirt, Zeitschrift für Politik und Wirtschaft, 7. Jahrg. Nr. 21, Berlin, 24. 2. 33, p. 1.
[56] Toni Stolper, Ein Leben, p. 315.

only a third of its value. Toni Stolper gives an apt description: an act of terror "sorgfältig legalistisch verkleidet"[57] With the help of Hjalmar Schacht, at least part of the proceeds were transferred abroad, thus saving Stolper from total lack of means.[58]

The farewell for him and the Volkswirt staff was traumatic. Lilo Linke, Gustav and Toni Stolper recorded the dramatic events of the time. The sudden arrest of Carl Landauer casted an additional shadow: "Many years of common effort for a work of which we all had been proud had come to an end".[59] "Seit Sonntag Nacht in Freiheit", Stolper writes to his old friend Paul Neumann in Vienna. A week full of horror, where he was prepared for death any moment, lay behind him: "Zu fünf Uhr war das ganze Volkswirt-Personal zu trauriger Abschiedsfeier nach Dahlem geladen. Es waren wieder ein paar erschütternder Stunden, nach den Aufregungen jener Stunden kaum mehr zu ertragen. Ich richtete an jeden einzelnen ein paar Abschiedsworte, Landauer [meanwhile out of custody, S.W.] erwiderte, Katona bekam einen Weinkrampf, die Mädels heulten fast alle".[60] Walking through the garden with Lilo Linke after the reception, he looked at his house, built only 4 years earlier. His hopes so suddenly shattered, he is caught by overwhelming grief and scepticism: "now we have to start again from the very beginning in an other part of the world. Shall I have the strength to pull through? I am no longer young, I can't be transplanted without being deeply wounded".[61] The nightmare receded only beyond the German borders, "Gustav Stolper findet zu einer herrlichen Freiheit gegenüber seinem Schicksal zurück",[62] where "unser kräftiges neues Leben all diesen üblen Spuk einer tragischen Zeit hinweg fegte".[63] In July, Lilo Linke received a letter from Marienbad. In high spirits, Gustav Stolper talks about promising negotiations well under way all over Europe. With sound career prospects ahead, he will be made the representative of several major European banks in New York. He speaks of a possibility that the Hitler-catastrophe might give his life an upward push. This is to become true within the next 14 years in abundance never dreamt of.[64]

---

[57] Toni Stolper to Clemens Lammers, May 18, 1948, Stolper papers, NL 186 vol. 1, Bundesarchiv, Koblenz.

[58] Toni Stolper, Ein Leben, p. 318ff.

[59] Lilo Linke, Restless, p. 432.

[60] Gustav Stolper to Paul Neumann, July 5, 1933, Stolper papers, NL/1168, vol. 28, Bundesarchiv, Koblenz.

[61] Lilo Linke, Restless, p. 423.

[62] See: Theodor Heuss, closest friend of Stolper and direct witness to the events to Dr. Franz Reuter, one of the Aryanizers who acted on behalf of Hjalmar Schacht, May 12, 1948, Stolper papers NL 186/116, vol. 1, Bundesarchiv, Koblenz.

[63] Toni Stolper to Clemens Lammers, May 18, 1948, see footnote 60.

[64] Gustav Stolper to Lilo Linke, letters to a friend, July 17, 1933, Stolper papers, NL 186/65 fol. 1, Bundesarchiv, Koblenz; nature, scope and source of the letters, see the following text; Gustav Stolper's American years, see: Joachim Radkau, Die Deutsche Emigration in den USA, Ihr Einfluß auf die amerikanische Europapolitik, 1933–1945, Düsseldorf, 1971.

On January 1, 1956, Lilo Linke answered Toni Stolper's letter of December 5, 1955. She was about to write a biography of her husband and asked Lilo for Gustav Stolper's letters. Toni agreed on Lilo's insistence on keeping some letters of an intimate nature. Some of the correspondence of the years 1929–1933 had been lost due to the war, was interrupted for the same reason or, this applies to the years 1933–1939, had to be sent from England to Ecuador.[65] Toni Stolper copied the letters and censored them, although incompletely. The originals seem to be lost. There are 54 letters, 22 of which are from 1933, written in English from 1944 onwards. The result resembles a multi-facetted mirror, not least because the reader is forced to see through Toni Stolper's glasses. Their correspondence confirms the intimate closeness between Lilo Linke and Gustav Stolper all the same. In 1933, at the moment of departure into exile, Toni and Lilo were the two persons Gustav Stolper relates to most closely.[66] Gustav and Lilo are debating politics with enthusiasm. The letters show again Gustav Stolper's precise analysis of events and their future consequences. Phases of depressive instability take hold of Stolper. The threat of war on the horizon, the "Anschluß" of Austria, the "Munich agreement", and the desperate situation of relatives and friends back in Europe recall the shadows of the past. On September 18, the Gestapo had tried to arrest Stolper. His House and his bank account were confiscated.[67] He comments on the Röhm-affair: "Alle Welt weiss nun endlich, dass sie es nicht mit einer Regierung sondern mit Gangsters zu tun haben".[68] Stolper is deeply worried about the fate of his first wife caught in Paris after the German occupation,[69] and about Elly and Theodor Heuss: "most of my old friends are dead, murdered, executed or suicides…"[70]

Full of gratitude, he talks about the miracle of his own rescue and his commitment to save Jewish refugees.[71] The feeling of being uprooted, the common fate of the exiles, his lack of English which he feels to be a glass barrier,[72] to prevent him from putting roots down recedes soon: "Hätte ich erst die Macht über die Sprache mir wiedererobert, ich traute es mir zu, in kurzer Zeit diesen faszinierenden Kontinent zu erobern".[73] Stolper's letter dated Easter 1936[74] tells a success story: "…lies es einfach als das Selbstgespräch eines reifen Mannes, dem das Glück vergönnt ist, sich aus einer Weltkatastrophe ein höheres Mass von Freiheit und

---

[65] Lilo Linke to Toni Stolper, January 3, 1956, Toni Stolper collection, box 5, general correspondence L – O, Leo Baeck Institute, New York.
[66] Gustav Stolper, letters to, September 29, 1933.
[67] Ibid. September 21, 1933.
[68] Ibid. July 14, 1934.
[69] Ibid. September 30, 1940.
[70] Ibid. July 1, 1945.
[71] Ibid. November 15, 1936; November 14, 1938.
[72] ibid. December 13, 1933.
[73] Ibid. October 28, 1933.
[74] Ibid. April 16, 1936; and Toni Stolper, Ein Leben, p. 377; Toni Stolper conceals the fact that Lilo Linke is the addressee.

Sicherheit zu retten, als er je besessen hat. Grund genug von der Besorgnis frei zu sein...Ich brauche heute niemanden mehr, der mich nicht vielmehr brauchte. Meine Lebensbasis ist, soweit es sich um materielle Dinge handelt, im letzten Jahr so breit und gesichert geworden, dass nach menschlicher Voraussicht ich und meine Familie nie wieder Geldsorgen haben und ich irgendwo auf dieser gastlichen Erde in Freiheit und Unabhängigkeit das Leben zu führen in der Lage bin, das mir meine körperlichen, geistigen und seelischen Kräfte zu formen gestatten. Dass ich drei Jahre nach dem kompletten Zusammenbruch soweit gelangt bin, erfüllt mich viel eher mit demütigem Staunen als mit Selbstgefühl".

In the beginning, Lilo Linke earned her living working on a chicken farm. Encouraged by Storm Jameson, she wrote her first book: "Tale Without End". The English text, edited with a preface by Storm Jameson, was published in 1934 by Constable in London and Alfred A. Knopf in New York. It is dedicated to Gustav Stolper: "for G.S. to thank him". The book gives an account of her journey through France.[75] This is France seen from below. It is the sphere of the lower classes, of hard work and social distress. She visited a dusty coal-mine in the North, the battle fields of Verdun, the harvest of seaweed in Brittany, the wine-harvest in southern France and the Lyon silk weavers. She accompanied a doctor working amidst the misery of a Paris slum for 4 weeks. She visited the prostitutes of Marseille, a night shelter for men, and signed up on a Mediterranean trawler for 5 days. This woman is bursting with vitality. She is absolutely fearless and has a distinct social conscience. A couple of years later, she will be learning midwifery[76] to assist Indian women in remote villages in childbirth. The book received benevolent reviews: "Today (for, sic) every American who ventures an opinion on today's news from Germany, 'Tale Without End' should be required reading. It stands for the very best of the republic that is now dead".[77] In 1935, her autobiography "Restless Flags",[78] dedicated to Margret Storm Jameson, was published. It received praise in the media, The New York Times being among them and a friendly review written by Friedrich Stampfer for the "Neuer Vorwärts", the SPD-weekly in exile.[79] With this book, the author recounts to herself the process of her growing self-awareness. Another important aspect is the effort to enlighten the Anglo-American reader as to the cause of the Weimar republic's failure and the threat Hitler poses to all of Europe. In the face of appeasement as the prevailing public opinion in England, Lilo Linke believed enlightenment to be a painful necessity. Adolf Lowe, émigré in London, later teaching at New York's School of Social Research, who explains the socio-political

---

[75] The exact year is not known, it is either 1930 or the second half of 1932.

[76] She asks Toni Stolper to send her teaching materials: Lilo Linke to Toni Stolper March 1, 1949, Toni Stolper collection, box 5, general correspondence L – O, Leo Baeck Institute, New York.

[77] Harold Strauss, in: The New York Times Book Review, August 12, 1934, New York.

[78] See: footnote 14.

[79] John Chamberlain, New York Times Book Review, April 7, 1935; New York Times, April 9, 1935; Neuer Vorwärts, Sozialdemokratisches Wochenblatt, June 6, 1937.

cause of appeasement in his "Essay on Contemporary Britain",[80] names the disputed point: "it can't happen here".[81] The political uproar following the "King and Country Debate", which took place in the time-honoured Oxford Debating-Society on February 9, 1933, only 10 days after Hitler assuming office, illustrates the atmosphere.[82] The Oxford Union carried the motion: "that this country will under no circumstances fight for its king and country" by 275 to 153 votes.

In his letters to Lilo, Gustav Stolper comments time and again on appeasement with anger and contempt. He refers to Lilo's political activities in England: "vielleicht kannst Du segensreich wirken",[83] clearly regarding her relations to top Labour politicians like Arthur Henderson, William Gillies and Aneurin Bevan. He accuses the Labour Party of intellectual and moral collapse and to pass on to Hitler during the party convention at Hastings: "was England vor dem Faschismus rettet, wird nie und nimmer die Labour Party sein, der Schutz der englischen Freiheit liegt bei den Konservativen". In all probability, Lilo must have informed Stolper on the following event: On his return from the Saarland, the British journalist Harrison Brown had written a letter[84] documenting the appalling torture of the SPD-politicians Ernst Heilmann and Fritz Ebert, son of the late German president, at Börgermoor concentration camp,[85] He suggests the British foreign secretary to make these atrocities public during the forthcoming League of Nation's summit in Geneva, hoping the anticipated diplomatic stir might be helpful to win the poor victims' release. At the Labour Party conference at Hastings, a German émigré approaches Henderson via Storm Jameson and Lilo Linke. On behalf of German trade union officials, he asks Arthur Henderson to help his German comrades. "Nothing, no emotion of any sort warmed a face the colour of a fishmonger's slab. I heard him say stiffly, 'what do you expect me to do'?" "Pilate", remarks Storm Jameson, having been a witness to this conversation.[86] A couple of weeks later, Lilo Linke tried anew to draw the attention of the leading Labour figures William Gillies, Arthur Henderson

---

[80] Adolf Lowe, The Price of Liberty, An Essay on Contemporary Britain, London 1937, quote from the 1948 edition, p. 12.

[81] The allusion to Sinclair Lewis' novel of the same title seems to be quite on purpose.

[82] See: Martin Ceadel, The 'King and Country' Debate, 1933: Student Politics, Pacifism and the Dictators, in The Historical Journal, vol. 22, No. 2. (June, 1979), p. 397–422.

[83] Gustav Stolper, letters to, October 20 and 21, 1933; November 18, 1933, September 21, 1938; November 14, 1938.

[84] Harrison Brown to Arthur Henderson, October 2, 1933, IO/GER/3/59, National Museum of Labour History, Manchester.

[85] See: Wolfgang Langhoff, Die Moorsoldaten, and respectively: Wolfgang Langhoff, Rubber Truncheon Being an account of thirteen month spent in a concentracion camp. Translated from the German by Lilo Linke, foreword by Lion Feuchtwanger, London 1935.

[86] Storm Jameson, Journey, vol. I, p. 322.

and George Lansbury to the documentation.[87] Lilo Linke was, if only marginally, involved in the "Save Ossietzky" campaign. Unflustered by Stolper's poisonous invective against Ernst Toller – "Typ des Literatur-Prostituierten",[88] Toller and she looked after Ossietzky's daughter Rosalinda during her temporary stay at Dartington boarding school.[89] Even in old age, Rosalinda von Ossietzky-Palm vividly remembers Lilo Linke to be of a type, the "neue, befreite Frau".[90]

In the years to come, Lilo Linke established herself as a writer, publishing short stories and reports of her journeys in a host of mainly leftist papers, among them the feminist magazine "Time and Tide", the preferred media of a network of British women writers during the inter-war years.[91] Others were "News Chronicle" and Kingsley Martin's "New Statesman and Nation". She travelled through Italy in 1938,[92] and to France with Gustav Stolper in 1938[93] and with Storm Jameson in 1937.[94] In 1939, she published "Cancel All Vows",[95] a novel set in the Paris émigré community. Robert Neumann writes a favourable review in "Das Neue Tagebuch".[96] Her next book is about her journey all over Turkey in 1935.[97] She travelled by ship, by railway, hitch-hiking, by lorry and on mule's back. Kemal Ataturk's new Turkey is widely seen as a laboratory of the modern age and thus as the focus of public interest. A number of journalists visit Turkey at the time, among them were Gustav Stolper's friend Dorothy Thompson, whom Lilo knew since Berlin days,[98] whom she probably held up as an example and who figures regularly in Gustav Stolper's letters. Among the German exiles Lilo met in Turkey is Wilhelm Röpke who put

---

[87] Lilo Linke to William Gillies, December 10, 1933, IO/GER/3/78, National Museum of Labour History, Manchester; William Gillies to Lilo Linke, December 11, 1933, IO/GER/3/79, ibid. visiting card of Lilo Linke with Lansbury's recommendation to Arthur Henderson, without date, IO/GER/3/59, ibid.; see also: Eugen Max Brehm to Karl Holl, November 10, 1993, property of Karl Holl, Bremen.

[88] Gustav Stolper to Lilo Linke, letters to, November 18, 1933.

[89] Lilo Linke to Ernst Toller, July 5, 1934; Ernst Toller to Lilo Linke, July 12, 1934, Harry Ransome Humanities Research Center, University of Texas, Austin.

[90] Rosalinda von Ossietzky-Palm to Karl Holl, October 22 and 27, 1991, property of Karl Holl, Bremen.

[91] See: footnote 6.

[92] Storm Jameson to Hilary Newitt Brown, April 28, 1938, in: Margaret Storm Jameson: In Her Own Voice, in: Jennifer Birkett, Chiara Briganti, ed., Margaret Storm Jameson, Writing in Dialogue, Cambridge 2007, p. 180; this volume carries a couple of wrong names and dates!

[93] Gustav Stolper, diary, March 28 and 29, 1937, Stolper papers NL 186, vol. 78, Bundesarchiv, Koblenz.

[94] Storm Jameson, Journey, vol. I, p. 358.

[95] Lilo Linke, Cancel All Vows, London 1938.

[96] Robert Neumann, Miniaturen, Lilo Linke, in: Das Neue Tagebuch, vol 25, 6th year, June 18, 1938.

[97] Lilo Linke, Allah Dethroned, A Journey through modern Turkey, London, 1937.

[98] Gustav Stolper, letters to, November 5, 1933.

photos for her book at her disposal.[99] The first stimulus to her Turkey project may well have been two very informative essays by Hans Hermann Aderholdt,[100] correspondent of "Frankfurter Zeitung" in Constantinople at the time, published in the Volkswirt.[101] Intelligent analysis of the socio-political and economic changes and sound, yet albeit careful, comparison of Ataturk's educational dictatorship with Hitler's tyranny make interesting reading. Thus, she received the attention of the Royal Institute of Foreign Affairs and subsequently an invitation to give a lecture on Turkey at Chatham House.[102] In 1939, when Turkey holds a leading position in the focus of British strategic interests in the Near-and-Middle-East, she is asked to contribute to the anthology "Hitler's Route to Baghdad"[103] and to give a talk on the same subject on the BBC.[104] From 1938, she is a member of the PEN-Club.[105] In June 1939, Lilo Linke left England and travelled to Columbia, Ecuador and Bolivia, resulting in "Andean Adventure, a Political Study of Columbia, Ecuador and Bolivia".[106] From September 1940, she stayed in Ecuador and became an Ecuadorian citizen in 1945. Meanwhile, she had to start her life all over again for the third time, with difficulty, mostly near subsistence level. Without knowledge of Spanish, she earned her living teaching English. Social work to help the local Indian population, who live in extreme poverty, was a matter dear to her heart.

Only after the war in 1945 or 1946 was there a reunion with Stolper in Mexico. "Magic Yucatan, A Journey Remembered"[107] captures the impressions of this trip. In 1946/1947, Lilo Linke travelled to Europe, to London and to Paris where she worked for UNESCO.[108] Soon she decided to go back to Ecuador for good. She felt an alien in Europe. She was longing to continue her social work – a programme focussing on illiteracy, hygiene and adult education – for the indigenous population.[109] She took her 15-year-old nephew along to educate him, an experiment

---

[99] Lilo Linke, Allah, p. XII.

[100] See: H.H. Aderholdt: Heike B. Görtemaker, Ein deutsches Leben, Die Geschichte der Margaret Boveri, München 2005, p. 104f.

[101] Hanns Herman Aderholdt, Die Türkei von Heute, Der Deutsche Volkswirt, no. 37, June 10, 1932, p. 1219–1222; ibid. Türkische Wirtschaft, D.D.V., no.40, July 1, 1932, p. 1318–1322; Lilo Linke had known the Aderholdts since Berlin days and met them again in Turkey.

[102] Lilo Linke, Social Changes in Turkey on March 4, 1937, published in the Institute's paper of the same name: vol. 16, no. 4, July 1937, p. 540–563; on the importance of Chatham House, see: Andrea Bosco Cornelia Navari, Chatham House and British Foreign Policy 1919–1945, The Royal Institute of International Affairs During the Inter War Period, London 1994.

[103] Lilo Linke, Modern Turkey, in: Hitler's Route to Baghdad, prepared for the international research section of the Fabian Society, Barbara Ward, ed., London 1939.

[104] On December 6, 1938.

[105] Hermon Ould to Lilo Linke, October 28, 1938, HRHRC, Austin, Texas.

[106] London, New York, Melbourne, Sydney, 1944.

[107] Ibid. 1950.

[108] Lilo Linke to Hans Joachim Schoeps, December 20, 1946, NL.148 (H.J. Schoeps papers) Lilo Linke, Staatsbibliothek Preußischer Kulturbesitz, Berlin.

[109] Ibid. April 10, 1948.

ending in failure.[110] Over the years, she started publishing in Spanish. As a staff member of "El Commercio", Quito's leading daily, she enjoyed a high reputation for her regional studies.[111] This is also true for her more than 2,000 articles on Ecuador and its people, well researched on countless trips to remote parts of the country, like a canoeing tour on the Amazon.

Gustav Stolper's sudden death on December 27, 1947 found Lilo totally unprepared. They had already made plans for their next meeting.[112] Three days prior to his stroke, he writes to Lilo: "In 1948 I have to go through my 60th Birthday – which means I have to start thinking on the liquidation of my life. How I'll do it God only knows. It is too absurd".[113] Does he assess his life and his relationships? 1947 has put enormous strain on Stolper. With the third Hoover Mission, he had travelled throughout the devastated Germany. The result was the US government's cancellation of the "Morgenthau-Plan", a decision which paved the way for Germany's economic reconstruction. Lilo received the news of Gustav Stoper's death the same day she got his last letter, which is full of praise and encouragement for her work and future plans in Ecuador. "Ich hätte seine Hilfe so sehr gebraucht…Ich will aus meinem Leben etwas Gutes machen…daß auch darin der Gustl weiterleben wird".[114]

She paid tribute to her mentor Gustav Stolper and understood his encouragement to be a legacy for the future, which she was willing to fulfil. In 1933, Gustav Stolper had written to Lilo: "Mein eigenes Leben von Kindheit an hat von der Enge immer wieder und weiter in die Breite geführt. Über Abenteuer und Not und Kampf. Eine andere Lebenslinie als Lebenslinie kann ich mir überhaupt nicht vorstellen".[115] This is equally true for Lilo Linke. She died of a heart attack on April 27, 1963 on a flight from Athens to London.

---

[110] Lilo Linke, Wo ist Fred?, Hamburg 1963.

[111] Lilo Linke, Ecuador Coutry of Contrasts, London 1954, on behalf of the Royal Institute of International Affairs; Lilo Linke, People of the Amazon, London 1963, published posthumously.

[112] Lilo Linke to Toni Stolper, December 31, 1947, Toni Stolper Collection, box 5, general correspondence L – O, Leo Baeck Institute, New York.

[113] Gustav Stolper letters to, December 21, 1947.

[114] December 31, 1947, Toni Stolper Collection, box 5, general correspondence L – O, Leo Baeck Institute, New York.

[115] Letters to, October 31, 1933.

Chapter 10
How to Fight Unemployment? A Review of the Strategy Discussion in "Der Deutsche Volkswirt", 1930–1932

Hans Frambach

In this study, the different positions are discussed of how to fight unemployment at the time of Heinrich Brüning as Reichskanzler of Germany that means the years from 1930 till 1932. Central are the contributions in "Der deutsche Volkswirt" which was edited by Gustav Stolper, a well-known journalist, economist and politician. In their articles, Stolper and his co-editor Carl Landauer contributed very much to the public discussion of economic policy. Famous authors such as Friedrich August von Hayek, Oskar Morgenstern, Wilhelm Röpke, Alexander Rüstow and Joseph Schumpeter published in "Der Deutsche Volkswirt" – one of the leading and probably the most influential economic and business weekly at that time. It can be regarded as an excellent source to portray the economic policy of the Brüning era. The direction of the weekly was a liberal one, backing the policy of Brüning critically – it "warmly supported, and probably rather influenced" the laissez-faire view of the Brüning government, some authors say (Garvy 1975, p. 398; Klausinger 1998, p. 187; 2001, p. 242; Röpke 1933, p. 429). This paper includes some modern theses and insights and by putting them into a new context it tries to clarify some issues.

H. Frambach (✉)
Department of Economics, Schumpeter School of Business & Economics,
University of Wuppertal, M. 14.33, Gaußstraße 20,
42119 Wuppertal, Germany
e-mail: Frambach@wiwi.uni-wuppertal.de

10.1 The Economic Situation

The decline of the Weimar Republic can be attributed to three catastrophes during the period from 1918 to 1933 (Stolper et al. 1964, 128–144):

- The military defeat in 1918, spawning the German Republic.
- The currency erosion of 1923; the social consequences of the ensuing inflation were dramatic, despite even the 1923 currency reform.
- The world economic crisis at the beginning of the 1930s.

The years from 1929 to 1932 were the years of the world economic crisis, which had its origin in the United States of America. The reasons were the following:

- A failed monetary policy: rising interest rates to slow down the stock rates.
- Expansion and modernization of the production sector was financed by public credits, not the least also financed by reparation payments of the World War I.
- Durable products were mass-produced, accompanied by a rise of the number of employees and of wages. People believed in a never ending state of economic growth. Wild speculation in the stock markets occurred.
- The overinvestment in the industrial and farming sectors led to an oversupply of goods, markets were saturated. Consequently, prices plummeted, workers were dismissed.
- October 1929 is a cornerstone at the beginning of the crisis. After a rise of stock prices – stocks had often been bought by lent money – the value of stocks slumped weakly at the beginning of October but fell rapidly after many firms had to suffer profit losses and one bankruptcy proceeding followed the other. During the next 3 years, industrial production and national product dropped to the half of their former level. Stores and factories closed, cities collapsed, mass unemployment followed.
- Germany was caught by the crisis in winter 1929/1930. The United States stopped promised credits and at the same time demanded the redemption payments. In connection with the structural problems of the German Economy of the 1920s – high real wages, low investment, little technical progress, heavy taxation on firms and high social security payments – the production and incomes fell and unemployment soared (in winter 1929/1930 three million workers were unemployed).
- The grand coalition finally broke up in 1930. The state of the Weimar Republic, weakened by its unstable political situation and its inability to compromise, anyway, was burdened additionally by the national budget, which was dwindling away. On 30 March 1930, Heinrich Brüning was appointed Chancellor of the Republic, commissioned with the task to end the crisis as soon as possible. Governing by means of the emergency decree of the 8 December 1931 – the emergence decree according to article 48 Reichsverfassung was an unparliamentarily instrument, a legal rule for extraordinary states of emergencies; Stolper (1930b, p. 1327; 1931b, 339, 341; 1932f, p. 364) called it a "clear breach of the

law" and an "abuse" – the Brüning government established a deflationary policy comprising different means, for example, (Stolper et al. 1964, p. 138):

- The reduction of fixed cartel prices by 10%
- The reduction of wages, salaries, rents, loan interests and prices to the level of 1927 prices, at the most by 10%
- A gradual reduction of the interest rate to 6% for all kinds of loans – an interest rate of 6% still being a high rate at that time
- The reduction of rents of old buildings by 10%
- Maintenance of the exchange rate instead of devaluation
- Enforcing the payment of tax liabilities
- A moratorium on short-term external debts (an agreement in summer 1931 to freeze payments between foreign creditors and German debtors supported by strict rules and restrictions in the sale and purchase of currencies)

- In 1931, the German banking system collapsed because its equity capital was very small (one result of the inflation a decade before) and because of the withdrawal of American loans – a substantial financing instrument. Therefore, the state was compelled to use its money reserve to keep the payment transactions of the economy alive.
- It was Brüning's plan to balance national budget by consistently applying a cost-cutting policy and by suspending the reparation payments. What happened in reality was a rise in the rate of unemployment (in February 1932 to 33%, i.e. six million people), a decrease of purchasing power, a drop in taxation revenues, a decrease of public expenditures by one third, a decrease of demand, a decrease of production to 50% of the level of 1928, bankruptcy of many firms, financial difficulties for many banks.
- On 30 May 1932, Brüning was released from his position as Chancellor (and replaced by Franz von Papen) because his deflation policy and the strong restriction of public expenditures to balance the budget at decreasing incomes and rising expenditures appeared to large parts of the population to be without any result.
- As an aside, the unpopular measures that Brüning took hoping to stimulate the economy are often regarded as the very factors that prepared the political grounds for the appointment of yet another Reichskanzler just 10 months later: Adolf Hitler on 30 January 1933.

Combining the different facts and lines of reasoning to assess the economic policy of the time between 1929 and 1932, we quickly arrive at the widespread view to put the blame for the economic causes of the collapse of the Weimar Republic on the deflationist policy of the Brüning government, in addition to its refusal to fight unemployment by programs for public work (e.g. Klausinger 2001, p. 241). In retrospect from a Keynesian point of view, at least three measures seem to be appropriate to solve the problems at that time:

1. Expansion of expenditures instead of additional savings
2. Devaluation of the exchange rates instead of keeping them fixed
3. Respite of tax liabilities instead of collecting the debts

It is easy by hindsight to justify an expansive economic policy as the adequate measure to solve the problems of the crisis. But it is much more interesting to ask for the reasons why such popular means had not been applied. This is the content of the so-called Borchardt thesis, according to which Germany operated in the way it did because a policy of expansion was not feasible. Against the specific background of the catastrophic experiences with the inflation less than 10 years ago, devaluation and deficit expansion of the national budget would have been perceived as a new inflation. In other words, the decision for the deflation policy was due to economical and political constraints, allowing no alternative measures such as, for example, a job creation scheme.

10.2 Measures to Fight Unemployment as Proposed by the German Economists

At the beginning of the 1930s, theoretical thinking about the economic problems in Germany was dominated by classical theories of the business cycle, based on the notion of overinvestment. Famous proponents of these theories were Friedrich v. Hayek and Joseph Schumpeter (Klausinger 1995, pp. 103–107). The strict defeat of expansionist instruments was derived from these theories, whose guidelines can be summarized as follows:

- The existing disproportionalities in the production structure of an economy have to recede automatically due to market mechanisms. Waiting for this to happen is regarded as the only effective remedy.
- Expansive fiscal policy and especially a policy of low interests are regarded as harmful.
- The creation of credit and a devaluation of the currency are refused due to the threat of inflation, the traumatic complex of the German soul as Robert Friedländer-Prechtl (1931, p. 76) named it.

Under the premise of purging the economy of untoward developments and restoring capitalism to be fully operational, the structural features of the crisis itself are actually considered as being helpful (e.g. Schumpeter 1929, p. 847). Examples are as follows: the disposal of wage rigidities – not so much price rigidities – and the avoidance of state intervention in the price mechanism; the reduction of unemployment benefits; the striving for a balanced national budget; the maintenance of the gold standard; and, especially under the restrictions of reparation payments, encouragement of exports and restriction of capital imports (Klausinger 1998, 187; Machlup 1988, pp. 13–14, 30–31, 100–108).

The presumption of a natural healing process of a crisis based itself on a liquid money market, influencing investment through low interests in the capital market. In face of the economic crisis at the begin of the 1930s, the prerequisites to apply expansive policy measures – that is low interest rates, large capital supply, a flexible capital market – did not exist at all in Germany. Thus, the only practicable solution politicians could do in those times of capital shortage – which itself Stolper (1932e, p. 328) and Landauer realized as being proved by the high interest rates in the capital market – was seen, trenchantly formulated, in "doing nothing but keeping calmness and order and comforting the hungry people with the argument that every period of famine has always found an end" (Landauer 1931b, p. 635). Overcoming a crisis in a capitalistic economic system is seen, in a certain sense, as an automatic process (Stolper 1931b, p. 339; 1931c, p. 417; 1932d, p. 1637). One of the most important problems Stolper and Landauer suspected behind every step of this causation process was a lack of trust (e.g. Landauer 1930b, p. 1569; Stolper 1931c, pp. 416–417; 1932d, p. 1635), and this lack could not be substituted for by an expansive policy because that would aggravate inflation.

In opposition to the German and Austrian "overinvestment-view" stood some German theoreticians oriented towards Keynesianism. First, a group around Wilhelm Lautenbach – Walter Eucken and others called him the "German Keynes" (Eucken 1951, p. 34) – has to be mentioned, an economist and high-ranking official in the Ministry of economic affairs of the Brüning government. The group consisted of such famous economists like Hans Neisser and Wilhelm Röpke. Other leading German economists from the Universities of Heidelberg and Kiel, supporting Keynesian ideas were Gerhard Colm, Emil Lederer, Adolf Löwe (Adolph Lowe) and Jacob Marschak. They all emigrated from Germany after 1933. They advanced arguments emphasizing capital accumulation and technical progress (Hagemann 1999, p. 117).

The Keynesian theorists were vividly involved in the wage-employment debate since the end of the 1920s, which focussed particularly on the employment effect of wage cuts. They opposed the "classical" view of cutting wages as a successful means for fighting unemployment, and advocated public work programs. Commonly they rejected, for example, a deflationary wage policy since it was practised as the main means of crisis strategy by the Brüning government. Two phases of an economic depression, a primary and a secondary depression, were distinguished. The primary depression is seen as a process of natural consolidation in every capitalist economy. Such a process could never be directed by an expansive economic policy. The secondary depression is understood as a degeneration of such a process when the self-healing power of the market is insufficient to lead out of the crisis. In such a case, an economic policy of intervention becomes necessary. In this case even the stabilization of the money market would be insufficient to induce an economic upward trend; instead an ignition effect by an increased public activity is desirable. All the programs of pump priming and job creation were based on this idea of fighting the crisis (Klausinger 1998, p. 188). Of course, the existence of the secondary kind of depression was completely denied by Stolper and Landauer. They did not absolutely disapprove all the public programs to create jobs, but they warned of a mere substitution between employees and of crowding out effects. The kind of financing a job creation program was regarded as decisive. Financing through the budget only makes sense if consumption taxes are used or savings in public expenditure are realized (e.g. Landauer

1930b, p. 1567; Stolper 1930a, pp. 1292–1293; 1930b, p. 1328). A general principle necessary to apply is that expenditures must be covered by a balanced budget (e.g. Stolper 1930a, p. 1291). If this is not the case the balancing of the budget has priority (and this exactly was the true intent of the deflation policy). But if a job creation program has to be financed by loans, then the money should preferably be taken from foreign countries in order not to withdraw domestic capital from investment; precondition to all kinds of public investment is, of course, the productivity and profitability of the branch of industry (e.g. Landauer 1930a, p. 1538; 1930b, p. 1569). Pump priming only makes sense when entrepreneurial initiative is lacking (Stolper 1932c, p. 1603).

Since 1929, a flood of working papers, expert's reports and statements appeared concerning the question of how to overcome the crisis. The aims of the different political parties, the reparation payments and the different ways how to deal with them made an agreement on a quick solution impossible. Even economic theory was unable to agree on suitable measures. The difficulty was the unpredictable rapid course of events.

Two classes of existing proposals can roughly be distinguished:

1. By means of an expansion of the credit volume, the expenditures should be financed to activate the economic process. As an example, even in 1929 Ernst Wagemann, the director of the Institute of Business Cycle Research and president of the Statistical Reichsamt, and Wilhelm Lautenbach demanded an imbalanced budget to finance programs for securing the payment of unemployment aid, to initiate economic activity, to supply banks, etc., but the plan was rejected by the Ministry of Finance for reasons of adherence to the principle of a balanced budget (Staudinger 1982, pp. 87–88).
2. The other direction favoured a restrictive money policy not to endanger the reparation payments. Of course, the creditors of the foreign loans tried to prevent expansive measures because they feared a devaluation of the payments by inflation.

A lot of alternative plans existed to the program of the Brüning government, mostly in the form of public works programs as an expression of the expansionist policy (see e.g. Barkai 1977; Garvy 1975; Klausinger 1998, 2001; Korsch 1976; Landmann 1981; Röpke 1931; Wagemann 1932). They all were discussed in "Der Deutsche Volkswirt". The alternatives to the deflation policy commonly contained different ideas about job creation plans and they all approved public expenditures as an appropriate instrument to escape from the crisis. Differences existed in the way of how to finance the programs, for example, by tax increases, redistribution of expenditures, loans from foreign countries and money creation by the Reichsbank. Even within the Brüning government public works programs and wage subsidies, financed by the shifting of public expenditures or by new taxes, were discussed already in 1930. These plans – labelled in "Der Deutsche Volkswirt" as "Brüning" and "Dietrich" plans – were used by Stolper and Landauer for a general critique of the effectiveness and desirability of public works, contrasting them negatively with the structural solution of fiscal reform (Landauer 1930a, b; Stolper 1930c, 1931a; see also Klausinger 2001, p. 246).

- The increasing unemployment figures induced Reichsarbeitsminister Steigerwald in January 1931 to establish a committee for the unemployment question chaired by the former Secretary of Labour, Heinrich Brauns. The different views within the committee did not allow a unified final report. So, the first part of the report was characterized by different ideas of orthodox liberalism including proposals as the prohibition of additional income, the reduction of working time, the restriction of double wage earning and the dismissal of female white collar workers in the civil service with severance pay, when husbands are in work. A first relevant deficit-financed public works program was proposed in the second part of the report, which appeared in April 1931 under the title "fighting unemployment by means of job creation" ["Bekämpfung der Arbeitslosigkeit durch Arbeitsbeschaffung"]. The central idea was the strengthening of the productive forces by new capital and thus, to create new job opportunities. It was proposed to finance the plan by long-term foreign capital, because no capital should be taken from other branches. Parts of the German short-term debts to foreign countries were to be consolidated by the government through raising a foreign loan so that the improved liquidity situation would enable banks to finance the public works program. This proposal was friendly discussed in an issue of "Der Deutsche Volkswirt" by Rudolf Joachim (1931) without arousing a further debate. The currency crisis made this proposal of a foreign loan obsolete and the programs had to rely on support by the German Reichsbank, for example, by its promise to rediscount the bills used for finance (Klausinger 2001, pp. 244–245).
- In September 1931, Hans Schäffer, a permanent secretary in the Ministry of Finance, proposed further alternatives to overcome the economic crisis based on a discourse between different ministries and the reflection of the Brauns report. Schäffer favoured the slowing down of the crisis by reducing the costs for firms and at the same time stabilizing prices for goods (Meister 1991, pp. 297–303).
- A quite similar idea to the Brauns report was proposed in the Lautenbach plan, discussed in the secret conference of the List society in September 1931. Not restriction but increase in performance was realized by Lautenbach as the natural way to overcome the crisis; this, in face of the "paradoxical situation" that, in spite of decreased production, demand falls behind supply and a tendency to a further decrease of production is initiated. The most important task of economic policy is to activate the unused production capacities. To reach this aim the state is asked to create new economic need, which means nothing else than capital investment. As examples, public works like road construction and the improvement of the railways are mentioned. With such a policy of investment and credit, the disproportion between demand and supply would be disposed and the production directed to the proper aim. Short-term indebtedness to finance consumption expenditures is refused. In an article under the title "Pump priming or inflation"? [Ankurbelung oder Inflation?] Landauer (1931d) criticized the plan. The defence of Neisser (1931), "Ankurbelung oder Inflation? – Eine Entgegnung",

evoked Landauer (1931e) to reply. The plan failed because agreement could not be reached with the Reichsbank and the government, the negative impression of the sterling crisis was too close. (Only 1 week after the conference the British government and parliament discharged the Bank of England of the duty to back the sterling by gold reserves. Against this background, it is understandable that the gold backing of the Reichsmark was impossible to be given up).

- A similar plan to that of Lautenbach was the WTB plan from German trade unions as of 1931/1932 (named after its protagonists Wladimir Woytinsky, Fritz Baade and Fritz Tarnow). They demanded concrete and active measures by the public sector – a real economic initiative. The central idea was to employ one million people. The creation of jobs was assumed to revive the consumer good industry and thus itself create new jobs. Furthermore, it was thought to award contracts by the Reichsbahn, the Reichspost, municipalities and other public corporations. The costs to finance the public works were estimated at two billion Reichsmark. A foreign currency loan by the Reichsbank to finance at least parts of the program was taken into account. The plan was based on the idea to issue long-term loans with low interest rates for debenture bonds, which should be paid out by, for example, the Reichskredit Corporation and be discountable at the Reichsbank. Because of the limit to a sum of two billions and the great unexploited production capacity, inflationary threats had not been feared (Schneider 1975, pp. 225–234). The WTB plan was fundamentally criticized by Stolper (1932a) and Landauer (1932a, b); at least to Woytinsky, an opportunity was given to reply with an article (Woytinsky 1932).

- A further important plan, proposed by Wagemann in his 1932 book "Geld- and Kreditreform", recommended the restructuring of the German banking system (Wagemann 1932, pp. 22–44). For example, he proposed to give the Reichsbank law more flexibility. The means of payment should be distinguished in so-called producer and consumer money – a distinction introduced by Adolf Wagner, which was completely misunderstood by Wagemann, as Stolper pointed out; Landauer et al. (1932, pp. 43–44). Consumer money, that means all coins and banknotes up to 50 Reichsmark, is insignificant for international money transactions. Thus, consumer money should be uncoupled from the gold and foreign currency backing and covered by public loans by an amount of three billion Reichsmark (Landauer et al. 1932, p. 40). The producers' money should still be linked to the backing rules. Wagemann pursued three goals by the issuing of government loans: (1) the relief of the public sector from maturity dates; (2) the relief of banks from frozen credits; (3) the relief of the Reichsbank from bills of payment (Wagemann 1932, pp. 22–32). In effect, such restructuring would have given the Reichsbank the opportunity of expanding the money supply by open market operations and thus to consolidate the public debt and inject liquidity into the banking system. The Wagemann plan was almost unanimously rejected by the scientific community, including a negative assessment in "Der Deutsche Volkswirt" which reached its climax in the so-called Anti-Wagemann, a book consisting of four Deutsche Volkswirt articles written by Landauer et al. (1932). In this book, the different Wagemann suggestions are assessed as absurd, daring,

outrageous, incredible, strange, wrong, unacceptable, etc. The Brüning government rejected the plan vehemently because it again feared a considerable danger of inflation, which, of course, stood in absolute contrast to its deflation policy. Furthermore, the government feared damage to the reparation policy. Foreign countries could easily get the impression that the German government tries to evade the reparation payments by increased credit creation.
- The Studiengesellschaft für Geld- und Kreditwirtschaft offered plans containing expansionist views like the devaluation of the Reichsmark. The plans of the Studiengesellschaft as well as those of Dräger, Friedländer-Prechtl (the plans of Heinrich Dräger and Friedländer-Prechtl were – unintendedly – used in the Sofortprogramm of the NSDAP propagated by Georg Strasser) and Gottfried Feder were dismissed because of their anti-liberal and anti-capitalistic attitudes, and sometimes their naivety (e.g. Landauer 1930c, p. 1767; 1931a, c; Stolper 1932b, p. 1147).
- After Brünings dismissal, some moderate expansionist programs were realized by his successors. The Papen plan fell back upon some of the ideas already proposed by Wilhelm Lautenbach, supplemented by an ingenious construct of tax vouchers. However, it stopped the direct implementation of public works. The latter was the reason why the v. Papen plan was less sceptically reviewed in "Der deutsche Volkswirt" than other plans (Landauer 1932c; Stolper 1932c); additionally, it was positively estimated by Rüstow (1932). The Schleicher plan, whose measures were in some way continued and reinforced by the Nazi regime, was criticized by Stolper (1932e) in the usual way, meaning the "usual" critique on public works and the danger of inflation.

10.3 An Assessment of Brüning's Economic Policy

Was Brüning right with his remark of the "failure a hundred metres before the goal is reached"? The advocates of a long-term policy aimed at a stabilization of the national budget and a flexibility of prices and wages as the prerequisite of an economic recovery. The deepest point of the crisis was passed in summer 1932, Brüning had just been dismissed. The decline of production and employment halted as did the credit crisis and the decrease of deposits. The prices of important raw materials and of certain stocks began to rise again. But nobody could really say that the crisis had been overcome. Despair spread in face of the still desolate economic situation. The masses increasingly believed in radical positions from the political right as well as the left which deemed the Republic of Weimar unable to solve the crisis. Consequently, the end of the political system of Weimar was initiated and the ground for a radical system prepared.

At this point of discussion, the debate of the Borchardt thesis comes into play. The thesis states that an expansive policy was simply not enforceable for economic and political reasons; deflation policy seemed to be the only practical solution. Borchardt analyzed the manoeuvring space for an expansive policy along two questions (Borchardt 1982, p. 166): (1) What would have been the right time for a policy of counter-steering? (2) Had suitable means of counter-steering been available? Concerning the first question, Borchardt argues that it was impossible for the Brüning government to take the initiative because of the following facts (Borchardt 1980, pp. 319–322; 1982, pp. 166–167):

- Experiences of the former crises of the 1920s were supposed to show that a sharp fall in economic development is always followed by a stronger upward trend.
- A downward swing is in tendency self-enforcing. But economic theory did not know this at that time.
- Experiences with such economic crises, which only could lead to equilibrium by an anti-cyclical finance policy, were rare.
- As a first realistic time of the Brüning government to act Borchardt mentions the beginning of the Austrian-German bank crisis and the release of the sterling exchange rate (both in summer 1931). He traced it back to the fact that the crisis had the character of a worldwide structural crisis of the national and international economic order. Worldwide a change of view was only beginning to happen that a crisis does not necessarily have to be followed by an upward trend (Borchardt 1980, p. 321; 1982, pp. 169–170).

In answering the second question of the availability of means, Borchardt refers to the technical and political disposition and to the impact of potential means. A first point is that the suggested means were of rather theoretical than practicable character. An example is the theoretical claim to finance higher expenditures by the Reichsbank, but in practice the Reichsbank law and the rules of the Young plan restricted the awarding of the credit volume. A further example is the proposal of the Brauns commission to increase employment by foreign loans. In reality, France was the only country with sufficient reserves. Brüning's problem was one of domestic policy. Adopting means used in France before the September 1930 elections would have been perceived as collaboration with the "enemy". France, on the other hand, contrary, wanted the issues of loans combined with strict security conditions (in particular, to continue the reparation payments according to the Young plan). And not enough: Hindenburg threatened to resign in case of borrowing. Borchardt applies these arguments to explain Brüning's complete constraints to adopt an expansive money policy (Borchardt 1980, pp. 322–325; 1982, pp. 170–174).

Referring to the political availability of means, Borchardt argues that it was the aim of Brünings deflation policy to prove Germany's insolvency and thus the inability to pay reparations (Borchardt 1982, p. 172). Within the population the horror of 1923s hyperinflation and its impacts was still very well intact, and the minority government was not backed by the leaders of the social democratic party regarding the question on expanding public expenditures (Borchardt 1982, p. 173).

In terms of the potential impacts of the measures, the sheer size of the programs simply was not sufficient to fill the arithmetic lack of demand (Borchardt 1980, p. 326; 1982, p. 174).Consequently, Brüning had no real alternatives to the policy he implemented, and thus acted to the best of his knowledge – the Borchardt thesis seems to be proved.

Although most of Borchardts results have been confirmed, some different insights can be drawn from works about Weimar's foreign trade and reparation policy (Ritschl 1998, pp. 68–70). Borchardt indicates the difficulties the Reich had in receiving loans from foreign countries and the unfeasibility to finance reflationary programs by credit expansion. He traces the causes of the crisis back to the economic wrong turns of the years before. The quotation of "the crisis before the crisis" marks this development.

Let us combine the crisis of the early 1930s with the desolate economic situation of the late 1920s, emphasizing the relationship between the conditions of the Young plan in the early 1930s and the Dawes plan in the late 1920s. The Young plan was the last reparation plan arranging Germany's financial commitments on the basis of the Treaty of Versailles. On 17 May 1930, the date on which the plan was decided to become effective was dated back to 1 September 1929. An average annuity of approximately two billion Reichsmark was determined of having to be paid back vastly in foreign exchange. The payments were planned until 1988 but stopped already in June 1931 by the Hoover moratorium and abrogated in July 1932 at the conference of Lausanne. The Dawes plan, coming into effect in 1924, was the first reparation plan which really resulted in payments for France. At the same time the American capital market was opened to Germany and the Dawes-loan was drawn in form of short- and long-term loans which, of the order of billions, was given with 50% to the German private and the other 50% to the public sector. This was the reason for the economic growth of the golden twenties of the Weimar Republic. In spite of a balance of trade deficit, there was enough currency to repay the annuity of the plan (Ritschl 1998, pp. 51–54; 2001, pp. 15–16).

But since 1927, the Wall Street Banks and the US Treasury Department were filled with disquiet that Germany could be over-indebted: Since 1924 foreign loans at a total of more than ten billion Reichsmark came into Germany but most of it was not spent on investments. On the contrary, German local authorities financed their expenditures through these means, for example house building, amusement parks, roads, etc. (e.g. Holtfrerich 1985, p. 132). The question also appeared to which kind of debt priority should be given in a potential crisis: the private debts or the public reparation payments. It absolutely was a German strategy to play off one kind of debt against the other. As the reparation expert Hans Simon put it even in 1927: "The greater our private debts, the smaller our reparation payments" (Heyde 1998, p. 38). During the late 1920s, the current account was in deep deficit, Schuker labelled it "American Reparations to Germany" (Ritschl 1998, p. 63). In Germany, worries were that with the Dawes plan the first normal annuity of 2.5 billion Reichsmark was due in 1928; and if the economy should develop too positively, a welfare index in the plan was designed to determine a higher sum, which in turn could exceed Germany's solvency.

Taking these aspects into account, the Borchardt thesis can be interpreted in a different light. Borchardt's thesis of the dilemma during the crisis is correct if the approaching debt crisis is seen against the background of the Young plan. But Borchardts thesis of the crisis before the crisis depends on the German debt inebriation of the middle of the 1920s. Because of the American loans – and after subtracting the reparation payments – there were still enough means to finance high wages and a generous social policy; by the way, this aspect was also critically mentioned by Stolper (1930d, p. 407). At this point, it just can be suspected what different development the world economic crisis could have taken if the credit policy of the 1920s had been carried on much more carefully (Ritschl 1998, pp. 60–63, 66–68). After all, Brüning (as well as "Der deutsche Volkswirt;" Stolper 1930d, p. 407) had even criticized in 1926 the costs policy, behind the background of the reparation payments, as a heavy burden on the future. From modern point of view, one has to agree to this critique (Morsey 1974, pp. 365, 369–371). The question appears important, if political stabilization, the golden years of Weimar, ever had been possible without the American loans (Ritschl 2001, p. 16). But to achieve stabilization, the emergency decree was used already in 1923, and later on in 1930, because there was no majority in the Reichstag to realize the Young plan. It clearly was a mistake of the government to strive for no parliamentary majority to justify the different measures of deflationary policy and to impose the emergence decrees instead.

Of highly political character, too, was the limited scope of the German budget, money and credit policy allowed for by the Young plan. Fulfilling, at best, revising or renegotiating the Young plan could only mean to give it top priority in German politics. Another policy than the Brüning government practised could not seriously be taken into account. Any other more actively built economic policy would probably have caused a unilateral breach of the Young plan – and this would have equalled a capitulation to the program of foreign policy of the extreme right (Ritschl 2001, p. 17). Given the Young plan as it was, the best strategy was to run the deflationary policy on the one hand, meaning to do the payments, but on the other hand to carefully start a revision of the Young plan without provoking foreign countries into countermeasures. As long as the Young plan burdened the German balance of payments, the more difficult was the receipt of new foreign loans. The thesis is that Brüning made no deflation policy to force the revision of the Young plan; on the contrary, he made deflation policy as long as a revision was not in sight. The aim of the deflation policy was to restore Germany's solvency in the long-run, to have a free trade of credits and goods after the depression and to get more foreign loans after the cessation of the reparation payments (see, e.g. Landauer 1931d, pp. 1707–1708). Even in spring 1932, Brüning hoped for such loans. A fifth emergency decree was planned to issue loan authorizations [Anleiheermächtigungen] of 1.5 billion Reichsmark. And after the desired end of the reparation payments with its currency burdens the way was paved for a credit expansion, as Schumpeter suggested (Schumpeter 1932, pp. 739–742). After the Nazis had raised an objection against the project at the Reichsschuldenausschuss, and the committee indeed identified a violation of the constitution, the project failed (Ritschl 2001, p. 14).

This interpretation matches the account of Landauer (1930b, pp. 1568–1569): Landauer absolutely voted for financing the economy by foreign loans because such loans would not take away capital from the German economy. But he raised two objections to this type of financing, which made it impossible to be realized: (1) it was doubtful whether foreign countries would have given long-term loans to Germany; (2) it was doubtful whether the German economy would take advantage of such means at all, because of the lack of capital expenditure requirements.

10.4 Summary and Conclusions

During his whole period in office, Brüning was in an absolute predicament: *Politically*, he depended on the minority government tolerated by the social democratic party and on the favour of Hindenburg. Assuming that deflation policy aggravated the crisis, it has to be taken into account that exactly this deflation policy was expected by the Allies to secure the value of the reparation payments. *Economically*, he was in a downward movement: investments went into capacities instead technologies, the development of the wages, the loss of territories, other burdens and the current reparation payments. The consequence was a general erosion of the belief in democracy. The different ideas of an anti-cyclical economic policy, if sufficiently completed at all, were hardly applicable because of restrictions like a lack of a homogeneous understanding of adequate principles of economic policy and theory, including their impacts, international contracts, the reservations and resistance of the creditor countries, the Reichsbank law, the fear of inflation in the population, and Brüning's goal to dispose reparation payments lastingly by substantiation of Germany's insolvency.

Even with an anti-cyclical economic policy, it is questionable whether the volume of proposed measures would have been sufficient to overcome the crisis and consequently to prevent democracy from failure.

Opposing the argument that increased investment would have solved the economic problems of that time, it is stated that the existing capital stock was not run to capacity and, therefore, that no private investment was to be expected. The core of the problem was not a capital shortage but the reasons why the existing capital stock was not used for accumulation and consumption (Meister 1991, pp. 104–105). Thus, the productivity of the capital stock becomes decisive, and not to what degree the capital stock is run to capacity. In the 1920s, investments were used primarily to increase production capacities and not to develop new technologies. This made the German production too expensive in the international competition and gave reasons for the mass redundancies. Additional state activities, measured by an increased ratio of public spending to GNP, were made responsible for the reduction of economic growth, insofar as the structure of public expenditure was diverted from investment to consumption. (By the way, this is a central criticism of Borchardt by Holtfrerich; Winkler 1992, p. 137). While Borchardt argues that the development of the wages was not neutral to cost (self-financing), Holtfrerich claims an increase of wages with productivity (Meister 1991, pp. 123–127). Quantities of goods at too high prices indicate a distortion of the equilibrium of supply and demand – the fundamental problem of those times (see, e.g. Stolper 1932d, p. 1635).

Losses caused dismissals, dismissals led to decreasing consumption und this, in turn, to further losses ending in a "feedback loop", a vicious circle. The only way out could just be the reduction of production costs. Today we know that the decrease of wages is not the only measure to reduce production costs: what is needed is the increase of investments in new technologies to strengthen the productivity forces of the capital stock.

Many historians interpreted Brüning's deflation policy as an attempt to show Germany's economic inability to afford the reparation payments. Although the deferral of debt repayment was even negotiated at the Hoover-moratorium, the decision was made after Brüning's dismissal (e.g. Meister 1991, p. 122; Morsey 1974, p. 373).

Anton Erkelenz, a high-ranking official of the "liberal Gewerkvereine", former member of the Reichstag, and chairman of the German Democratic Party, commented on Brüning's deflation policy later as a "rightful attempt to release Germany from the grip of reparation payments, but in reality it meant nothing else than committing suicide because of fearing death. The deflation policy causes much more damage than the reparation payments of 20 years" (commentary on emergency decree, 8 December 1931). Even in December 1931, he warned about the deflation policy to set 95% of the population against the government and thus to work for Hitler (see, e.g. Stolper 1932b, p. 1147). Fighting against Hitler is fighting against deflation, the enormous destruction of production factors.

Stolper had different insights at different times, changing his opinion in time. He was an adherent of a system of liberalism and democracy, fighting against all types of political radicalism. To give a prediction at the beginning of the 1930s of what would happen or not in the following years, has a highly arbitrary character. Assertions such as that he "contributed unintentionally to those obstacles that eventually appeared to be insurmountable" (Klausinger 2001, p. 263) are difficult to hold. For me it is certain that the editors of "Der deutsche Volkswirt" not only represented the mainstream opinion on German economic policy of their time, but also in doing so they also contributed to the best of their knowledge to the vital questions of their era. In some aspects, they were more right and in others wrong. Opinions and convictions turned but were always embedded into the fundamental conviction of liberalism and democracy.

References

Avraham Barkai, 1977. Das Wirtschaftssystem des Nationalsozialismus. Der historische und ideologische Hintergrund 1933-1936, Köln, Wissenschaft und Politik.

Knut Borchardt, 1980. Zwangslagen und Handlungsspielräume in der großen Wirtschaftskrise der frühen dreißiger Jahre: Zur Revision des überlieferten Geschichtsbildes, M. Stürmer (Ed.). Die Weimarer Republik. Belagerte Civitas, 2. ed., Königsstein/Ts., Athenäum, Hain, Scriptor, Hanstein, pp. 318–339.

Knut Borchardt, 1982. Wachstum, Krisen, Handlungsspielräume der Wirtschaftspolitik, Göttingen, Vandenhoeck & Rupprecht.

Walter Eucken, 1951. Unser Zeitalter der Mißerfolge. Fünf Vorträge zur Wirtschaftspolitik, Tübingen, J.C.B. Mohr (Paul Siebeck).
Robert Friedländer-Prechtl, 1931. Reichsmark schützt den Sparer, Wirtschaftswende 2 (14. October 1931).
George Garvy, 1975. Keynes and the Economic Activists of Pre-Hitler Germany, Journal of Political Economy 83, pp. 391–405.
Harald Hagemann, 1999. The Analysis of Wages and Unemployment Revisited: Keynes and Economic 'Activities' in Pre-Hitler Germany, L. Pasinetti and B. Schefold (eds). The Impact of Keynes on Economics in the 20th Century, Elgar, Cheltenham, pp. 117–130.
Philipp Heyde, 1998. Das Ende der Reparationen. Deutschland, Frankreich und der Youngplan 1929 – 1932, Paderborn, Schöningh.
Carl-Ludwig Holtfrerich, 1985. Amerikanischer Kapitalexport und Wiederaufbau der deutschen Wirtschaft 1919 – 1923 im Vergleich zu 1924 – 1929, M. Stürmer (Ed.). Die Weimarer Republik. Belagerte Civitas, 2. ed., Königsstein/Ts., Athenäum, Hain, Scriptor, Hanstein, pp. 131–157.
Rudolf Joachim, 1931. Arbeitsbeschaffung – Das zweite Gutachten der Brauns-Kommission, Der deutsche Volkswirt 5 (32), pp. 1068–1071.
Hansjörg Klausinger, 1995. Schumpeter and Hayek: Two Views of the Great Depression Re-examined, History of Economic Ideas 3, pp. 93–127.
Hansjörg Klausinger, 1998. Die Alternativen zur Deflationspolitik Brünings im Lichte der zeitgenössischen Kritik. Ein neuer Blick auf die Borchardt-These, Wirtschaft und Gesellschaft 24, pp. 183–216.
Hansjörg Klausinger, 2001. Gustav Stolper, Der deutsche Volkswirt, and the Controversy on Economic Policy at the End of the Weimarer Republic, History of Political Economy 33 (2), pp. 241–267.
Andreas Korsch, 1976. Der Stand der beschäftigungspolitischen Diskussion zur Zeit der Weltwirtschaftskrise in Deutschland, G. Bombach, H..J. Ramser, M. Timmermann and W. Wittmann (eds.). Der Keynesianismus I. Theorie und Praxis keynesianischer Wirtschaftspolitik, Berlin, Springer, pp. 9–132.
Carl Landauer, 1930a. Arbeitsbeschaffung, Der deutsche Volkswirt 4 (45), pp. 1535–1538.
Carl Landauer, 1930b. Ankurbelung, Der deutsche Volkswirt 4 (46), pp. 1567–1570.
Carl Landauer, 1930c. Das nationalsozialistische Wirtschaftsprogramm, Der deutsche Volkswirt 4 (52), pp. 1764–1768.
Carl Landauer, 1931a. Dummheit oder Verbrechen, Der deutsche Volkswirt 5 (18), pp. 571–575.
Carl Landauer, 1931b. Der Ursprung der Krisen, Der deutsche Volkswirt 5(20), pp. 635–637.
Carl Landauer, 1931c. Neue nationalsozialistische Wirtschaftstheorien, Der deutsche Volkswirt 5 (34), pp. 1141–1145.
Carl Landauer, 1931d. Ankurbelung oder Inflation?, Der deutsche Volkswirt 5 (51), pp. 1707–1711.
Carl Landauer, 1931e. Replik [to Neisser], Der deutsche Volkswirt 6 (3), pp. 84–85.
Carl Landauer, 1932a. Arbeitsbeschaffung, Der deutsche Volkswirt 6 (29), pp. 944–948.
Carl Landauer, 1932b. Replik [to Woytinski], Der deutsche Volkswirt 6 (32), pp. 1049–1050.
Carl Landauer, 1932c. Wirtschaftspolitische Entscheidungen, Der deutsche Volkswirt 6 (48), pp. 1571–1573.
Carl Landauer, L. Albert Hahn, Gustav Stolper, 1932. Anti-Wagemann. Drei Kritiken, Berlin, Verlag des Deutschen Volkswirts.
Oliver Landmann, 1981. Theoretische Grundlagen für eine aktive Krisenbekämpfung in Deutschland 1930–1933, G. Bombach, K.-B. Netzband, H.-J. Ramser and M. Timmermann (eds.). Der Keynesianismus III. Die geld- und beschäftigungstheoretische Diskussion in Deutschland zur Zeit von Keynes, Berlin, Heidelberg, New York, Springer, pp. 215–420.
Fritz Machlup, 1988. Führer durch die Krisenpolitik, repr. ed. 1934, Viena, Manz.
Rainer Meister, 1991. Die große Depression. Zwangslagen und Handlungsspielräume der Wirtschafts- und Finanzpolitik in Deutschland 1929–1932, Regensburg, transfer Verlag.
Rudolf Morsey, 1974. Brünings Kritik an der Reichsfinanzpolitik 1919–1929, in: E. Hassinger, J. H. Müller and H. Ott (eds.). Geschichte, Wirtschaft, Gesellschaft. Festschrift für Clemens Bauer zum 75. Geburtstag, Berlin, Duncker & Humblot, pp. 359–373.

Hans Neisser, 1931. Ankurbelung oder Inflation? – Eine Entgegnung, Der deutsche Volkswirt 6 (3), pp. 80–84.
Albrecht Ritschl, 1998. Reparation Transfers, the Borchardt hypothesis, and the Great Depression in Germany, 1929–1932: A guided tour for hard-headed Keynesians, European Review of Economic History 2, pp. 49–72.
Albrecht Ritschl, 2001. Knut Borchardts Interpretation der Weimarer Wirtschaft. Zur Geschichte und Wirkung einer wirtschaftsgeschichtlichen Kontroverse Vortrag, gehalten auf der Jahrestagung 2001 der Ranke-Gesellschaft, Essen, 17.11.2001.
Wilhlem Röpke, 1931. Praktische Konjunkturpolitik. Die Arbeit der Brauns-Kommission, Weltwirtschaftliches Archiv 334, pp. 423–464.
Wilhlem Röpke, 1933. Trends in German Business Cycle Policy, Economic Journal 43, pp. 427–441.
Hanns-Joachim Rüstow, 1932. Nochmals: Das Wirtschaftsprogramm, Der deutsche Volkswirt 6 (50), pp. 1637–1640.
Michael Schneider, 1975. Das Arbeitsbeschaffungsprogramm des ADGB. Zur gewerkschaftlichen Politik in der Endphase der Weimarer Republik, Bonn-Bad Godesberg, Verlag Neue Gesellschaft.
Hans Staudinger, 1982. Wirtschaftspolitik im Weimarer Staat. Lebenserinnerungen eines politischen Beamten im Reich und in Preußen 1889 bis 1934, Bonn, Verlag Neue Gesellschaft.
Joseph A. Schumpeter, 1929. Grenzen der Lohnpolitik, Der deutsche Volkswirt 3 (26), pp. 847–851.
Joseph A. Schumpeter, 1932. Weltkrise und Finanzpolitik, Der deutsche Volkswirt 6 (23), pp. 739–742.
Gustav Stolper, 1930a. Der Ausweg, Der deutsche Volkswirt 4 (38), pp. 1290–1294.
Gustav Stolper, 1930b. Die Entscheidung, Der deutsche Volkswirt 4 (39), pp. 1327–1329.
Gustav Stolper, 1930c. Halbe Selbsterkenntnis, Der deutsche Volkswirt 4 (44), pp. 1503–1505.
Gustav Stolper, 1930d. Wo stehen wir?, Der deutsche Volkswirt 5 (13/14), pp. 403–408.
Gustav Stolper, 1931a. Dietrichs Plan, Der deutsche Volkswirt 5 (16), pp. 507–509.
Gustav Stolper, 1931b. Zwischen Hitler und Marx?, Der deutsche Volkswirt 6 (11), pp. 339–342.
Gustav Stolper, 1931c. Wo stehen wir?, Der deutsche Volkswirt 6 (13/14), pp. 411–418.
Gustav Stolper, 1932a. Arbeitsbeschaffung, Der deutsche Volkswirt 6 (21), pp. 671–674.
Gustav Stolper, 1932b. Die antikapitalistische Sehnsucht, Der deutsche Volkswirt 6 (35), pp. 1147–1149.
Gustav Stolper, 1932c. Wirtschaftsprogramm, Der deutsche Volkswirt 6 (49), pp. 1603–1606.
Gustav Stolper, 1932d. Krisenwende, Der deutsche Volkswirt 6 (50), pp. 1635–1637.
Gustav Stolper, 1932e. Arbeitsbeschaffung, Der deutsche Volkswirt 7 (11), pp. 327–330.
Gustav Stolper, 1932f. Wo stehen wir?, Der deutsche Volkswirt 7 (12/13), pp. 363–370.
Gustav Stolper, Karl Häuser, Knut Borchardt, 1964. Deutsche Wirtschaft seit 1870, Tübingen, J.C.B. Mohr (Paul Siebeck).
Ernst Wagemann, 1932. Geld- und Kreditreform, Berlin, R. Hobbing.
Heinrich August Winkler (ed.), 1992. Die deutsche Staatskrise 1930–1933, München, Oldenbourg.
Wladimir Woytinsky, 1932. Arbeitsbeschaffung – Eine Erwiderung, Der deutsche Volkswirt 6 (32), pp. 1047–1049.

Chapter 11
Der Deutsche Volkswirt After *Gleichschaltung* (1933–1935)

Helge Peukert

11.1 Introduction

In the following, we will analyze major (more or less) scientific contributions in *Der Deutsche Volkswirt* from 1933 to 1935. We will focus on the leading articles in the journal after *gleichschaltung*. Every number contained about two to four more or less brief articles (on average three pages). We have not considered the business reports and other, more descriptive and empirical shorter contributions.

The selected topics are as follows: (1) How should the new national economic science be conceptualized? (2) How should the ideal new economic and social order look like? Respectively, the criticisms of mainstream economics and the old economic order will be included and more general philosophical considerations will also be taken into account. We omit the numerous articles on special subjects (e.g., housing, reorganization of banks, etc.).

The rejection of socialism, bolshevism, and communism is mentioned in most articles and will not be repeated separately when discussing the articles. We will also leave out the more or less neutral descriptions of the state of affairs and the programs of the government (see e.g., the report of the finance minister, count Schwerin von Krosigk, on the tasks of fiscal policy in 5.1.1934, 585–587). We only mention in passing, that some well-known representatives of the private sector made contributions in favor of National Socialism. One example is Krupp von Bohlen und Halbach's introduction (Special edition to No. 30, 27.4.1934, 7) to the exhibition "German people – German work," where he praises the blood and

---

H. Peukert (✉)
University of Erfurt, Nordhäuser Street 63, 99089 Erfurt, Germany
e-mail: helge.peukert@uni-erfurt.de

cultural roots and promises a participation in the German work battle.[1] Another example is Fritz Thyssen (10.11. 1933, 233–235), who argues against independent private banks in favor of a quasi public, corporative, embedded banking.[2]

If we try to conceptualize the field of discourse, we may first mention the remark of Neumark[3] that all economic science fluctuates for about two millennia now between a more individualist and a more collectivist orientation. In a neutral way, the new National Socialist economic reasoning may be understood as a move toward collectivism. A second set of dichotomies to distinguish economic analyses and the research of institutions is offered by Rutherford,[4] who distinguishes between formal and antiformal, individualist (methodological individualism) and holist approaches (emergent properties), rationality (homo oeconomicus) and rule following (norms matter), evolution (spontaneous order) and design (ordered economy) and efficiency (assumption of markets) vs. reform (necessity of interventions for political, social, or other reasons).

The implicit analytical question of our investigation will be in how far a switch from the left to the right pole of Rutherford's dichotomies took place or if the authors muddled through clear statements or posited themselves consciously somewhere in between. We will summarize this question in the conclusion.

It should be mentioned that the editors of the journal, especially G. Stolper, tried to influence the public discourse before *gleichschaltung*. As only one example we mention his alarming article "clearness" (7.10.1932, 11–12) after the fall of Brüning. Stolper leaves no doubt that Germany was at the crossroads, a free economy and parliamentarianism were in earnest jeopardy. The basic relationship between individual and society and between the state and the economy was at stake, in Stolper's view finally a spiritual question. Therefore, he proposes the inauguration of an open-minded, liberal-democratic political association beyond party cleavages, an association for economic and political education *(Bund für wirtschaftliche und politische Bildung)*, which should hold public meetings and debates to recalibrate the old questions of the limits and impact of the state and the relationship between power and economic laws. The journal may have failed in the identification of the economic nature and the consequences of the great depression but what the political

---

[1] "Wenn Herr Ministerpräsident Göring in seinem Aufsatz von dem soldatischen Geist der Pflichterfüllung, der Pünktlichkeit, der Verantwortlichkeit für das Ganze und der Nutzbarmachung dieses Geistes für die friedliche Arbeit spricht, dann kann ich als Führer der deutschen Industrie die darin liegenden Imperative nur aus vollem Herzen unterschreiben."

[2] "Nur so ist das nationalsozialistische Ziel einer Überwindung der reinen Zinsherrschaft, einer Dienstbarmachung von Geld und Kredit für die eigentlichen produktiven Aufgaben zu erreichen" (10.11.1933, 235).

[3] Neumark, F. "Zyklen in der Geschichte ökonomischer Ideen." *Kyklos*, 28 (1975), 257–285.

[4] Rutherford, M. *Institutions in economics*. Cambridge: Cambridge University Press, 1994.

dangers are concerned Stolper leaves absolutely no doubt (see also the declaration of the *Bund* in 28.10.1932, 103–104).[5]

11.2 Otto Donner's and Alfred Sohn-Rethel's Contributions

The first interesting article was written by Otto Donner. He first worked for the statistical national bureau *(Statistisches Reichsamt)*. After his habilitation he taught in Hamburg. After 1945, he went to the US and worked as a lecturer. At this time he was also the German representative at the IMF.

In his fundamental article (28.7.1933, 1221–1223)[6] on the preconditions and consequences of public works, he first explains the nonfunctioning of the automatic business cycle recovery mechanisms due to historically specific circumstances (reparation payments, the international credit crunch etc.). Therefore, an external intervention by the state via public investments (Keynes' multiplier effect is explicitly mentioned) is necessary to increase the profits of investors and ameliorate the psychological situation. Public investments may not be viable *(rentabel)* but they are productive. A necessary precondition is the end of the deflationary price movement and a generous money supply. Increasing prices and costs may impede the export position of a country, which has therefore to devaluate its currency. It is interesting to observe that Donner does not make clear-cut theoretical decisions with respect to the reasons of the crisis, the working of the monetary mechanisms or the question longer-run multiplier effects vs. short-run booster *(Initialzündung)*.[7]

But it cannot be said that he had no theoretical economic agenda. He fully accepted the basics of neoclassical economics and the supply-demand logic, but he did not presuppose the assumptions of equilibrium in a double sense: full-employment and the smooth working of the adaptation mechanisms need not hold in reality. This flexible view is also dominant in his article on a functioning capital market (15.9.1933, 1443–1445). He first states that for some years now the interest rate on capital markets

---

[5] See also Stolper's realistic analyses of the political process and the enduring dangers of national socialism (11.11.1932, 167–169), his admission of the positive influence of public works in a narrow framework (16.12.1932, 327–330), Rüstow's ordoliberal commitment for a strong state (11.11.1932, 169–172), the report on the meeting of the *Verein für Socialpolitik* in Dresden with a clear statement in favour of free trade (16.12.1932, 330–332), T. Stolper's article on anticapitalism (23.12.1932, 386–390), Röpke on autarky (6.1.1933, 437–439), Stolper's article on the coup d'état (3.2.1933, 563–566, and 10.2.1933, 599–600), the excellent analysis of the logic and contradictions of a corporative state by C. Landauer (3.3.1933, 698–701, and 10.3.1933, 731–734).

[6] See the reprint in Bombach, G. et al. (eds.). *Der Keynesianismus II*. Berlin: Springer, 1976, 61–65 (the year of publication is not mentioned in Bombach et al., only volume and number).

[7] For an historical and economic history overview of the deficit spending proposals see e.g. Korsch, A. "Der Stand der beschäftigungspolitischen Diskussion zur Zeit der Weltwirtschaftskrise in Deutschland." Bombach, G. et al. (eds.). *Der Keynesianismus I*. Springer, Berlin, 1976, 9–132.

is too high. Because of the international special circumstances (the gold standard, reparations, etc.), the rate would not sink naturally so that the private economy has no incentives to invest. The natural rate cannot be defined theoretically but the historical more or less adequate rate was about 4% for fixed interest securities. This reasoning demonstrates his historical approach. An essential point is the recovery of confidence which – in his view – necessitates a temporary stabilization of the state via public (mainly communal) credit.

In another, long article on the intellectual reorientation of economic policy (13.10.1933, 53–55, and 20.10.1933, 100–103) the more questionable side of his pragmatism becomes obvious when he states that the old political order with parliamentarianism is gone. But he keeps a certain critical distance in mentioning that the traits of the new economic system have not been developed yet because urgent and pressing questions of the day like mass unemployment had to be solved. He also presents some rhetoric against the free play of the anonymous market forces. He argues like critical institutionalism or the historical school but puts it into a national socialist language.[8] It should be mentioned, however, that Donner never explicitly shared a national socialist aggressive view (e.g., against Jews or other groups, but see his praise for National Socialism on page 54). He mainly refers to Keynes (somewhat questionable) article on national autarky in *Schmollers Jahrbuch* in the same year and he also includes quotes from Keynes' *On Money*.

He mentions Keynes' liberal worldview and cites him extensively, but he does not share his "fundamentalism" that neoclassical economics is logically untenable. He somewhat downplays the difference between Keynes and the new order: He draws – as an Englishman – similar consequences whereas in Germany many think that a more revolutionary language is warranted. For Donner, the interest-exchange rate-commodity exchange adaptation mechanisms do not work anymore because the countries do not let them work and to some degree for good reasons. The emergent, developing countries accept the credits of the capital rich developed countries but they do not accept the imports of their commodities and impose tariffs which put the capital exporting countries under deflationary pressure. This is a new constellation because the emergent countries began to produce manufacturing goods themselves. So a new stage of development began. According to his pragmatism, a broadening of the corridor of the gold intervention points or a change of the currency regime (paper standard) could solve the problem.

In the second part, he does not only argue that because the production structures became more similar the net disadvantage of nontrade became smaller. He also holds that some reasons in favor of national self-sufficiency exist and guesses that the old idea of free trade will never dominate again. Surprisingly, he first only offers the alleged voluntaristic tendency of a rising international inclination to integrate all national forces. His second argument is more or less old institutionalist,

---

[8] "Der Instinkt des Volkes aber, darüber kann kein Zweifel bestehen, weist in eine andere Richtung, bäumt sich gegen das Unterworfensein lebendiger Menschen unter die 'Marktlage' und unter die anonymen Kräfte von Angebot und Nachfrage" (13.10.1933, 53).

referring to an article in *Der Volkswirt* by Fricke,[9] he points out that e.g., the conditions of profitability of private investors depend on the full scale of national and international investment conditions. There is no noneconomic policy.[10] The ideal would be to have a constant level of investment. If the private economy could not hold the level the state should fill the gap. In a later article, he identifies the problem of a crowding out (high or rising level of the interest rate due to public credits) and proposes therefore the direct provisioning by the central bank (direct increase of the money supply) or the institutionalization of a fond for national work with active open market management of the central bank (5.1.1934, 590–592).

Donner also delivered an article (22.12.1933, 513–516) for the series on the banking commission in the journal. In his view, the central bank should actively manage the money supply but the private banks had a tremendous discretionary leeway if the credits were taken cashless (nonexistence of a minimum reserve at the time in Germany). He pleads for the introduction of a minimum reserve and for the active use of the open market policy to guarantee an adequate (and not inflationary) money supply. Besides Jessen (see below), Donner is the only author of the economic deficit spending group in Germany who wrote articles in the journal.

Surprisingly, A. Sohn-Rethel wrote most pages in the time period under consideration here because he is usually known as a (methodological) Marxist.[11] In fact, he was in close contact with some members of the Frankfurter School (Adorno, Benjamin) and he was member of the British communist party until 1972. His major theoretical work had a certain influence after the leftist revolt in 1968.[12] His dissertation under E. Lederer in 1928 was already an early critique of marginal utility approaches.

But he also had another side. In the years 1931–1936, he worked in a more or less inferior scientific position for the *Central European Economic Organization (Mitteleuropäischer Wirtschaftstag)*, a lobby organization of the leading German export industries.[13] Two longer articles deal in a neutral way with the Italian Donau memorandum, the other with the viability of an Austrian-Hungarian customs union (13.10. 1933, 57–60, and 2.3.1934, 945–949). The more interesting article was on the origin and function of the corporative *(ständische)* policy (13.7.1934, 1835–1839, and 20.7.1934, 1883–1888 and his reply to R. Pfälzner in 14.12.1934, 467–469).

Corporative trade policy is a substitute for nonorganized, free trade, based on private competition. The new trade policy is based on bilateral, corporative agreements

---

[9] There were only very minor citations of authors in *Der Volkswirt* to other authors in the journal.

[10] "Jede seiner wirtschaftspolitischen Maßnahmen ändert die Bedingungen des Marktes und mit ihnen die Rentabilitätsvoraussetzungen. Er kann deshalb unmöglich an die Rentabilitätskonstellationen gebunden werden, wie sie sich unter dem Zufall der historischen Entwicklung ergeben" (20.10.1933, 102).

[11] *Geistige und körperliche Arbeit*. Frankfurt: Suhrkamp, 1970.

[12] *Warenform und Denkform*. Frankfurt: Suhrkamp, 1978.

[13] *Industrie und Nationalsozialismus: Aufzeichnungen aus dem "Mitteleuropäischen Wirtschaftstag,"* ed. and intr. by C. Freytag. Berlin: Wagenbach, 1992.

between governments on the trade parameters (quantity, price, quality, etc.). In an empirical and historical first part, he shows that already many agreements of this sort existed, especially in Europe. Certain symbolic words of the new order are used (the white race, the *Liberalisten, Reichsnährstand*). He interprets this as a long-run necessity because of the structural antagonism in capitalism between the free competitive structure in the agricultural and raw material branches on the one, and the cartelized, embedded *(gebunden)*, and organized structure in the industrial sector on the other side. Two different logics operate and impede an equilibrated situation. A return to a competitive order is impossible because the industrial sector is advanced and dominated by modern big industry with specific cost structures (high fix costs and interrelated techniques) which necessitate organization (Schmalenbach's argument, who is no mentioned by Sohn-Rethel) and makes quick adaptations to market expansions and contractions almost impossible. So an organization of agriculture and the raw material sector by the state is necessary because in contrast to the big industries the dispersed peasantry cannot perform this task. He cites Keynes but his way of arguing seems to be inspired by Marx in that there exists a necessary and deterministic transformation of free markets via an organized system, foreshadowing his later thesis of subsumption *(Subsumtionstheorem)* and the contradiction between the logic of distribution and the logic of mass production.

If this organizational work will not be undertaken, chaos, state socialism, or even bolshevism will result. Fortunately, National Socialism prevented them.[14] Very early their leaders understood that quota systems were necessary for international trade to prevent disastrous conflicts.[15] International trade policy has to follow an embedded, organized, and nationally oriented path. But he also points out that some sectors of the economy do not need to be organically synchronized by the state (maybe he means the branches and companies which he worked for). He strongly rejects the allegation that he prefers a planned state economy.

Like Donner, he emphasizes that a corporative policy in international trade is a new synthesis, which rejects unregulated competitive market mechanisms as well as the expropriation of the capitalists. In response to a criticism in the journal, he underlines the value neutrality of his analysis and the objective analytical character of his reasoning. Sohn-Rethel obviously justifies the National Socialist policy and salutes their exchange via agreements policy and gives a theoretical (quasi Marxian) justification of the historically inevitable.

---

[14] "Sie [die Wende] ist in Deutschland das gewaltige Werk des Nationalsozialismus gewesen" (13.7.1934, 1839).

[15] "Seine Führer [des Faschismus] waren nämlich schon sehr frühzeitig von der Ueberzeugung durchdrungen, dass die Konkurrenzkämpfe zwischen den großen Industriestaaten über kurz oder lang zu einer festen quotenmäßigen Aufteilung der umstrittenen Märkte, vor allem in Europa, führen werden" (20.7.1934, 1885).

11.3 Erwin Wiskemann, Sombart's Reply, and Jens Jessen

E. Wiskemann is one (besides Jessen maybe the only) of the few convinced national socialists with a broader economic background knowledge. In 1933, he became professor in Königsberg, in 1935 he changed to Berlin. He supported an historical school approach and tried to show that a national socialist economic science was possible and the climax of the German special development *(Sonderweg)* in economics.

In an article on science and practice in economics (14.7.1933, 1163–1165, and 6.10.1933, 11–16), he first rejects the liberal criticism of the hermeneutical method called *Verstehen*. Abstract economic laws and mathematics as the master science are rejected. He refers to Sombart, List, and Dilthey. The cultural background is essential and nonarbitrary because the history and the spiritual forces of a people have a very specific makeup, which cannot be chosen or changed and which defines objectively its path of development. It is interesting to note that Wiskemann's critical part (against formalism) and basic apology of a historical, cultural, and institutional approach has an intellectual level. But the "constructive" part is a mere repetition of national socialist ideology.[16]

We will skip the following proposals for educational reform[17] and mention only the definition of the role of the entrepreneur in the new regime.[18] He surely rejects unlimited free enterprise but also the primitive formula that a social should prevail instead of an individual orientation *(Gemeinnutz geht vor Eigennutz)*. He pleads in an imprecise way for a synthesis: The entrepreneur has to accept the principle of profitability but he has also to keep in mind the people's interests.

In a second article, Wiskemann asks if an economic normal state *(Normalzustand)* exists and can be defined (13.4.1934). He states that the allegation of a normal state presupposes a normative ideal (he refers to Plato and e.g., G. Myrdal's methodological critique). Liberalism pretended a harmony of interests, which was only

---

[16] "…worauf kein anderer als Adolf Hitler immer wieder hinzuweisen nicht müde wird, dass die Geschichte aller Völker auf *bestimmten* natürlich-biologischen und geistig-sittlichen Grundkräften beruht, die in ihrer Fortentwicklung vom geschichtlichen Bewusstsein erfasst werden können, und die dem politischen Willen bestimmte Aufgaben diktieren und *bestimmte* Entscheidungsmöglichkeiten anheim stellen" (6.10.1933, 12).

[17] See also 17.5.1935, 1519–1521; and in the same vain A. Ringer on the education of the economist in 29.9.1933, 1513–1515.

[18] We will not discuss his article on the importance of economic history (24.8.1934, 2100–2102) in which he argues with Weber, Sombart, Jecht, Gottl, and others in favour of economic history and the deplorable neglect in the recent past. The function of economic history in the new regime will be to make sure the historical roots of a people and allows to give examples of heroic behavior.

a justification of private profit making. National Socialism with its biological basis of blood and soil supersedes normative arbitrariness and sets the tasks for the state and the community without impeding individual will power and initiative. Essential is the self-realization in the fight for survival, he mentions Nietzsche's will to power in this context.

Jens Jessen was also a convinced national socialist. In 1930, he became member of the NSDAP. In 1934, He became director of the Institute of world economy in Kiel (successor of Harms) and editor of the *Weltwirtschaftliches Archiv*, but he was substituted in 1934 by A. Predöhl and had to be professor in Marburg. The first edition of his *Volk und Wirtschaft* (1935) had been severely criticized in the *Völkischer Beobachter*. But in 1935 he became professor in Berlin where he could not institutionalize a major national socialist research center with Wisekmann. In 1939, he became editor of *Schmollers Jahrbuch*, and in 1940 he held the organizing chair of the economics group in the Academy of German Law *(Akademie für Deutsches Recht)* where regime critical economists met. In the mid-thirties, he became more and more critical of the regime and held contact with Stauffenberg and the group of Beck and Goerdeler. In 1944, he was decapitated after the attempted assassination of Hitler.

He wrote an interesting programmatic article on the German way of economic policy (24.11.1933, 325–327), which contrasts to Wiskemann's much more ideological contributions. He admits that the new order is conceptually only at the beginning in the economic sphere but an obvious tendency will be the inward orientation of the economy in the future, a "return to ourselves" to stop the external forces, which cannot be influenced. An essential element will be the reequilibration of agriculture and industry. In the short run, the reduction of the international division of labour will influence productivity negatively. This can only be circumvented in the longer run by technical progress. A certain substitutive effect will also be reached by an expansion of economic activity to the unpopulated German east.

A related problem concerns the necessary increase of the use of raw materials in the process of expansion. Here, substitution by German raw materials and technical substitution must play a role. A further point is the elimination of unemployment, here Jessen holds that only a reagriculturization can solve the problem. He asks: Or should elementary settlements at the outskirts of the cities be preferred? Can they be integrated in the exchange circuit of the formal economy? How should the necessary productive credit creation be organized? What about the further division of GDP between investment and consumption? Finally the most important aspect is the spiritual attitude of the people. As Sombart remarked (see later), a lot of decisions have to be made even in the framework of the new order. In contrast to Wisekmann, Jessen is less ideological and asks relevant practical questions, but without answering them.

The journal asked Sombart to reply to Wiskemann's aforementioned article and in two parts Sombart put forward his points of view (10.8.1934, 2009–2011, and

17.8.1934, 2055–2057).[19] In the first paragraph, Sombart asserts that his view coincides to a large degree with Wisekmann's. But his reasoning and the last sentence of the article make clear that he totally rejects Wiskemann and the new regime. He states that only a formal or a cultural economics is possible according to his arguments in *Die drei Nationalökonomien*.[20] A third approach à la Wiskemann is not possible.[21] "Not even in the Third Reich." He shares with Wiskemann the rejection of formal-mathematical economics and he pleads (like Wiskemann who holds a naturalistic fallacy) for the difference between values and factual statements. But then he negates Wiskemann's thesis of the absolutely predetermined character of economic policy: Even in the new regime different emphases could be set, between industry and agriculture, equal pay or wage differentials, etc. He further rejects the focus of analysis on the economy of the own country, a broader, more international perspective is warranted. He further reiterates Gottl's view of economic systematic elements sui generis (needs, households, factors of production, etc.), so that not everything is relative in economics, but certain basic categories hold for all economic systems.

He introduces his master term of the economic system, which defines possible combinations of systematic dichotomies. He also criticizes Wisekmann for his opinion that all science must be practical in the first instance. In fact, fiscal economics, business science, and economic policy have a practical orientation. But economics as such is – like all other sciences – determined by theoretical ideas. It cannot give practical answers and has insofar a certain ascetic character. But it can ask questions and put debates into conceptual frameworks to make them more rational and to make clear the limits of the planned economic policies. Sombart makes no concessions. As a major proponent of the historical school, his article demonstrates that the propagation of an historical approach does not go hand in hand with the promulgation of national socialist ideas. The article also falsifies those who argue that Sombart supported National Socialism at least for some time. This view seems to be definitely incorrect.

The low enthusiasm for Sombart as a companion of National Socialism is also apparent in Jessen's review (7.12.1934, 414–415) of Sombart's *Deutscher Sozialismus*.[22] Jessen appreciates Sombart's critique of the rationalistic method and

---

[19] We will not discuss Sombart's further article on the probable development of public and private companies in the German economy (20.12. 1935, 527–529). Sombart argues that not much will change and that the difference between public and private is often exaggerated. The main difference is between free and regulated, irrespective of the public or private formal arrangement. Her underlines that the future of mankind will be decided according to the neither capitalist nor socialist economic systems in which soul and not spirit dominates (self-sufficiency, agriculture, and handicraft). This is in clear opposition to the official pros and cons in the new regime.

[20] 3rd ed. Berlin: Duncker und Humblot, 2003.

[21] "Zwischen diesen beiden Möglichkeiten, eine Wirtschaftswissenschaft aufzubauen, haben wir zu wählen. Eine dritte gibt es nicht. Auch nicht im Dritten Reich" (10.8.1934, 2011).

[22] Charlottenburg: Buchholz und Weißwange, 1934.

the highlighting of the necessity of a leader (of leaders). Jessen does not discuss the book in detail but he criticizes the detachedness and the lack of concreteness and the practical economic consequences which should be drawn. He also strongly dislikes Sombart's thesis that a nation can be a nation without a deep we-consciousness. The article shows that Sombart was not considered as a brother in mind by convinced National Socialists like Jessen.

11.4 The New Business Economics

Wilhelm Kalveram is mentioned several times in the history of the faculty of economics in Frankfurt. But his adaptation to the new national socialist creed is not referred to. He held a chair in business economics (especially banking) since 1924 and retired in 1945 but he represented the chair since his death in 1951.[23]

He offered two articles on business science in the corporative state (27.10.1934, 142–145, and 3.11.1934, 195–197). He vividly castigates the decay of the liberal world and its moral principles. The almost absolute freedom of the individual lead to an asocial, over-mechanized world, combined with scepticism, nihilism, egotism, materialism, with a dominating profit principle and the mergence of trust and power to strong social groups (cartels, trade unions, etc.). The unity of the live process was broken. He presents a synopsis of criticism of the old world but he surprisingly admits that liberalism set free the incredible will power and engagement of individuals, which was necessary for the progress of civilization.

The exact and causal approaches in business science up till now followed this trend with the natural sciences as the ideal. It should not be abolished but transformed, the object would remain the same (the complex organism of companies), as well as the methodology: risk problems, profitability- and cost-analyses should be central after reorganization. Like Wiskemann, he does not want to abolish the entrepreneur. But he, as a leader (a *Führer*, he frequently cites A. Hitler's *Mein Kampf*) in economics, should consider the interests of the state and the people. In how far this is reconcilable with the profit motive is not discussed. But we see again the search for a compromise. Material prosperity is important, but eternal ideals make life distinct.[24]

As mentioned, major classical problem areas should remain, but the scope be enlarged and the firm should be put in the context of corporative organization principles, which he hastens to differentiate from a planned economy. How, e.g., the prices should be determined is only explained *ex negativo:* not by central decree and not by supply and demand. An organic price harmony should be fixed inside the

---

[23] Schefold, B. (ed.). *Wirtschafts- und Sozialwissenschaftler in Frankfurt am Main.* Marburg: Metropolis, 1989, 318–319.

[24] "Würde und Weihe empfängt es [das meschliche Handeln] erst durch die Hinwendung zu den über seinem begrenzten irdischen Dasein stehenden ideellen ewigen Gütern" (3.11.1934, 195).

economic corporatives, respecting the eternal values of the people's community. Another apology of the national socialist educational plans in economics and business science is formulated by the well-known E. Niklisch (25.5.1935, 1573–1574). He argues against the old liberalist tendency and fully appreciates the new educational principles based on the people and higher values.

11.5 Concepts and Principles of the New Order

Besides the contributions of the better known economists, a couple of authors, partly young economists, or people with political functions, contributed to the question how the new economic order should look like. Some articles were mere heroic rhetoric (see e.g., G.M. von Astfeld in 19.1.1934, 673–674, who asks for a frontier soldier attitude in labour relations). A systematic delineation of the new politics cannot be found immediately after *gleichschaltung*. Instead, we find articles on the new role of the trade unions (21.4.1933, 813–816, and 5.5.1933, 867–868), the American technocratic movement (5.5.1933, 873–875), and agricultural cooperatives (19.5.1933, 934–937, and 26.5.1933, 961–962).

The question of leadership was discussed several times in the journal. A longer article was written by H. Reupke, an executive member of the *Reichsstand der Deutschen Industrie* on the principle of leadership in the economy (26.1.1934, 673–674). In the liberal past, paternalist leaders like A. Krupp with social concerns for the employed played a role besides the mere money makers.

A true leader must have an inner calling. An economic leader, as an expression of private initiative (private property is considered as an essential element in National Socialism), must integrate efficiency and a sense of honor. Historical examples (ancient Germans), the medieval relationship of obedience and trust, and the parallels to the military sphere (companionship, the nature of fighters, etc.) are drawn. Intermediate institutions are called for, e.g., a *Vertrauensrat*, where employers and employees are associated, which should help to fix adequate wages.[25] On a higher level, the leaders of the companies should be organized in a council of leaders and according to the corporative principle the intermediate organizations should also find representation on higher levels (e.g., the branches).

A new type of the entrepreneur is also developed in W. Jost's article (4.5.1934, 1349–1351). The undertaker is the leader of his company. An essential element is the new spirit. But the new order also allows the interdiction of investments (if they are too speculative or considered less necessary). But the entrepreneur is not degraded to a mere executive function, he should consider the meaningful integration of his undertakings into the total production structure. So he may consider investments, which would have been outside his horizon in the old order.

---

[25] The *Vertrauensrat* was the substitute of the abolished *Betriebsrat* which had legally defined rights.

Discipline in the company should be based on mutual trust and understanding. He pleads for an ordered competition *(veranstalteter Wettbewerb)* in which fraud, boycott, etc. are excluded. Fair play is an essential moral component of the new order. Sometimes a conscious price policy by the state seems necessary. But usually the prices should be set by market forces in so far as the companies act in concert with the above mentioned ethical standards.

But also a slightly more interventionist perspective exists. H.R. Fritzsche e.g., the press speaker in the economic ministry, highlights the new directive on price increases (1.6.1934, 1541–1543), which forbids the private fixing of minimum prices, and price increases in general for necessary goods of everyday life in so far as the input prices did not rise. In a general remark, he argues that the state has to identify the needs in the economy and direct the companies in the just way.[26]

Often new terms were created to describe the qualitative structure of the new order. H. Marschner and G. Ziegler (6.4.1934, 1170–1173) used the term "duty bound freedom" *(pflichtgebundene Freiheit)* to underline the combination of personal initiative and duties vis-à-vis the workers, competitors, the economy, and policy (see also K. Guth in 15.2.1935, 877–880). Only a fair competition should be accepted. Cartelization, monopolization, dumping, the artificial curtailment of supply, and in general the exploitation of a superior market position are not allowed. The means of production should remain in private property but the owner is only a trustee of society. Against liberalism, the primacy of politics is underlined. The entrepreneur should not act against the policy directives to pursue his personal profit interests.

The question of the just price was a constant concern. K. Mahn (21.7.1933, 1193–1195, and 20.4.1934, 1261–1263) first shows how difficult the finding of a just price may be and gives an overview on the different meanings e.g., the *justum pretium* in the middle Ages. The just price may be defined as the price in accordance with the political aims of the system. But somewhat in contrast the author hastens to add that this is not to say that the prices will be administered by a public organ. Usually the price finding process can be left to the market, intervention is only necessary in the case of cartels, or if a quantitative imbalance between supply and demand occurs. Also the marginal suppliers should not automatically fall out of the market in the adjustment process because this may lead to the complete breakdown of the respective market. He differentiates between four levels of intervention: (1) Interventions that leave the market processes themselves intact (interest rates set by the central bank); (2) The indirect influence of supply and demand, e.g., the prohibition of certain investments; (3) Enforced collusion of companies to bundle production or the setting of prices; (4) The suspension of the market process by minimum or

---

[26] "Im nationalsozialistischen Wirtschaftssystem, in dem der Staat Führung und Regulativ innehat, stellt dieser das Bedürfnis fest und ruft kraft seiner Autorität zur Deckung des vorhandenen Bedarfs, zur Nachfrage auf ... So regulieren ... nicht Angebot und Nachfrage die Wirtschaft, sondern die Nachfrage und das Angebot sind die Aeußerungen des wirtschaftlichen Lebens, das von der autoritären Führung des totalitären Staates ausgeht" (1.6.1934, 1542–1543).

maximum prices. The logic of intervention should be to use the less interventionist mechanism as possible and to use the principle with the highest degree of market conformity.

It would be wrong to define the just price according to the existing production costs. This could impede technological progress. He mentions the examples of the radio for the masses *(Volksempfänger)* and the car for the people *(Volkswagen)* where a lower price was enforced. Administered prices need not be uniform over the whole branch or industry, they may be firm specific. Finally, he mentions that the instruments of price regulation and control are still in its infancy.

In foreign trade, a moderate position was taken. The preferential treatment in the liberal area was abandoned for good reasons but also the nationalist autarky and tariffs after the World War I is rejected (see Schlotterer in 30.11.1934, 371–373). Self-sufficiency is not the aim but mutual agreements (principle of reciprocity) between nations and long-run exchange relationships among private companies, intermediate organs. Representations of industry should also play a role.

Surprisingly, two articles can be found which reject O. Spengler's thesis of the betrayal of technique. Spengler argued that the white dominating countries should not export technical equipment to the inferior colored people (leapfrogging). They would loose their advantageous position. Because of low wages and long working hours, the colored people could start competition in the manufacturing sector and impair the economic situation of the hitherto advanced countries. In W. Weniger's view (29.3.1935, 1170–1173), this is pure nonsense and an expression of a materialist reductionism. If the advanced countries live in a technically inclined culture, the export of technical equipment will not impede their long run position on the world markets. If they will loose their position in the future due to the exports then they cannot be helped anyway. A concise criticism of Spengler is also offered by W. Jost (22.12.1933, 517–519) who castigates his aristocratic backwardness and primitive determinism (liberalism leads to nihilism and bolshevism). Spengler's economic proposals: No exports of technical equipment and the drastic reduction of the wage level are vividly criticized and parallels to his hated liberalists (L. Mises) in the wage question and the negative view on the role of trade unions are pointed out.

Some authors tried to give a more precise description of the corporative structure of society. Th. Hupfauer (responsible for corporative affairs in the NSDAP) first castigates the mistakes of the old order (3.11.1933, 191–194): Profit orientation, greediness, the polarization of incomes, the economy as an end in itself, parliamentarianism as an expression of the liberal-individualist idea of the equality of all people, etc. Instead, National Socialism favors the principle of achievement: The value of a person is evaluated according to what the person has done for the community. The corporatives should be organized according to industry, commerce, and handicraft with its subdivisions. The corporatives are responsible for all social institutions, labour protection, insurance systems, etc. The article is not very precise about the further details. The final appeal shows the search for synthesis (or ambiguity?): The social should dominate the individual orientation *and* everybody what (s)he deserves! *(Gemeinnutz geht vor Eigennutz, Jedem das Seine!)*

Finally, the articles on the social component should not be dismissed. K. Seesemann wrote about the work service *(Arbeitsdienst)* as a transformation mechanism to supersede the crisis (2.2.1934, 761–763). The international economic crisis destroyed the property of the middle and lower classes. The task now is to create new property in their hands. The solution could be the aforementioned settlements, which should only be paid for 20% of the real value. The work service should, at least to a certain degree, build the necessary constructions. But attention should be paid to the problem that workers of the regular labour market could be crowded out if all work were down by the work service. But it is better to work for the work service instead of being unemployed. As a consequence some industrial production should be relocated close to the settlements so that, e.g., new canal routes must be developed. The settlements would have the positive by-effect to strengthen the deeply routed relationship of the settlers to the German soil. A plea for a longer period of notice *(Kündigungsfrist)* is asked for by an unknown C.D. (1.12.1933, 376–378).

11.6 Contributions of Members of the Later Resistance: Goerdeler, Dietze, and Lampe

Three contributions by members of the later resistance to Hitler could be found.[27] Goerdeler (at the time mayor of Leipzig) contributed a – politically very neutral – article on the new German municipal decree (1.3.1935, No. 22, and 8.3.1935, 1031–1034). He does not criticize the regime, his overview is merely descriptive. He underlines the need to reduce the debts of the municipalities and the strict rules for new credits (ability to pay the annuities, etc.). He explains the necessity of serious accounting rules and highlights many details, e.g., what happens in case of compulsory execution. In an anonymous article, his work as price commissioner is appreciated, especially his willingness to enforce price stability and his flexibility what the question of the just price (replacement cost or cost price, *Wiederbeschaffungs –* vs. *Einstandspreis*) is concerned (16.11.1934, 281–284).

Janssen summarizes Dietze's biography as follows[28]: In 1927, he became professor in Jena. In 1934, he opposed the agricultural policy of the new regime. After Hitler's seizure of power he became successor of his teacher Sehring in Berlin. The opposition against the *gleichschaltung* of the German speaking economic association *(Verein für Socialpolitik)* elected Dietze in 1935 for president. In 1936, Dietze was dismissed in Berlin and had to go back to Jena. He was sentenced a first time in 1937

---

[27] We will not present more biographical or other details here, because they are well documented. On the German resistance see the overviews by e.g. Rüther, D. *Der Widerstand des 20. Juli auf dem Weg in die soziale Marktwirtschaft.* Paderborn: Schöningh, 2002; and Goldschmidt, N. (ed.). *Wirtschaft, Politik und Freiheit.* Tübingen: Mohr Siebeck, 2005.

[28] Janssen, H. *Nationalökonomie und Nationalsozialismus.* Marburg: Metropolis, 1998, 524–525.

when he acted publicly as a member of the confessing church *(Bekennende Kirche)* against the new regime. In 1938, he changed to the University of Freiburg and was member of the opposing Freiburg circle.

Dietze's article in the journal is missing in Janssen's bibliography (26.1.1934, 723–725). It deals with the reagriculturalization of Germany. It starts with Sombart's proposals and some empirical material. According to the new regime, a self-sufficient food situation is necessary. Other countries try to oppress German via a curtailment of food supply. Hitler is quoted. To strengthen national unity and coherence, a stronger and broader basis for the peasantry is necessary. An educational initiative is necessary to implement the spiritual ideas of the new regime, if the peasants do not fulfill their obligations, expropriations could be undertaken. All this sounds very ideological and repressive[29] and does not fit into the biographical sketch of Janssen and others. Dietze in fact mentions that the *Reicherbhofsgesetz* put high duties on the peasants and opened the way to expropriation. Nevertheless, it is not easy to read a critical attitude between the lines.

Lampe contributed three parts of an exceptionally long article on economic science and economic policy.[30] Lampe argues that a distinction between primitive liberalism and the existence of economic laws have to be made. Especially the new state is dependent of competent economic advisers. The economy has its own laws and they have to be known to be able to influence the economy. Lampe proposes a technocratic or decisionistic model of expertise: the theorist informs what be economically correct or efficient but does not interfere in the preponderance of political decisions. They can inform about the material welfare losses, which can then be compared with the value of idealist goals. He tries to present economics as a general logic of choice with no presupposition of the egotist homo oeconomicus. The mover of the market economy is finally the consumer. He directs the production process. But the unhampered market processes have deficiencies, or market failures. One is due to different start chances. A natural monopoly may produce rents without achievement.

A second problem refers to the identification of the origin of price changes (relative price changes vs. changes in the price level). Wrong directions of the production process may take place (this is in principle an open door for manifold interventions). Another aspect concerns technological progress, which may work too quickly (devaluation of the existing production structure). A strong state above the interest groups is necessary to lead the market economy.[31] Intermediate

---

[29] "weil bei maßgebenden Mächten der Wille vorhanden ist, das deutsche Volk zu knechten, wir also um der Erhaltung unseres politischen Daseins und um der Wiedererringung unserer Freiheit willen darauf bedacht sein müssen, uns nicht dem Hunger als wirksame Waffe auszusetzen … Damit mündet die Frage Reagrarisierung, wie alle nationalsozialistische Wirtschaftspolitik, in entscheidende Erziehungsaufgaben ein" (26.1.1934, 724–725).

[30] 26.4.1935, 1381–1384; 10.5.1935, 1478–1481; and 17.5.1935, 1526–1529.

[31] "Nur ein *über den Kämpfen stehender Schiedsrichter*, der die Spielregeln der 'freien' Marktwirtschaft und alle ihre Mängel kennt, wird es vermögen, mit fester und dennoch behutsamer Hand die Marktwirtschaft *so* zu steuern, dass Veredelung der Konkurrenz erreicht wird und freie Marktwirtschaft sich idealer Marktwirtschaft zum wenigsten nähert" (10.5.1935, 1481).

organizations (like the *Arbeitsfront*) can help to reduce frictions. Institutions such as central banks, employment offices, a patent law, etc. are necessary directive institutions. A pure theory of the market economy has to be abandoned instead of "productive interventionism." A certain critical distance cannot be derived from the text. The author seems to be willing to propose a regulated economy for the new regime.[32]

11.7 The Headline Articles

Every number of the journal was introduced by a short article of one page (marked with O(tto).M(eynen)., F(ranz).R(euter)., or H.B.). Usually they pick up new laws or refer to recent important speeches. Their tendency was obviously National Socialist because of the early *gleichschaltung* of the journal. Nevertheless, the headline articles had a specific trait, which deserves mentioning: It almost always took the side of business and opted for a "liberal National Socialism." It can therefore be stated that the main tendency of the journal before *gleichschaltung* had been preserved to a certain degree.

One headline article deals with the change of the editors (7.7.1933, 1). The achievements of the former editor are highlighted but it is also mentioned that the party policy orientation of the journal was very one-sided. The journal will adapt the new order but as the new editors Otto Meynen and Franz Reuter underline, it will not pursue a "mechanical *gleichschaltung*." It will report in a reliable and objective way, the many foreign readers are explicitly mentioned. The journal will not engage in politics. It will become the number one journal on economics in Germany. A new emphasis will, e.g., be put on the practical reports of business cycles. Criticism of the economic policy of the government is possible in the confines of the existing order. But a commitment for national socialist policy (uniting the country) follows. The journal will mediate between the economy and the still unclear, hasty activities *(unklar, stürmisch)* of the new political forces in power. The principal of leadership, which is so important in the political domain, will also play a major role in the economy (entrepreneurship).

In one article (3.11.1933) it is stated that under the new regime a certain reluctance vis-à-vis new theoretical research was observable and that National Socialism does not produce a new economic system like Marxism. German socialism is not of a political-constructive-organic nature but in essence it is an ethical principle. A strong state and strong personalities in the economy can be reconciled. Surely, some rhetoric can also be found: A certain natural order exists, which is deeply ingrained in the people.

---

[32] "Jeder Theoretiker, der alte Meister ehrt und ihr Werk in stetem Dienstbemühen gegenüber nationaler Wirtschaftswirklichkeit fortentwickelt, wird Annäherung von Wirtschaftspraxis und–theorie als dringende Gegenwartsaufgabe pflegen" (19.7.1935, 1529).

In another article (12.1.1934), the anonymous author deals with the proposals to nationalize major banks and insurance companies. He vividly rejects both. It is pointed out that historically a lot of bad experiences have been made with nationalizations and hasty actions are no good advice. Further, nationalizations are a typical measure of the political enemy. Hitler is cited with his commitment to strong personalities. This is used as an argument against nationalization. The basic orientation of National Socialism is that the state should lead the economy but nor direct it. Over and over again the educational and ethical character of the new regime is mentioned (see e.g., 19.1.1934). One reason may be that the author(s) want to minimize the (necessary or envisioned) structural changes, which go hand in hand with the new order.

The law for the preparation of the organic build-up of the German economy is put in the same context (16.3.1934). The fight for a new spirit is underlined. Major institutions of business will exist further on *(Industrie- und Handelskammern)*. The author underlines that in the longer run a free economy with strong leaders is envisioned and that competition, the free play of economic forces, will – in a modified form and after a period of transition – be conserved as one of the most powerful forces in the economy.

One article (27.4.1934) appreciates the activities of the state to bring people into work. But these measures can only be temporary. The financial burdens on mass consumption must be reduced to accelerate growth. An example is the special income tax for the German *Arbeitsfront*. A devaluation of the currency is rejected (production of bad money). According to the author, autarky is even forgotten by those who wrote long books on it in the past. Cooperation with foreign countries is necessary and possible if Germany will not enforce its ideals upon other nations.

But a certain disagreement may have existed among the editors of the journal because another article (8.6.1934) argues against the liberalist tendency to comment on a stronger and enlarged structure of the national raw material basis with a dismissive gesture.

Another topic is (the import of) raw materials (25.5.1934). It is asserted that a control must be exercised and cannot be left to the market. But this control should be left to the self-governed organs of industry. A national commissioner for raw materials is admitted.

After the inauguration of the New Plan *(Neue Plan)* ambivalence came up (5.10.1934): Is the New Plan the march into a planned economy or is it still based on institutions with important market structures. The author argues that existing control structures have a tendency to multiply and intensify and will produce more and more tasks and bureaucracy. This is a brief example of public choice arguments. The author underlines that in history a planned economy never succeeded, especially in more complex economies.[33]

---

[33] "Die Geschichte der Menschheit kennt kein Beispiel, dass die staatliche Planung auf den großen und lebenswichtigen Gebieten des Wirtschaftslebens, wenn sie über vorübergehende Notwendigkeiten hinaus durchgeführt wurde, Erfolg hatte. Zentralverwaltete Wirtschaft muß naturnotwendig letzten Endes alle persönlichen Kräfte verdrängen und ersetzen oder überhaupt den Versuch aufgeben, den ungeheuer vielgestaltigen Prozeß des modernen Wirtschaftslebens in seinen zahllosen Einzelheiten planmäßig zu leiten" (5.10.1934, 1).

Another article is a plea for intellectualism and economic theorizing: Good will and political correctness are not enough for an economy with complex interrelationships (12.10.1934). Also in the debate on price increases the journal had a clear opinion (2.11.1934). The man in the street often has a wrong impression, profiteering by price increases is almost inexistent. The problem for companies is that the price setting rules of the state lead to a quick shrinking of the stocks. Finally products which can be sold must represent a correct price because supply and demand obviously match.[34] This is an affirmation of the equilibrium creed of "liberalism."

Another article argues against the abolition of cartels (16.11.1934). A big company would be able to force a small company into bankruptcy. A cartel prevents this and guarantees workplaces. What is needed is first of all confidence of the state and the people vis-à-vis entrepreneurship. It is also argued (12.7.1935) that Marxism, mechanization, and rationalization almost abolished the freedom and responsibility of the entrepreneurs. Fortunately, in National Socialism the personal leadership function is revalued.

Some articles in 1935 leave the impression that the ideological and aggressive components became stronger. In one article (26.7.1935), the permanent questions of foreigners and the foreign press due to some "occurrences" in Berlin (at the *Kurfürstendamm*) is criticized, pogroms against Christians and Jews are only imagining things. Instead, pogroms happened in Ireland. These are only political attacks by other countries but the Germans stand united behind the leader and will change the balance of power in their interest.[35] On the occasion of the party convention in Nuremberg (13.9.1935), the speech of Hitler is reiterated: His strictness in declaring fight to the enemies of the regime. Only the leader decides if fight or education should be used (this is mentioned in the context of alleged infringements). The ruthless following of principles of iron is necessary for defense against internal and external enemies.[36]

---

[34] "Der Käufer bezahlt die einzelne Ware überall und immer so hoch, wie sie ihm nützlich oder angenehm ist. Deswegen wird sich der Preis zuletzt stets nach Angebot und Nachfrage bestimmen. Seine Anpassung daran kann man aufhalten und regulieren, nicht aber auf die Dauer verhindern" (2.11.1934, 1).

[35] "Je stärker es im übrigen auch der böswilligen Auslandspresse erschwert wird, die absolute Geschlossenheit und Einmütigkeit des deutschen Volkes in Zweifel zu ziehen, je stärker Deutschland in den Augen der Welt zur nationalen Verkörperung von Ordnung, innerem Gleichgewicht und Einigkeit wird, um so erfolgreicher kann die Außen- und Wirtschaftspolitik des Führers und seiner Mitarbeiter unserem Volke in der kommenden Auflockerung der gegenwärtigen Kräfteordnung Geltung, Wohlstand und Frieden zurückgeben" (26.7.1935, 1).

[36] "Die entschlossene Anwendung der eroberten Gewalt gegen Feinde drinnen und draußen, diese rücksichtslose Befolgung eiserner Prinzipien wird damit begründet, dass nur sie Deutschland vor dem Versinken in die an vielen anderen Stellen bedrohlich erkennbare Gefahr eines bolschewistischen Chaos zu bewahren vermögen" (13.9.1935, 1).

11.8 Conclusions

It is worth mentioning that between 1933 and 1935 no major aggressive or racial National Socialist propaganda could be found besides some terminology (like the white race). Only in the last numbers of 1935 this seems to change. Negative comments on other countries are mostly missing. For example, the war preparations of other countries are discussed in a neutral way (H. Bauer in 19.7.1935, 1954–1957), as well as the debate on work programs in England between N. Chamberlain and L. George (E. Wölfflin in 26.7.1935, 1996–1998).

Let us come back to the set of dichotomies to distinguish economic analyses and the research of institutions according to Rutherford[37] and distinguish between formal and antiformal, individualist (methodological individualism) and holist approaches (emergent properties), rationality (homo oeconomicus) and rule following (norms matter), evolution (spontaneous order) and design (ordered economy), and efficiency (assumption of markets) vs. reform (necessity of interventions for social or other reasons). The interesting result is that many authors put an emphasis on the right side of the dichotomies but at the same time tried to reconcile both sides: The practical side of economics under the new regime was underlined but we also found strong statements for theoretical investigations. It was often alleged that the economy must be reembedded into the whole structure of society but at the same time the logic of supply and demand was accepted. At least in the early years, there was room for discussion: Are the laws of markets the final arbiter, can the equilibrium points be influenced by institutional design, how strong may the instruments (from market conformity to mere interventionism) be applied?

Self-interest as a norm was rejected and the ethical component was underlined (rule following) but at the same time many authors supported the necessity of rational economic behavior (profitability principle etc.). Markets should definitely not be left to themselves (against liberalism), but their bounded efficiency was appreciated. Market failures were identified and remedies were proposed and the general principle of the primacy of the policy underlined. This last principle may seem to be a contradiction to the acceptance of markets and limited interference but for us it is an objective problem of all modern societies: primacy of politics or the self-regulation of markets. Usually, an always ambivalent compromise will result in practice.

Because of the moderate right wing dichotomy focus a natural affinity to the criticism and historical emphasis of the historical school existed. But as we have seen (the example of Sombart) their main representatives dissociated themselves very quickly and were rejected by the Nazi movement. A really profound discussion on method did not take place. A theoretical rising star, a high level theorist of the new order, could not be identified in the journal. Instead, a surprising overlap of more or less critical thinkers of the new order is discernible.

---

[37] Rutherford, M. *Institutions in economics*. Cambridge: Cambridge University Press, 1994.

It could be noticed that the journal took a liberal stance inside the framework of the new order. Besides rhetoric, it almost always was on the side of business and defended its freedom of action (on the basis of a new moral) and the marvelous working of the price mechanism when they commented new laws and regulations (the corporative restructuring, the price fixing, etc.). But besides the static arguments for free markets the journals also incorporated the new ideas of productive credit creation and deficit spending (but as the authors of the journal point out: Within limits). In so far it put specific emphases despite *gleichschaltung*. What autarky is concerned there was even a certain opposition to the main trend. It did not comment critically the aggressive actions and viewpoints of the new regime. If we would only know the social and economic reality of National Socialism via the journal the repressive and increasingly totalitarian aspects would almost get unnoticed. Even the men of the later resistance accepted the rules and framework of the new regime, critical aspects (if existing) were very much hidden between the lines.

We cannot pick up the discussion here if the contributions at the time led to a coherent alternative economic structure in theory and practice.[38] To a certain degree the questions of e.g., in how far the market processes should be shaped and influenced was also fundamental and hotly debated in the concept of the later social market economy or today in the debate on globalization and harmonization in the EU. A coherent approach between individualism and collectivism, free and regulated markets has never been developed. Its practical design depends on the circumstances, normative statements, assumptions on historically specific behavior, etc.

We do not share Kruse's opinion[39] that in National Socialism an ideological-theoretical concept was totally missing compared with the other approaches just mentioned. Instead, we share the view that a comprehensible economic reshape was envisioned[40] and that a certain theoretical ideal type of the future economy and society, a third way between capitalism and planned economy, was developed.[41] This is also exemplified by the contributions in the journal discussed here.

Woll and Janssen point out as main elements of the new order: The concept of race; the unity of the people; the primacy of politics; the economy should be embedded; liberalism leads to slavery; a limited self-sufficiency is warranted; private property is accepted, but only in the confines of an ordered competition; profits are legitimate, but e.g., interest is only partially acceptable.

It is interesting to notice that some (more or less "liberal" minded) authors of the journal, Sombart, and Lampe shared company in supporting the existence of economic basic facts and tendencies ("laws") and the independence of theoretical research. Unfortunately, an alliance of open-minded economists who went beyond

---

[38] See the overview in Peukert, H. "Nationalökonomie und Nationalsozialismus." *Jahrbuch für Wirtschaftsgeschichte*, 2 (1999), 215–228.

[39] Kruse, Chr. *Die Volkswirtschaftslehre im Nationalsozialismus*. Freiburg: Rudolf Haufe, 1988.

[40] Barkai, A. *Das Wirtschaftssystem des Nationalsozialismus*. Frankfurt: Fischer, 1988.

[41] See Woll, H. *Die Wirtschaftslehre des deutschen Faschismus*. Munich: Oldenbourgh, 1994. Janssen, H. *Nationalökonomie und Nationalsozialismus*. Marburg: Metropolis, 1998.

their neo/anti/classical horizon did not exist before National Socialism came to power. What may an intelligently designed deficit spending program with work for the unemployed have prevented?

Today we are not in a much better situation: An international rainbow coalition of the insightful would be necessary to save the biosphere. The problem is the opposite to the expansionary necessity in the 1930s: A contraction of material throughput and emissions is warranted but mankind seems to be evolutionarily programmed in a different way. National Socialism has taught us: Catastrophes are possible, half-hearted compromises with a wrong regime make guilty.

Chapter 12
Gustav Stolper's Influence on U.S. Industrial Disarmament Policy in West Germany, 1945–1946

Nicholas W. Balabkins

This paper was first presented at the 20th Heilbronn Symposium in Economics and the Social Sciences, June 21–24, 2007, Heilbronn, Germany

Our Heilbronn Symposia has for years used the traditional threefold format. Speakers survey the available literature of the Symposia's focus. They provide a critical rendition of the topic in terms of contemporary economic theory. And they assess how useful the legacy of an author is for contemporary theory or policy making.

The first part of my paper deals with Gustav Stolper's life in the U.S. from his arrival in New York City in 1933 to his role in the Herbert Hoover Mission to West Germany in the bitter winter of 1947. Stolper died in New York at the end of 1947 at the age of 59. The basic source for this part of the paper is the reliable volume by Toni Stolper, his wife, called *Ein Leben in Brennpunkten Unserer Zeit* of 1960. In addition, a few remarkable essays on Stolper by Heinz Rieter, Hansjörg Klausinger, Karl Häuser, and Wolfgang Stolper, along with a book by Harald Hagemann and Claus-Dieter Krohn, have provided solid information on Gustav Stolper's teenage years and his editorship of *Der deutsche Volkswirt* up to 1933.

For the second part of my paper, I have used books and articles readily available on the American policy in occupied Germany.

In the third part, I probe some of the unintended consequences of the early Morgenthau-inspired economic policy in terms of economic growth theory. Stolper's legacy is presented at the end of my paper.

N.W. Balabkins (✉)
Lehigh University, Bethlehem, PA, USA
e-mail: nib2@Lehigh.EDU

12.1 What Made Stolper Tick?

Gustav Stolper grew up in a humble home. His ancestors hailed from Eastern Europe, but Gustav was born in Vienna. The youngster was a precocious lad with a wide range of interests, music being one of them. He learned early the sting of the Pan-German anti-Semitism in Vienna, but he paid no attention to the violent ideology of racial bigotry. He spent his time reading books, studying and playing piano, and eschewed Zionism and socialist agitation.

As a teenager, Gustav Stolper decided to become a journalist. In 1906, he entered the University of Vienna, where he studied law and economics. In 1912, he received his doctorate and started working on the editorial board of the *Der sterreichische Volkswirt*.[1] From his early days as a journalist, Stolper knew that practice without theory was no more acceptable than theory without practice. His role model was the *London Economist* in terms of topics, analytical presentation of subjects, and elegant language, marked by brevity, clarity, and precision.[2]

Following the end of the World War I and the disintegration of the Austro-Hungarian Empire, Stolper was not happy to live and work in the truncated remnant of Austria. In 1925, he moved to Berlin and founded a business weekly, *Der deutsche Volkswirt*.[3] In six short years, Stolper's Volkswirt became the best business weekly in Germany. Alas, in the parliamentary elections of 1932, German voters filled the Reichstag with National Socialist deputies, and in January of 1933, Hitler was elected Chancellor of Germany. Stolper knew he had to flee Germany as quickly as he could if he wanted to remain alive. The Nazis were preaching the doctrine of race war against Jews, converted to Christianity or not, and Stolper knew that the eradication of all Jews was possible in the near future.

While residing in Berlin, Stolper had become acquainted with many immigrants from Soviet Russia and had learned from them about the Soviet concentration camps and the massive purges of the Soviet intelligentsia. For more than a decade, he had observed how the Communists had been eliminating the bourgeois and entrepreneurial class. He abhorred Stalinist Russia and all Soviet institutions.[4]

---

[1] Rieter, Heinz, (1998), "Der deutsche Volkswirt 1926 bis 1933," in *Studien zur Entwicklung der okonomischen Theorie XVII*, p. 98.

[2] Stolper, Toni, (1960), *Ein Leben in Brennpunkten unserer Zeit, Gustav Stolper, 1888–1947*. Tubingen Rainer Wunderlich Verlag, p. 38.

[3] Stolper, Toni, p. 179.

[4] Holl, Karl, (1999), "Stolper, Gustav" in Hagemann, Harald und Krohn, Claus-Dieter, (eds.) *Biographisches Handbuch der deutsch-sprachigen wirtschaftswissenschaftlichen Emigration nach 1933*, München, K.G. Saur, p. 694.

12.2 Stolper's Transplantation to the U.S

Gustav Stolper arrived in the U.S. in October of 1933, at the age of 45. He read and spoke quite a bit of English, but the switch from German to English was daunting. Stolper retained his badge of nonnative American, while learning to write respectful English prose. Without having attended American high school, the native American pattern of speech cannot be learned. Without having been exposed to American university education, he had difficulty absorbing colloquialisms, puns, and idioms. How does an immigrant learn the paradigm of staccato, Hemmingway-style English? That is, how does one learn to follow consciously and purposefully the rule of noun, verb, object, and adverb sequence to avoid dangling participles?

Stolper brought to the U.S. a detailed and well-tested editorial experience and a thorough grounding of geopolitics, law, wartime economics, and jurisprudence. He also knew intimately the international banking community and many bankers on a personal basis. Alas, all of his training and experience was transplanted to the U.S., which was suffering from the most severe economic depression in its entire existence.

He brought with him to the U.S. the proceeds from the sale of the *Der deutsche Volkswirt*, so he was not exactly destitute. He could take his time, visit his acquaintances, and determine how best to establish himself in this country. Initially Stolper played with the idea of launching the American version of his German language business weekly. But with unemployment reaching 25%, this turned out to be a pipe-dream. Even his friend and much-admired academic economist, Joseph A. Schumpeter, teaching at Harvard, was skeptical. So Stolper started publishing economic situation reports on Europe and the U.S. in English for subscribers. With his astute sense of observation and his analyses of the balance sheets and income statements of banks and businesses, Stolper published 201 economic reports in the U.S. and was able to make a comfortable living.

He also became a much respected public speaker. The French are known for saying that it does not matter what you say provided you say it in proper French. Americans, however, are much more tolerant in this regard and they paid close attention to what Stolper had to say, regardless of his German accent. Stolper became quite friendly with the influential journalist Walter Lippmann and also with Allen Dulles, Alvin Johnson, Parker Gilbert, and other foreign affairs specialists. But he discovered soon enough that American liberals were much further left than himself,[5] and that many just about adored Soviet-style socialism.

Upon arrival in New York City, Stolper met many of his former acquaintances and friends looking for jobs. The Rockefeller Foundation had generously financed 170 German-speaking economists, but academic jobs were scarce. Many of these

---

[5] Stolper, Toni, pp. 344–347.

immigrant scholars were Jewish, and they knew that all Ivy-League universities were closed to them at that time. In the fall of 1933, the "University in Exile" was founded in New York City, later called New School. This institution provided many teaching jobs. In no time at all, the intellectual potential of its faculty became an integral part of the brain trust of the *New Deal*.[6] A few of these refugees were anti-New Deal economists, like Ludwig Mises.

The Japanese attack on Pearl Harbor in December of 1941 opened up new opportunities for Stolper. In November 1942, for instance, he spoke at the annual meetings of the American Academy of Political Science, discussing the nature and functions of the transportation system during the war. He was particularly anxious to explain the existing transportation bottlenecks in the Third Reich.[7] A year earlier, in February 1941, he took part in a round-table discussion of the war aims of Nazi Germany organized by *Fortune* magazine.[8]

By 1943, the wartime propaganda, cast in black and white terms, was already advocating a permanent weakening of Germany after the end of the war. Stolper was alarmed by the derisive "anti-Prussian fanaticism" in the American mass media. He was particularly upset by the venomous attitude of the influential journalist Walter Lippmann, New York intellectuals and academics.[9] The wartime "pro-Soviet" attitudes were projected into the glorious, cooperative postwar years, almost forever and ever, provided Germany remain weak, disarmed, and pastoral. During the war, Americans shipped tons of food, medicines, and 550,000 heavy GM and Studebaker trucks to the Soviet Union, but the Soviets had not publicly acknowledged these lend-lease shipments. Nor have they expressed any thanks for them. Stolper was baffled by such ungratefulness of the Soviet ally. Nor had he forgotten the massive Soviet purges of the 1930. The American love affair with the wartime Soviet ally can be amusing reading today by scanning the issues of the American *Life* magazine of the World War II years. Furthermore, the American Ambassador in Moscow, Joe E. Davis, wrote a book, *Moscow Mission*, in which he extolled the virtues of the Red Army and praised to the sky the "nice Soviet allies."[10] The well-known American journalist Dorothy Thompson turned out pro Soviet articles on a daily basis. After the presidential elections of 1944, in which FDR won his fourth term as U.S. president, Stolper became unhappy with FDR's Secretary of the Treasury, Henry Morganthau. He had what his wife, Toni, dubbed in German, a "böse Bedeutung," or, in English, a "bad premonition."[11]

---

[6] Hagemann, Harald and Krohn, Claus-Dieter (1999) "Emigration der Wirtschaftswissenschaften – Einleitung," in Hagemann, Harald und Krohn, Claus-Dieter, (eds.) *Biographisches Handbuch der deutschsprachigen wirtschaftswissenschaftlichen Emigration nach 1933*, München, K.G. Saur, p. XXVIII.

[7] Stolper, Toni, p. 346.

[8] Stolper, Toni, p. 418.

[9] Stolper, Toni, p. 424.

[10] Stolper, Toni, p. 430.

[11] Stolper, Toni, p. 433.

The September 1944 Quebec meeting between Churchill and FDR, and the announcement of a postwar "pastorization" plan for defeated Germany had shaken Stolper to the core.[12] Later on, in the spring of 1945, at the Yalta conference, the spirit of deindustrialization of defeated Germany was shocking for Stolper. At the end of the war, wide sections of the U.S. population were in awe of Soviet Russia and nothing was harsh or punitive enough for the destroyed Third Reich.[13] Alas, in retrospect and hindsight, the American public and mass media had totally missed the Soviet expansionist ambitions in Europe and Asia. Peaceful coexistence with the loyal wartime ally after the unconditional surrender of the Third Reich was a happy pipe-dream of the American public, mass media, and academics.

12.3 The Essence of the Morgenthau Plan

The Morgenthau Plan called for a complete destruction of the German metallurgical, chemical, and electrical industries within 6 months after the cessation of hostilities. All factories should be razed, blown up, or dismantled and sent to the victorious countries as *reparations in kind*. All German mines should be closed. Germany was to become an agricultural country.

Morgenthau claimed that without heavy industry, Germany would never again wage war.[14] It is known that this Carthagenian proposal was officially accepted by President Roosevelt and Prime Minister Churchill at the Second Quebec Conference in September, 1944, as the program for postwar Germany.

The public reception in the U.S. of the Morgenthau Plan was adverse, but not entirely unfavorable. Although the American government never formally adopted this blueprint in its original form, its basic principles nevertheless dominated the official and unofficial thinking of policy makers in Washington, and in the U.S. Military government in its occupied zone of Germany.

The Potsdam Conference, held 3 months after the unconditional surrender, outlined most of the wartime Allies' policy goals. The Potsdam document called for a drastic reduction of German heavy industry. Postwar Germany was to have only "peaceful industries" and a highly developed agriculture. Germans were to be farmers and dairymen, not engineers, chemists, and steelmakers. The Potsdam blueprint called on the Allied Control Council in Berlin to work out a "level of industry" plan within 6 months to indicate the industries to be left in Germany and to earmark firms and capital equipment for reparations.

---

[12] Stolper, Toni, pp. 433–434.
[13] Stolper, Toni, p. 443.
[14] Morgenthau, Henry (1945) *Germany is Our Problem*. New York: Harper & Brothers.

In 1945, Americans were in favor of a thorough deindustrialization policy of the defeated Third Reich without regard to the economic and political consequences such a policy might have on Europe.[15] By way of contrast, to the British representatives on the Allied Control Council, such punitive attitudes of the Americans amounted to "utter lunacy."[16] They held that postwar Germany without industry would paralyze the entire Western European economy. From long experience, the British knew that extreme and punitive measures were futile in international affairs. They showed preference for moderation. The British members of the Allied Control Council in Berlin spent much time and effort in opposing the more extreme policy measures of some overzealous Americans. In over-all policy terms, the British aimed essentially at two things: the preservation of the wartime alliance and the prevention of Germany's starting another war.

12.4 Part II: The Directive of the Joint Chiefs of Staff, JCS 1067

After the Morgenthau Plan was officially withdrawn, Morgenthau nevertheless continued to have a strong influence on the planning process of German occupation. The secret JCS 1067 directive issued by the Joint Chiefs of Staff to General Eisenhower in April 1945, became the early "bible" of the American occupation policy in its zone of Germany. It was a diluted version of the Morgenthau Plan.

JCS 1067 did not require the destruction of all German industries and the flooding of all mines, but it limited industrial activity to a level needed to prevent "disease and unrest."[17] In terms of this policy document, the U.S. occupation authorities were instructed to build a strong Europe with a weak, partially deindustrialized Germany. The objectives for the initial postdefeat period were industrial disarmament, demilitarization, denazification, and decentralization of German administration through regional and local autonomy.

Industrialization disarmament was to be practiced in three forms: reparations in kind, i.e., removal of German plants and equipment; outright destruction of German production facilities and statutory neglect of plants and equipment. The U.S. Military Governor was required to impose "controls to the full extent necessary to achieve the industrial disarmament of Germany." He was forbidden to take "steps (a) looking toward the economic rehabilitation of Germany, or (b) designed to maintain or strengthen the German economy." Only minimum production of iron and steel, chemicals, nonferrous metals, machine tools, radio and electrical equipment,

---

[15] Balabkins, Nicholas (1964) Germany under Direct Controls. *Economic Aspects of Industrial Disarmament*. New Brunswick, NJ: Rutgers University Press, p. 21.

[16] *The Economist*, CIL. 321, Sept. 8, 1945.

[17] U.S. (Department of) State, (1947) *Occupation of Germany: Policy and Progress, 1945–1946*. Washington, D.C., Government Printing Office, pp. 28–42.

automotive vehicles, heavy machinery, and important parts thereof was permitted. This minimum level of industrial operations designed to prevent widespread disease and unrest was undefined and ambiguous. The initial postsurrender period in the American zone of occupation was designed to weaken the German industrial base as thoroughly as possible.

To cripple permanently, the German preeminence in physics, chemistry, and engineering and to eliminate German technological "know-how" as a factor of industrial war potential, JCS 1067 spelled out in great detail ways and means for "technological disarmament." Paragraph 31 stated as an additional measure of industrial disarmament, the U.S. Military Governor would adopt the following measures in the U.S. zone of occupation:

(a) Prohibit all research activities and close all labouratories, research institutions … except those considered necessary to the protection of public health.
(b) To exclude from further research activity any persons who previously held key positions in German war research.

However, thousands of the most able minds of the technological elite of the Third Reich went to the United Kingdom, the U.S., and the Soviet Union. The U.S. Military had to smuggle the German rocket specialists into the U.S. to prevent the American mass media from decrying that the U.S. is allowing the Nazi war criminals to enter the U.S. Among such immigrants was Werner von Braun, a man who spearheaded the space program of the U.S. James Michener had articulated this process of technological transfer in his much read novel, *Space*.

In this stringent form, the JCS 1067 probably determined the U.S. policy for a few months in 1945.[18] In the winter months of 1945–1946, Americans discovered that the Soviet wartime ally has an expansionist agenda in Europe. In the Soviet occupied zone, they quickly had erected a Stalinist-type totalitarianism, including Soviet-style concentration camps. Privately owned means of production disappeared and one-party "democracy" became the norm.

The JCS 1067 was formally repudiated in July of 1947. Alas, as long as JCS 1067 was not formally revoked, the lower administrative echelons in the U.S. Military Government had to enforce its harsh provisions. Since instructions of JCS 1067 were commands, the rank-and-file administrators frequently interpreted its provisions rigidly and applied them zealously.

Some of the U.S. and U.K. Military Government officials were kindly disposed toward socialist and communist ideas. They had seen the horror scenes of the liberated Nazi concentration camps, and they believed that the Soviet way is the way of the future. They were idealists who had never known or heard of the human costs of building socialism in Soviet Russia. They had never experienced Stalinism and had never lived in Soviet-Style societies. Some of these U.S. Military government

---

[18] Zink, Harold (1957) *The United States in Germany, 1944–1955*. Princeton, NJ: D. Van Nostrand & Co., pp. 92–96. See also, Clay, Lucius (1950) *Decision in Germany*. New York: Doubleday, pp. 72–73, and Balabkins, N., *op cit.*, pp. 13–17.

officials moved to live in the Soviet zone of occupation. For instance, an American officer of the U.S. Military Government, George S. Wheeler, who was in charge of the denazification program, went to live in Czechoslovakia.[19] The case of Stefan Heym is particularly revealing in this regard. He was a German-born immigrant who settled in the U.S. in 1933. In 1939, he joined the American Army and eventually rose to the rank of an officer. He served in the U.S. Military Government, and he flouted his socialist creed in word and deed in the newspapers he edited. Soon enough, he was sent back to the U.S., where he resigned his commission, gave up his U.S. citizenship, and settled in the Soviet-occupied zone of Germany. His German-language book, *Nachruf*, reveals how this enthusiastic believer in socialist creed, after decades in DDR, had to learn the hard way what Soviet-style socialism is about on a daily basis.[20] Another example of similar experiences was that of a German-born British army colonel by the name of J rgen Kuczynski.[21] He also left the British zone of occupation and settled in the Soviet zone, where he resided for four decades. As a student in Göttingen, I heard once a story that Kuczynski walked into the Soviet *Kommandandura* in Karlshorst, East Berlin, as an English colonel and walked out as a Red Army general!

To a number of American Military Government officers, the postwar economic policy was unique, incomprehensible, and ran counter to the normal policy objectives in economic life. Industrial disarmament policy meant lowering the capacity of postwar Germany to produce goods and services. One disillusioned American official admitted that "the task of deliberately reducing production and holding down the standard of living...went contrary to all habits of thought in the western world."[22] And in the view of *The London Economist*, the Allied Industry Plan of 1946 was "without exaggeration, a plan for dislocation and impoverishment. It is negative, restrictive, and basically unworkable."[23] It was the greatest machine-smashing action ever attempted in peacetime. It was designed to bring about economic retrogression in postwar Germany.

The objectives of the American industrial disarmament policy changed in mid-July 1947, when the U.S. Military Governor of the U.S. zone of occupation, General Lucius Clay, was instructed to proceed with the economic reconstruction to achieve a self-sufficiency of the combined US/UK zones of occupation. The new Directive, JCS/1779, conceded that under the First Level of Industry Plan of 1946, Germany could neither become economically viable nor contribute her indispensable part to the economic rehabilitation of Western Europe.[24]

---

[19] Wheeler, George S., (1958) *Die Amerikanische Politik in Deutschland 1945–1950*. Berlin: Kongress-Verlag, p. 13.

[20] (1995) Frankfury/Main, Fischer Taschenbuch Verlag, 842 pp.

[21] Kuczynski, J rgen (1972) *J rgen Kuczynski, Die Erziehung des J.K. zum Kommunisten und Wissenschaftler*. Berlin und Weimer, Aufbau Verlag, pp. 401–416.

[22] Ratchford, B.U. and Ross, W.D., (1947) *Berlin Reparations Assignment*. Chapel Hill, The University of North Carolina Press., p. 69.

[23] *The Economist*, vol. CL, 532 (April 6, 1946).

[24] U.S. Department of State (1950) *Germany, 1947–1949: The Story in Documents*. Washington, D.C. Government Printing Office, pp. 33–41.

On August 29, 1947, the U.S. and U.K. Military Governments released a new document entitled, *The Revised Plan for Level of Industry in the Anglo-American Zones*. It provided for the retention of sufficient industrial capacity roughly to approximate the 1936 level of aggregate output and aimed essentially at two objectives: (a) to provide for a self-sustaining economy of the Bizonal Area and (b) to enable this area to make an economic contribution to the rehabilitation of Western Europe. However, the industrial equipment and entire plants, declared in excess of the permitted level, were to be removed in the form of *reparations in kind*. Accordingly, in the fall of 1947, the British and American Military Governments published a list of industrial plants or portions of them to be dismantled as reparations. For the Bizonal Area of Germany, 682 industrial plants were scheduled for dismantling.[25] From the heavily industrialized British Zone, 496 plants were on the removals list, the majority of which were either steel producing or steel processing plants. Even after the onset of the Marshall Plan in 1948, out of 157 plants dismantled, 118 were engineering plants. The reparations program ended in 1951.

It did not take long to prove that the American attempt to build a strong Europe with a weak Germany was a chimera. The American and British zone of occupation could not produce enough food to feed its population. Without imported food, mass starvation in the U.K., the U.S., and even the French occupied zones was inevitable. It was estimated that the food produced in the British and American zones of occupation at that time came roughly to 1,000 calories, per person, per day, or 30% less than the 1,550 calorie ration for the "normal" consumer. All food that was distributed was subject to rationing, at fixed wartime prices. However, 1,000 calories or often less was "too much to die on and too little to live on," as the saying went at that time.

During the first year of occupation, roughly 2,000,000 tons of food were imported to prevent famine in the Ruhr. How do you prevent famine and unrest among the hungry, freezing, and hopeless Germans? Many American officers saw the millions of fleeing refugees and expellees from Eastern Europe and the Soviet-occupied zone of Germany. Every escapee was ready to kiss the boots of every American soldier for having escaped the Communist paradise. To avert mass starvation, Americans came up with the "Government and Relief in Occupied Areas" appropriations, which financed the shipments of American food to occupied West Germany. At the end of 1947, American expenses for providing such relief supplies to the western zones of Germany stood at $750 million and by the end of March 1948, the total sum was almost $1 billion![26] Under the pretext of preserving wartime Allied unity, American policy had intended to keep Germany weak. It did not work. Such a policy amounted to keeping Europe in rags. In 1947, it took months of Congressional hearings in Washington, D.C. to learn what was happening in occupied Germany and Europe. It took the Marshall Plan and $20 billion to clean up the Morgenthau legacy.

---

[25] U.S. (House of) Representatives. (Committee on) Foreign Affairs, (1947) *Plants and Parts of Plants Listed for Reparations from United States and United Kingdom Zones of Germany*.

[26] U.K. House of Commons Select Committee on Estimates (1946), *The Control Office for Germany and Austria: Expenditure in Germany*. London: HMSO, pp. IV–V. See also, Schlange-Schoeningen, H. (1955), *Im Schatten des Hungers*, Hamburg: P. Parey verlag, p. 140.

Gustav Stolper saw what the American-led occupation policy had wrought in occupied Western Germany and in Western Europe, and he was upset, to say the least. And so were a number of many sober, perceptive, and responsible U.S. government officials, senators, and congressmen, including President Harry S. Truman.[27]

On December 18, 1946, Gustav Stolper had a long conversation with the former U.S. President Herbert Hoover in New York. On January 20, 1947, he had a second meeting with Hoover and he became a member of the Hoover-Mission to Germany, consisting of Hugh Gibson, Tracy S. Voorhees, Dr. D.H. Fitzgerald, Dr. W.H. Sebrell, Louis P. Lochner, Frank Mason, and Herbert Hoover as Chief. Stolper was delighted that he finally will be heard where it counts. Four days before the trip, Gustav Stolper wrote for Herbert Hoover a short memo dealing with the serious food problem, the industrial disarmament problem of Germany, incarceration of thousands of German industrial managers, and the envisioned socialization of the entire Ruhr Valley industrial complex.[28] To make sure that this Presidential mission of Germany remained secret, untainted by the glare of an army of journalists, the plane took off from a small airfield on Long Island.

12.5 Part III: Stolper Takes on the American Deindustrialization Policy

Gustav Stolper was confounded by the U.S. policy of disarming German industry. To understand his objections, let us use a basic tool of Eco 101, called the *production possibilities curve*, which is built around the idea of universal scarcity. Given finite amounts of labour, capital equipment, and technology, a market-driven society has to face limits on what it can produce. If a society produces only machinery, it can produce no butter. On the contrary, if it opts to make only butter, it can make no machinery. The optimum amount of machinery and butter for this society is indicated in the next figure by the boundary line between T and B, which is called the *production-possibilities curve*. The trade-offs on it are indicated by points A and C. Being at point A or C means that more machinery can be produced only by sacrificing some butter production. Over time, more labour and better technology can expand an economy's capacity to produce more machinery and more butter. In such a case, the *production possibilities curve* will shift outward.[29]

America's policy of industrial disarmament, however, called for lower production of capital and consumer goods. Such a policy meant that Germany's production possibilities curve would shift downward, as shown by Fig. 12.1. No college freshman

---

[27] Stolper, Toni, p. 449.

[28] Stolper, Toni, p. 451.

[29] For an innovative discussion of this concept, see Hubbard, R. Glenn and O'Brien, Anthony Patrick, (2006). *Economics*. Upper Saddle River NJ: Pearson-Prentice Hall, pp. 39–40.

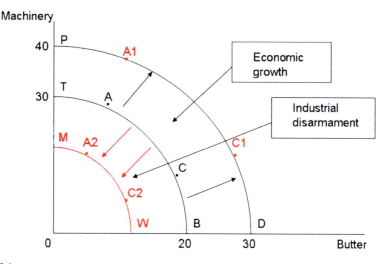

Fig. 12.1

today would entertain such an economic policy goal. This simple expository device of the production possibilities curve puts the short-sightedness of the industrial disarmament policy into sharper focus. In fact, this unique policy, a deified ideal for postwar Germany, was launched by the U.S. Secretary Morgenthau to reduce Gross Domestic Product in occupied Germany, in the very center of Europe, for quite some time into the future. It amounted to a policy of negative growth, and is likely to remain in the annals of history as an example of "utter lunacy" as the British called it.

After the end of the World War II, when decolonization of Europe's overseas empires was in full blast, all graduate students in economics in the U.S. were virtually force-fed the various versions of the Harrod-Domar growth model, which asserted that the rate of growth of output was equal to the national savings rate divided by the capital-output ratio. It was written as follows:

$$\left|\frac{\Delta Y}{Y} = \frac{S}{\beta}\right| \quad \text{where } S = \frac{S}{Y}; \beta = \frac{K}{O}.$$

Accordingly, in economic policy-making terms, an output growth rate of 5% a year, assuming the capital-output ratio for the economy as a whole to be three, required a national savings rate of 15%, per annum. This savings-centered growth theory was acclaimed by the tune-calling academic economists to have almost universal applicability. For example, massive capital investment in poor and underdeveloped countries, usually in material infrastructure facilities, financed by foreign aid, would provide a quick panacea for economics backwardness, social ills, and stagnation. Alas, industrial disarmament called for lower capacity of Germany designed to produce smaller amounts of machinery and consumer goods. It aimed at shifting its production possibilities curve inward. It's aim was negative economic growth, i.e., $-\Delta Y / Y$!

Industrial disarmament had been practiced in three forms: reparations in kind, i.e., removals of German plants and equipment to Allied countries; outright destruction of certain production facilities, known as war plants; and statutory neglect of industrial facilities. For several years, West Germans were not allowed to repair the bomb-damage to their industrial plants. The U.S. Military Governor was forbidden to take any "steps (a) looking toward the economic rehabilitation of Germany, or (b) designed to maintain or strengthen the German economy." The combined effects of wartime destruction and massive, virtually around-the-clock bombing raids, had resulted in heavy declines in immediate output, but destruction of plants was around 10%, as the U.S. Bombing Survey indicated after the war. However, postwar statutory neglect of the damaged plants, which were forbidden to repair even minor damages, made a dramatic impact. Ironically, through the outright destruction of industrial facilities as "war plants" and the removal of West German industrial facilities as *reparations in kind* turned out to be highly salutary for the West German economy. In 1951, reparations in kind were stopped, and West Germans were able to modernize their industrial plants and equipment with up-to-date facilities, on the double, so to say. John Stuart Mill (1806–1873) might have found this turn of events amusing. Mill wrote in the mid-nineteenth century that all capital equipment suffers, over time, from wear and tear, causing a country's existing capital stock to lose value gradually.[30] The removal, destruction, and statutory neglect of industrial plants and their replacement by more modern equipment with better technology gave our former enemy a competitive edge in the world market. If Americans had been really keen on punishing their former German enemies for starting the World War II, they should have imposed a reparations policy requiring the defeated Third Reich to buy America's used industrial plants and equipment. Such equipment would have had to be shipped to Germany. For instance, postwar German steel makers would have to buy the used Bethlehem Steel facilities from my home town in Bethlehem, Pa., and transport and install them in the territory of former Krupp or Thussen steel factories. Under such a policy, the defeated Germans would not have been able to launch their once famous and by now forgotten "German economic miracle" after the currency reform of 1948.

The American planners who strove to impose a policy of industrial disarmament had probably never read or had forgotten the first chapter of John M. Keynes's *Economic Consequences of the Peace* of 1919, in which the author sketched the interdependence among Europe's national economies. Imperial Germany's role in the nineteenth century as a chief wheel in this system of economic specialization and well-being was undermined by the Carthagenian features of the Versailles Treaty, which eventually produced hyper-inflation, the intractable "transfer problem," and eventually and indirectly, Nazism.

---

[30] Mill, John S., (1900) *Principles of Political Economy*, Revised edition. New York: The Colonial Press, pp. 74–75.

After a few short years of Morgenthauist economic policy in the Western zones of occupied Germany, its consequences were visible for all to see. Western European countries desperately needed German coal and steel. The Italians could not sell the vegetables they had previously sold in Germany. The Dutch wanted to sell vegetables for German machinery and coal, but the Western Allies refused to consider the offers, and the Dutch had to destroy considerable portions of their crop. Denmark offered 150 tons of lard a month; Turkey wanted to sell hazelnuts; Norway was ready to sell fish and fish oil; Sweden even offered considerable quantities of fats to alleviate shortages in the British zone in exchange for the toys of Nuremberg. But again nothing happened.[31]

These economic difficulties of Western Europe were compounded by political instability, especially in France and Italy. Washington feared that the Stalinist Soviet threat might spread to Western Europe and take possession of the Ruhr Valley, the industrial hub of Western Europe. To forestall that possibility, Congress passed a large-scale assistance program called the European Recovery Program, or Marshall Plan, which was to run from April 1948 to December 1951. It is forgotten today that, in February of 1948, Communists took power on Czechoslovakia and set up Soviet-type totalitarianism. During the World War II, in 1942, Keynes suggested that the Western Allies set up "a Reconstruction Fund to be supported by the United States, on terms of unprecedented generosity, as soon as Hitler was overthrown, to prevent the spread of communism in Germany."[32]

12.6 Working at Full Steam on the Hoover Mission in 1947

All his life, Stolper had an enormous respect for facts, not ideological fictions. He liked to get his journalistic feet wet and hands dirty, so to say. He knew that journalistic practice without theoretical underpinnings was no more acceptable than theory without practice. Stolper, like the Swedish Nobelist economist Gunnar Myrdal, knew that "facts kick and they kick hard." As editor of *Der deutsche Volkswirt* in Berlin and published of his *Economic Reports*, Stolper always employed the broad-based method of economic analysis, acquired from Joseph A. Schumpeter, and he loved veracity, as his wife Toni, forever emphasized.[33] Very much like Thomas Hobbes in 1651, in his *Leviathan*, Stolper knew that intellectual activities are not products of spontaneous thought, but reactions to outside stimuli. After all, Stolper knew intimately German history and its economic evolution, and wrote elegantly about it in his *German Economy, 1870–1940*.[34]

---

[31] Reported by Dr. Semler, Head of the Department of Economics of Bavaria. See Anlagen zum Kommentar meiner Erlanger Rede (1948), appendix 6.

[32] Harrod, Roy F. (1951) *The Life of John Maynard Keynes*. New York: Harcourt, Brace and Co., p. 489.

[33] Stolper, Toni, p. 410.

[34] (1940) New York: Reynall & Hitchcock. See also, Stolper, Gustav, Hauser, Karl and Borchardt, Knut (1967), *The German Economy, 1870 to the Present*.

12.7 The Hoover Mission in 1947

The appointment to the Hoover Mission was a pure fluke, as Toni Stolper had revealed.[35] Stolper had met John McCloy, then Under-Secretary of War, and the two talked at length, in the spring of 1945, of German things and concerns. On December 17, 1945, Stolper was asked to visit Herbert Hoover the following day at 5:30 PM at the Waldorf-Astoria.[36] A year later, on January 20, 1947, Stolper talked to Hoover for a second time, when he was made an economic adviser to the ex-President Hoover, who was the Chief of the Mission. President Truman wanted to find out "what was going on in Germany and what can be done about it?" Truman wanted to launch this mission quietly, away from the glare and noise of the mass media folks.

Once in Germany, Stolper was permitted to set his own agenda. In Berlin, he found his own private place to live where he met former acquaintances and friends. Hoover knew that Stolper would explore facts best if he were left alone and free from the interference from the U.S. Military government officials and journalists. Stolper was very busy, and he slept 4 h a day, as his wife reported.[37]

President Truman received the *First Hoover Report* on the food and nutrition situation in West German zones of occupation and Austria on February 28, 1947. The crucial *Third Report* was submitted to President Truman on March 18, 1947. It dealt with the necessary steps for promotion of German exports, so as to relieve American taxpayers of the burdens of relief and for economic recovery of Europe.

Stolper's role in collecting facts, presenting them, and calling for a major reversal of the U.S. policy was immense. In this report, President Truman was given to understand that Germany is an integral part of Europe and that war and peace industries are hard to separate.[38] In this report, Hoover wrote that "We can keep Germany in these economic chains, but it will also keep Europe in rags."[39]

It was *die Sternstunde*, the hour of glory, of Gustav Stolper. President Truman already knew of the danger posed to the U.S. by former World War II. He wanted to relegate to the dustbin of history the remaining relics of Morgenthauist legacy.

12.8 Stolper's Legacy to Economic Policy Makers

Our symposium rules require that speakers conclude their presentations with an assessment of Stolper's legacy to public policy making. It was more than 150 years ago when Thomas Carlyle (1795–1881) relegated economics to the status of "the

---

[35] Stolper, Toni, p. 448.
[36] Stolper, Toni, p. 449.
[37] Stolper. Toni, pp. 451–452.
[38] Stolper, Gustav (1948) *German Realities*. New York: Reynal & Hitchcock, p. 164.
[39] Hoover, Herbert (1947) *The President's Economic Mission to Germany and Austria, Report #3*. Parch 18, 1947, p. 15.

dismal science." For decades thereafter, economics has endured bad press, even though, in the popular mind, economists were powerful. But what part of economics is so objectionable? Is it *positive economics*, or economic theory, with its value-free study of "what is?" Is it *normative economics* with its postulates of what "ought to be," such as full employment, price and wage stability, egalitarian distribution of national income, and continuous economic growth? Or is it *policy-making economics*, which tries to find solutions to pressing problems through legislation?

In today's market-based and democratic society, economic policy-making is complex and elusive compared with the precision and value-free stance of economic theory. But as the *London Economist* reposted in the 1980s, only 5% of American economists are interested in policy-making economics. In fact, in the early 1990s, Isabell Sawhill of the *Urban Institute* of Washington, D.C., wrote that "Economists are often unaware of what is happening in the world of public affairs." As a result, both the quality of public decision-making and the role that economists play in it are less than optimal.[40] The popular textbook version of economic policy-making is simple but grossly inadequate. Once a congressman or senator sitting on a particular Congressional committee has drafted the outlines of what needs to be done, it becomes subject to a Congressional hearing managed by an army of Congressional aides. They select who is to testify, what to say, what to emphasize and what to exclude, and what to add to the final draft of the bill. The political push and pull, involving legions of lobbyists, shape the final version of the bill before congressmen and senators vote on it.

Traditional economic policy-making, as described in economic textbooks, calls for maximization of per-capita national income, regular growth of Gross Domestic Product, and reasonably fair distribution of national income. Alas, rational action is a good postulate for the classroom, but not in the political arena, be it Washington, London, or Berlin. Political passions and wishful "ought-to-be's" always result in a less than optimal economic policy-making process.

America's blueprint for deindustrializing the defeated and occupied Western zones of postwar Germany was a unique document in the history of economic policy making abroad. Deindustrialization was proposed in 1944 by Secretary Morgenthau and accepted by Franklin D. Roosevelt who, as U.S. President, had Constitutional authority over American foreign policy. Article II, Section 2, of the U.S. Constitution assigns to the president leading authority for foreign policy. No Congressional hearings were held on the matter. Later on, in the spring of 1945, the gist of the Morgenthau plan was written into the secret JCS 1067 Directive, again without Congressional oversight.

It was Gustav Stolper in early 1947 who warned senators, congressmen, and American military leaders that Morgenthau's deindustrialization policy could in no way revive war-destroyed and despirited Western Europe. The Soviet Union by 1947 had become a major threat to U.S. interests in Western Europe and the entire world. The economically morassed Western zones of Germany were largely responsible for

---

[40] "Policy Watch Note," (1992), in *Journal of Economic Perspectives*, vol. 6, p. 189.

the economic stagnation of Europe. Stolper pleaded that the Germany economy be released from Morgenthau's chains. He made his argument in his *Economic Report #3* of the Hoover Mission, which was submitted in early 1947 to President Truman, who was undoing what Roosevelt had wrought at the end of the World War II. It was Stolper's *Sternstunde*, a moment of glory for a naturalized American from Germany. It demonstrated, once again, that economics gets its cue from politics. With hindsight, today we can also say that a deindustrialized Germany, without industry and coal mines, would never have been able to pay more than $100 billion of "moral reparations" to its victims.

Index

B
Bauer, Otto, 5, 6
Bechtold, Chancellor Count, 35
Bismarck, Prince, 65
Bonn, Moritz Julius, 33, 52, 96
Brentano, Lujo, 39–43
Brüning, Heinrich, 109–111, 113, 114, 117–122, 126

C
Cole, G.D.H., 5

D
Der deutsche Volkswirt, 39–44, 50, 51, 57, 93, 96–98, 101, 107, 109–122, 125–145, 147–149, 159
Der Österreichische Volkswirt, 1–14, 16, 23, 25, 27, 31–36, 47, 73–90, 148

E
Emperor, 31–36, 60
Eucken, Walter, 49, 51, 52, 101, 113
Europeanization, 57–62

G
Gleichschaltung, 44, 125–145

H
Habsburg monarchy, 73, 76, 83, 88, 89
Hayek, Friedrich A., 2, 21, 22, 26, 48, 49, 74, 87

Heuss, Theodor, 50, 74, 96–98, 102, 103
Hitler, Adolf, 3, 4, 52, 70, 71, 76, 98, 101, 102, 104, 105, 107, 111, 122, 131, 132, 134, 138, 139, 141, 142, 148, 159

K
Katona, George, 74, 97
Keynes, John Maynard, 7, 8, 24, 49, 66, 127, 128, 130, 158, 159

L
Linke, Lilo, 3, 93–96, 98–108

M
Machine Age, 18, 26
Machlup, Fritz, 74, 112
Macmillan, Harold, 7, 11, 25, 49
Malthus, Thomas, 40, 41
Menger, Carl, 46
Miksch, Leonard, 51
Mises, Ludwig von, 2, 22, 23, 47, 48, 75, 88, 137, 150

P
Polanyi, Karl, 1–28, 74, 75

R
Roosevelt, Franklin D., 4, 10, 13, 25, 151, 161, 162
Röpke, Wilhelm, 48, 49, 87, 97, 106, 109, 113, 114, 127

S
Schacht, Hjalmar, 48–52, 97, 102
Schumpeter, Joseph A., 10, 48–50, 58, 74, 76, 84, 88, 96, 97, 109, 112, 120, 149, 159
Shah, 59, 60, 62
Sohn-Rethel, Alfred, 127–130
Sombart, Werner, 131–134, 139, 143, 144
Stolper, Gustav, 1, 31, 34–36, 48–52, 67, 69, 70, 73–83, 85, 87–89, 93–111, 113–117, 120–122, 126, 127, 147–162
Stolper, Toni, 50, 51, 73, 75, 94–104, 108, 127, 147–151, 156, 159, 160
Stolper, Wolfgang, 97, 147

V
Versailles, 35, 66–67, 70, 71, 119, 158

W
Weber, Max, 27, 131
World War I, 20–23, 26, 46, 77, 87, 95, 110, 137, 148

Y
Young Plan, 50, 70, 118–120